Both Your Houses

Minneapolis

First Edition April 2026
Both Your Houses: Iran, America, and the Wages of Unchecked Power
Copyright © 2026 by Massoud Amin. All rights reserved.

No parts of this book may be used or reproduced by any means, graphic, electronic, or mechanical, including photocopying, recording, taping or by any information storage retrieval system, without the written permission of the publisher except in the case of brief quotations embodied in critical articles and reviews.

10 9 8 7 6 5 4 3 2 1
ISBN: 978-1-962834-74-2

Cover and book design by Gary Lindberg

Both Your Houses

Iran, America, and the Wages of Unchecked Power

Massoud Amin

Minneapolis

Dedication

به همهٔ آنان که ماندند

For those who stayed —
who did not choose the fire,
and could not leave it.
For those who left,
and have been leaving ever since.
For every person, under every flag,
handed a war they did not start
and a bill they did not sign.
The plague falls on all the houses.
The people inside them did not build the feud.
May the distance close.
May their voices reach us—
in dignity, and in peace.

Contents

Epigraphs

"A plague o' both your houses! They have made worms' meat of me."

—William Shakespeare, *Romeo and Juliet*, Act III, Scene I Mercutio, dying after being wounded in the fight between the Montagues and Capulets

"Someone will come who will spread the light."

—Forugh Farrokhzad, "Someone Is Coming," from *Another Birth* (1964)

Also by Massoud Amin

Technological Leadership: Leading Through Complexity — Resilient Systems, Ethical Technologies, and Sustainable Futures

Smart Power: Digital Grids, Public Trust, and the Future of Energy

The Line That Holds: Building Resilient Leadership for a World in Transition

The Integrity Compass: Leading with Ethics in a Changing World

Resonant Threads: Poems of Love, Resilience, and Wisdom

Roots of Light: A Memoir Across Empires, and the Legacy Carried Forward

Author's Notes

I was born in northwestern Iran and came to the United States as a teenager, arriving just before the revolution that would remake the country I love and grew up in. I thought it was a temporary move. Instead, the years turned into decades. I built a life here in Minneapolis, Minnesota—a family, a career, a home—while carrying Iran inside me the way you carry blessings of love and beauty, but also a wound that has scarred over without quite healing.

I have known Iran from the inside—not as a tourist or analyst, but as someone who was formed by it. I carry it the way you carry the place where you first learned what the world was. Each return to Iranian culture, to its literature and its people, has confirmed the same thing: it is a civilization of extraordinary intelligence and creativity living with a gap between what it is capable of and what its circumstances have permitted.

In the winter of 2025–26, as Iran burned—first with protest, then with foreign bombs—and Minneapolis descended into federally imposed monitoring and fear, I found I could no longer separate the two identities I carry or postpone the reckoning they demand. This book began as a series of essays and op-eds, written in real time. It has grown into something larger: an attempt, through the lens of a systems scientist and an Iranian-born American, to understand how the two countries I love have come to this moment.

A note on this book's method. Every page reflects a single question: what best serves the cause of human dignity? I have written about systems, policies, historical forces, and documented events, drawing throughout on the international public record. I care deeply about Iran—precisely because I care about its people.

This book is organized into five parts. Part One establishes the moral framework. Part Two traces Iran's century-long struggle with the postwar economic architecture. Part Three chronicles the crises of 2022–2026. Part Four broadens the lens to include America and the international order. Part Five looks forward.

Throughout, I draw on history, on poetry I have written over a lifetime, on the essays I published in real time, on the best available reporting, and on a lifetime of studying how systems fail and what it takes to rebuild them. All errors of fact are my own. All errors of judgment will be judged by history.

A Note on Allegiance

This book was written by a Persian-American systems scientist who has spent his career as an independent scholar, unaffiliated with any political party, government, foreign interest, or ideological program—in Iran, in the United States, or elsewhere. That independence is not a posture. It is a documented fact for nearly five decades.

The argument this book makes addresses two kinds of failure simultaneously: the failure of any governing system when power operates without accountability, and the human cost that failure always exacts on civilians. The book applies that argument consistently, regardless of which government is under examination. It does not take sides with any state, faction, or opposition movement. It does not serve any government's interest in how Iran or its people are perceived.

This book will be accused by some of being an apology for one side. It will be accused by others of being propaganda. Both accusations reflect the reflex of those who require books to take sides in a feud. This book declines. The people made worms' meat by the quarrels of the powerful deserve something more honest than partisanship.

A Note on Form

This book was written during a war. Most books about wars are written afterward, when the dust has settled, and the record is complete. This one was not. The events it describes were still unfolding when the last pages were written. Some of what is asserted with confidence will be confirmed by time. Some will be revised. A few claims, made on the best available evidence in March 2026, may look different from a distance. These are the conditions of witness writing, and the author accepts it.

The form reflects the same condition. Different chapters demanded different kinds of attention—some analytical, some closer to testimony, a few holding both at once. A reader expecting a conventional policy book will find it uneven. A reader expecting a memoir will find it argumentative. It is both, and neither entirely. That is not a failure of discipline. It is what this moment required.

The core of the book—the documented sequence of decisions, the names of the people who died, the argument about what unchecked power produces—will not change. Everything else is the best account that could be given from inside the event.

I offer this book in the spirit of inquiry. Its purpose is literary, historical, and philosophical: to bear witness to what memory, resilience, and shared humanity look like when civilizations are tested; to document, as honestly as one witness can, what happened and why; and to ask what a more just and peaceful future might require of the people who must build it.

I engage the people of Iran—all of them, of every political view, generation, and walk of life—with the deepest respect. This book is written by a Persian-born American who left as a teenager and has spent forty-seven years carrying both countries inside him.

The tension between those two inheritances is not resolved in these pages. It is the lens through which they were written.

A Note on Sources and Evidence

Every factual claim in this book that bears on living persons, institutions, casualty counts, or allegations of official conduct is from one or more of the following categories of sources: official government transcripts or testimony; reports by credentialed international institutions (UN, IAEA, Amnesty International, Human Rights Watch, HRANA, IHRNGO); verified journalism from named outlets with documented editorial standards; published peer-reviewed analysis; or satellite imagery assessed by named institutions, where a claim rests on a single source (which is stated). Where sources conflict—as they inevitably do in events that are still unfolding—both are cited, and the dispute is named. The bibliography at the back of this book is organized to allow the reader to trace major claims back to their sources. Claims about official motive or intent are framed as inferences from the documented record, not as established facts, and are identified as such. Claims about civilian casualties in active conflict zones carry different levels of confidence: confirmed means verified by at least two independent sources; reported means from a single credible source pending verification; and contested means the figure is disputed between sources and the dispute is noted. This framework is the standard to which this book holds itself. Where it falls short, the author welcomes correction.

Method, Sources, and What I Refuse to Do

Every claim I make rests on the public record. I have not relied on private sourcing that could endanger people inside Iran. I have been deliberate about this. Words travel in ways their authors cannot predict, and some of the people whose names appear here, or whose names do not appear precisely because naming them would be dangerous, are still living in the country I am writing about.

Where numbers are contested or preliminary—casualty estimates in the first days of a conflict, protest death tolls under a blackout, intelligence assessments whose basis has not been publicly released—I say so. The confidence level matters. "Confirmed by multiple independent sources" is different from "preliminary reporting suggests" which is different from "disputed by the parties." I distinguish these throughout. The reader should hold them accordingly.

What I refuse to do: trade in rumors, endanger sources, claim certainty I do not have, or pretend that the most consequential facts are the ones most easily verified. The hardest truth in this story—that a diplomatic breakthrough was bombed, that children were in school when the strikes came, that the legal case for the war does not hold—is documented. The record exists.

A note on witness testimony: individuals cited in this book who are not public figures, or who face potential risk from identification, have been anonymized using one or more of the following methods: name changed, profession generalized, city or region made less specific, or identifying details composited across multiple sources. In each case, the underlying testimony has been verified, and the substance has not been altered. The standard applied is this: no detail has been preserved that could, in combination with others, allow a hostile actor to identify a private individual or endanger anyone still in Iran.

A Note on the Asymmetry and the Symmetry

I want to be precise about one important part of what I am arguing and what I am not in this book. The Islamic Republic of Iran and the United States government are not the same thing. I know this. They operate under different legal frameworks, levels of democratic accountability, relationships to civil society, and types of violence. The Islamic Republic has governed through a system that has restricted civil liberties and, as the documented record shows, used force against protest movements. The United States is a constitutional democracy with free elections, an independent judiciary, and a press that can and does criticize its government without its journalists being disappeared. These are not equivalent systems.

The symmetry I indict is specific: when institutional constraints fail, both systems produce the same outcome for civilians. Unchecked power treats people as expendable material. The United States government treated Iranian civilians as expendable when its strategic objectives required bombing them. It treated immigrant communities in Minneapolis as expendable when its domestic political project required their terrorization. The mechanisms differ by geography. The logic is identical: power insulated from accountability produces civilian suffering. That is the argument I am making.

I name both. I do not equate them. What I argue is that they share a specific logic: civilian disposability under unconstrained power.

Siavash in Ferdowsi's Shahnameh

Ferdowsi, the sage of Khorasan, composed the *Shahnameh* between 977 and 1010 CE and completed it on the eighth of March 1010. The poem is nearly fifty thousand couplets and is the national epic of Iran. The story of Siavash is among its most tragic and most instructive passages.

Siavash,[1] the prince of Iran, had fled his father's court not out of fear but out of conscience. Kavus, the Iranian king, had ordered him to break a peace treaty he had negotiated, execute hostages, and resume a war he had honorably ended. Siavash refused. He crossed into Turan, the land of Iran's enemy. Afrasiab, the Turanian king, received him warmly, gave him his daughter in marriage, and gave him land on which to build a new city.

But Garsivaz, Afrasiab's brother, envied Siavash's rise in the Turanian court. Through lies and fabrications, he poisoned Afrasiab's mind against the young prince. Piran, the wise counselor, warned against the execution. He was not heeded.

1 See Appendix: Poems of Witness, "Siavash"

Ferdowsi does not indict only Afrasiab. He indicts Kavus as well, the Iranian king whose unjust commands drove his blameless son from his homeland in the first place. Siavash was caught between two powers without conscience: the power that claimed to be his father, and the power that claimed to be his host. Both placed their own interests first. Both treated the innocent Siavash as the cost of their objectives.

Afrasiab feared Siavash's blood. He ordered it spilled on barren ground, caught in a golden bowl, kept from the living earth—because he understood, or half-understood, what Ferdowsi knew completely: that the blood of the innocent does not stay where power puts it. At that very hour, a plant grew. Only God knew how it grew.

Piran, the wise counselor, warned him: a crowned head is not to be severed; the avengers are already watching. Afrasiab ignored him. When power has already made its choice, the counsel of those who see clearly is the last thing it wants to hear. The counselors of 2026 warned too. The record shows it. The same silence followed.

This is the pattern the *Shahnameh* names, and that this book names too. Not one house. Both houses. In March 2026, the Iranian people were caught between the same two logics: a government whose citizens had lived without the civil freedoms they demanded, and a foreign power that treated those same citizens as acceptable losses in a strike package. The mechanisms differ across a thousand years. The logic is the same.

The young woman who stood in the streets of Tehran in 2022, carrying a sign that read "Woman, Life, Freedom," was the branch Siavash asked for. She was not asking any foreign power to liberate her. She was renewing the tradition held in the land itself. The bombs that fell on her city on February 28, 2026, did not answer her call. They interrupted it.

Siavash's blood fell to the earth, and a plant grew from the place where it landed. The Persians named that plant after him. The life that emerges from the ground against all odds is not forgotten.

A Note on Developments Since This Book Was Completed

On April 7, 2026, a Pakistani-brokered ceasefire brought forty days of strikes to a formal pause. The terms aligned more closely with Iran's opening position than with America's stated objectives. Tehran declared victory. The nuclear program—the stated objective of the war—is now more dispersed, more opaque, and harder to verify than on February 27, the day before the bombs fell. The Islamabad talks opened on April 10. Whether they produce a durable framework remains to be seen.

Nothing in those developments alters the argument of this book. They confirm it. The framework that was available on February 24—zero stockpiling, full IAEA verification, irreversible down-blending—was on the table the morning before the first bomb fell. The decision to reject it, and the forty days of documented costs that followed, are the record this book preserves. The table in Islamabad is where the work should have begun. It is better to reach it late than not to reach it at all.

This book's core argument—about the pattern of negotiations used as cover for military action, the limits of what ground forces can achieve, and the cost paid by civilians who had no voice in these decisions—is unaltered by these developments. It is, if anything, more urgent.

--Massoud Amin
Minneapolis, Minnesota
April 2026

PART ONE: THE PLAGUE

The Moral Frame and the Record

The war that began on February 28, 2026, was not the beginning of a crisis. It was the culmination of specific choices made by specific people, in full view of a public record that contradicts their stated justifications. Part One establishes the moral framework and opens the documentary record.

Prologue: Worms' Meat

At 1:15 AM on February 28, 2026, I was in Minneapolis when the alerts began to come in on my phone. The first was from a journalist I had been following who covered Iran. Then a second, from a former student. Then a news notification: US Strikes Iran. B-2 Bombers. Supreme Leader. My hands did not shake, which surprised me. I had been expecting something like this for months. What I had not expected was the feeling that came next, which was not fear or anger but grief—the specific, exhausting grief of watching something you had hoped would not happen, happen anyway. I sat at my desk in the dark and watched the missile trails draw white arcs across the night sky of Tehran on my screen. I was born in that city's orbit. I left when I was seventeen. It has never fully left me.

By the afternoon, Iran's state media confirmed what Israeli officials had already told reporters: Ayatollah Ali Khamenei, Supreme Leader of the Islamic Republic of Iran, who had held that position since 1989, was dead. Forty Iranian officials were also killed. Hundreds of missile sites were struck. The Strait of Hormuz was in chaos.

The world held its breath.

In Iran, the people who had been in the streets since December 28, 2025—driven there by economic collapse that, as Treasury Secretary Scott Bessent testified under Senate oath, had been deliberately engineered—now faced a terrible new kind of uncertainty. The country they were protesting in was under attack from the sky. The power that had always claimed to be their liberator was now dropping bombs on their cities. A girls' elementary school in Minab was struck. Schoolchildren were among the dead. The people of Iran were simultaneously targets of American economic warfare, caught in the violence of their own protest movement, and now caught beneath American and Israeli bombs. They had not asked for any of this. They had asked for a working economy and the ability to live in dignity.

I thought of Mercutio.

Shakespeare's dying swordsman does not curse one house more than the other. He makes a diagnosis: both houses have made him their instrument, and now both houses have made him their victim. "They have made worms' meat of me." The line is not a policy prescription. It is a moral accounting—the recognition that when power becomes a feud, when factions care more about defeating each other than about the people caught between them, the innocent pay the price.

That is precisely what has happened in Iran for more than a century. The Iranian people have been, again and again, the worms' meat ground between competing houses: the house of closed governance that has ruled them through fear and ideology, and the house of foreign power that intervenes in their affairs with the confidence of those who have always believed they know better. Both houses have claimed to love Iran. Both houses have, in the end, sacrificed Iranians to their own agendas.

I thought of the Persian word for what had happened: *tārājdi* (from tārāj, Persian: تاراج) which refers to plunder, pillage, devastation, or looting—the stripping of what belongs to others. The word carries more weight in Persian than in English. It is not merely theft. It is the act of those who believe that what they want is already theirs by right.[2]

2 See Appendix: Poems of Witness, "The Weight of Ash"

Chapter 1: The Architecture of a War – Method, Stance, and What Follows

One month earlier, in January 2026, between 3,000 and 36,000 Iranians died during the protest movement that swept all thirty-one provinces. Young people—students, nurses, engineers, teenagers who had grown up their whole lives inside Iran and decided, finally, that they would no longer accept the status quo—went into the streets. The economic conditions that put them there had been deliberately engineered. Scott Bessent, the United States Secretary of the Treasury, said so under oath: “President Trump ordered the Treasury to put maximum pressure on Iran, and it’s worked... their economy collapsed... hence we have seen the Iranian people out on the street.” The people in those streets did not know they were fulfilling a strategy designed in Washington. They knew only that they could not feed their families.

The range is not a failure of counting. It reflects what an information blackout does to the death toll. The lower figure represents cases documented by name by the Human Rights Activists News Agency (HRANA); the upper figure incorporates a statistical projection methodology that accounts for unverifiable deaths during communications shutdowns. Iran Human Rights (IHRNGO) documented at least 3,428 killed as of January 14, 2026. The range is the record of circumstances that made accurate counting impossible.

One month later, on February 28, the United States government and the Israeli government dropped bombs on Iran. One hundred and sixty-eight girls and fourteen teachers were killed when a strike hit the Shajareh Tayyebeh elementary school in Minab. They had nothing to do with the nuclear program or the geopolitical calculations being made seven thousand miles away in Washington and Tel Aviv. They were in school. They bled real blood. They died in the rubble of a building that had been standing that morning.

Simultaneously, in Minneapolis—the city where I have lived and worked for decades— federal agents were conducting what witnesses and local officials described as mass arrests in neighborhoods where immigrant families had lived for years. People were pulled from their cars at traffic stops, taken from workplaces, and separated from children who were American citizens. The administration called it enforcement. The families called it terror. The mechanism—armed agents of the state removing people from their communities by force, without meaningful due process, on the basis of their identity rather than individual adjudicated guilt—was recognizable to anyone who had lived under the Islamic Republic.

These are not different stories. They are one story about what happens when power stops answering to the people it governs and starts treating those people as a resource to be managed, a threat to be eliminated, or a population to be bombed into compliance. The architects of these operations occupy the same offices. Some of them are the same people.

★★★

The objective of Netanyahu and the hardline bloc in Israel was regime change in Iran—breaking Iran up. This has been consistent and deliberate. Netanyahu speaks of destiny and mandate in the same breath--messianic language that frames military action not as a reluctant last resort but as a historical calling. They found a willing ally in Trump to carry it out.

He withdrew from the JCPOA in 2018, imposed maximum pressure sanctions, and, after direct strikes on Iranian targets, urged Iran's leaders to stand down while warning of further force.

The evidence does not support the claim that these negotiations were conducted in good faith.

Trump and Netanyahu call it "pre-emptive." They say the strikes were necessary to prevent a war. It is the war they just started. Pre-emption requires evidence of imminent threat. That standard is central to the legal and strategic debate.

Congress did not issue a specific authorization for these strikes. Under Article I of the Constitution, war-making authority rests with Congress. Presidents rely on Article II powers for limited military action. Whether this action is lawful is disputed and will be tested politically and legally.

The result is renewed military confrontation across the Middle East. The risk now is escalation. Maritime routes in the Gulf become exposed. Energy markets react. Miscalculation becomes more likely.

Diplomatic options narrow. The path to a negotiated solution grows dimmer. It moves us into a civilizational war. The outcome may even be the fragmentation of Iran, as happened in Sudan, Syria, Somalia, and Libya.

The risks have risen. No one controls what comes next. The future is uncertain. We wait.

★★★

This is not only about protecting life, though that is the first duty. The objectives are concrete:

Stop a regional war before it spreads. Stop escalation before it becomes irreversible. Prevent the collapse of a major state into militia rule and fragmentation. Protect global energy routes and food supply chains that affect billions of people. Preserve constitutional order at home. Keep diplomacy alive so escalation can still be contained.

Those are the stakes.

Iran is not Libya. It is a country of nearly 90 million people, with hardened facilities, proxy networks, missile capacity, and geographic depth. If the state fractures, there will be no clean transition. There will be armed factions, outside intervention, refugee flows, and prolonged instability across the Gulf, Iraq, Syria, and Lebanon.

The Strait of Hormuz carries roughly one-fifth of the global oil supply. Even partial disruptions shock energy markets. Fuel and food prices rise. Fragile economies absorb the first blow. Political instability follows.

What follows is not a lament. It is a record of what the evidence shows works, and what it shows does not. The response I believe is necessary runs along six lines. First, an immediate mutual halt to further strikes— made public and enforced through existing military channels—to create the breathing room that no other step can provide. Second, the restoration of continuous nuclear monitoring: inspectors and data. Verification is the only instrument that has ever constrained Iran's nuclear program reliably; airstrikes have never been an effective substitution, and the evidence that they cannot is now conclusive. Third, Congress must debate and vote on authorization. War cannot proceed on executive decisions alone. Constitutional clarity is not a procedural formality—it is what separates a democracy from a government that makes war in the dark. Fourth, expanded coordination in the Gulf, including direct crisis hotlines between military commands, to reduce the risk that a misread signal or a commander's miscalculation triggers an escalation no one authorized. Fifth, defined and limited objectives, with no open-ended mission and no language of destiny or historical calling—a discipline of scope is the only thing that can prevent a military operation from turning into a generational entanglement.

Sixth, results judged by concrete outcomes: no widening conflict, no accelerated weaponization, open sea lanes, stabilized energy markets, and sustained diplomatic contact with every party that influences what comes next.

Escalation is fast. Control requires structure. Three weeks into this war, preventing a strategic shock from becoming a generational fracture is still possible. The window will not stay open.

★★★

Since February 28, I have watched the United States, the country I call home, strike Iran, the country where I was born and raised, at the behest and with the support of Israel.

I left for high school in New York in August 1978 as the revolution gathered force. I thought I would return, but instead, decades passed.

The state monitored daily life closely since the creation of SAVAK in 1957, with the help of the CIA and Israeli intelligence agency Mossad. More recently, citizens were not able to purchase a SIM card without a national identification card; financial transactions, medical care, and travel all required documentation. The system left little room for anonymity.

Ayatollah Ali Khamenei shaped Iran's direction for more than three decades. His government suppressed dissent. Many Iranians paid a high price. Few will separate their grief from their judgment.

Now the question is simple. What comes next?

The removal of Iran's senior leadership did not follow a conventional legal process. Iran has supported armed groups across the region. At the same time, the United States did not publicly present evidence of an imminent attack. Though Iranians—and outsiders—may meet news of Ayatollah Khamenei's death with celebration, does the end justify the means?

Leadership vacuums rarely stay empty. Inside Iran, reformist and hard-line factions will compete for authority, including over the

Revolutionary Guard. Outside the country, some will argue for the return of the former monarchy under Reza Pahlavi.

Economics will shape behavior as much as ideology. Iran holds major oil and gas reserves. The Strait of Hormuz remains a strategic artery for global energy flows.

History leaves a pattern. Iranians seek agency over their economy and daily life. Foreign intervention—from the early twentieth century through the 1953 overthrow of Dr. Mohammad Mossaddegh, planned by the CIA and British Intelligence—has deeply impacted the psyche of Iranians. Trust in outside powers does not come easily.

My hope is restrained but real. The people of Iran, at home and across the diaspora, deserve stability, dignity, and peace.

After the "regime change" wars in Iraq and Afghanistan, are those countries any better, and are the countries around them any safer? One would have thought that we had learned the lesson.

I am a systems scientist. I study how complex systems fail. I have spent more than forty years applying the tools of systems analysis to power grids, financial markets, and critical infrastructure, to the question of how a system that appears stable can collapse catastrophically when its warning signals are ignored, and its feedback loops are broken. The postwar economic architecture I describe in this book is not a metaphor. It is a systems failure with specific, identifiable mechanisms, and it is susceptible to specific, identifiable interventions—interventions that would eventually prevent deadly consequences for real people who bleed real blood.

But I am also a human being who was born in Iran, who left as a teenager, who has carried Iran inside him for forty-seven years, the way you carry a scarred wound. When I see what is happening to Iran—the bombs, the blackout, the children in the rubble—I am not processing it as data. I am processing it as grief. When I see what is happening in Minneapolis, I am not processing it as a policy question. I am processing it as recognition: I have seen this before. I know what this is. I know where it goes.

Here is the contract I offer the reader: a documented record of what produced this war: the CIA coup of 1953 that ended Iran's democratic government; the Shah's surveillance state built with American and Israeli assistance; the Iran-Iraq War that the United States enabled and prolonged with intelligence and chemical weapons precursors; thirty years of sanctions designed not to produce diplomacy but to inflict economic pain; and finally, the deliberate economic warfare that Scott Bessent described proudly under Senate oath. That chain of American decisions is documented here. It is the chain that led to the protests of December 2025, the diplomatic breakthrough that was bombed out of existence, and the deaths of more than 168 people—schoolchildren, teachers, and parents—at the Shajareh Tayyebeh school in Minab. The record is complete enough. It requires no embellishment.

And this record will not pretend that the bombs of February 28 were not also catastrophic in their human cost. The United States struck Iran while diplomatic negotiations were producing a breakthrough. It did so without congressional authorization. It did so based on an intelligence assessment that did not support the stated legal rationale. It killed civilians, including one hundred and eighty children. The legal case against the strikes is documented and serious. The moral case has been stated clearly by international law scholars, former diplomats, and members of Congress. The girls of Minab did not die so that anyone could be safer. They died because powerful men had a choice that was available to them, and they made it.

Two different systems of power. Two different governments. Two different ideologies. The same structure: power treating people as expendable weight in the service of its own continuation and expansion. A plague on both your houses. That is what Mercutio says when he is dying, stabbed in a fight he did not start, between two families whose feud was never his to inherit. It is what the people of Iran have been saying, in one form or another, for more than a century. It is what I am saying now.

The hypocrisy that animates this argument is specific. It is not the hypocrisy of a country that says one thing and does another—that is ordinary politics, predictable and almost forgivable. It is the hypocrisy of a country that condemns the Iranian government for killing protesters in January, then drops bombs in February that kill children in schools, and calls the first act a crime against humanity and the second act a defensive necessity. It is the hypocrisy of a government that uses the language of liberation to describe an action that was planned before the liberation of the Iranian people was ever a realistic outcome, and that will produce consequences—chaos, a failed state, nuclear breakout, regional conflagration—that make the liberation of the Iranian people less likely, not more.

Arguments need faces. Numbers need blood. Taha Safari needs to be named, not just counted. The girls of Minab need to be seen, not just tallied.

The people who will pay for what happens next are not the people who made these decisions. They are the people who had no choice. They are always the people who have no choice.

Chapter 2: The Contradictions – What They Said, and What the Record Shows

The most direct statement of the administration's reasoning came from Secretary of State Marco Rubio on March 2, 2026, speaking to reporters on Capitol Hill before a closed-door briefing with congressional leaders. His explanation, drawn from the official State Department transcript, deserves to be read carefully, because it is an example of circular reasoning as remarkable as any produced by a senior American official in recent memory.

Rubio's definition of the "imminent threat" that legally justifies preemptive war under both US constitutional law and the UN Charter:"There absolutely was an imminent threat, and the imminent threat was that we knew that if Iran was attacked—and we believed they would be attacked—that they would immediately come after us."

Let us parse this with care. The United States struck Iran to prevent an attack by Iran. The attack Iran was going to launch was in retaliation for an Israeli strike. The Israeli strike had not yet happened. The Iranian retaliation was therefore a response to a hypothetical action that had not occurred. The United States, in other words, struck Iran to prevent Iran from retaliating against the United States for an Israeli attack that Israel had not yet carried out.

This is not preemption in any legal or strategic sense that the term has ever carried. The logic reduces to this: three people standing in a room. One of them (US) hits a second one (Iran), then says: "I knew the one next to you (Israel) was going to hit you, and I knew that you were going to hit me in retaliation. So I hit you first."

Senate Minority Leader Chuck Schumer, who attended the briefing, was direct in his assessment: "I found their answers completely and totally insufficient. That briefing raised many more questions than it answered." Rep. Jim Himes, the top Democrat on the House Intelligence Committee, said based on administration briefings that the operation amounted to "a war of choice with no strategic endgame."

The fallacies and contradictions do not end with Rubio. They constitute a pattern throughout the administration's senior leadership in the days immediately following the strikes. The record is worth preserving because records are how accountability becomes possible.

On the question of regime change:

"This is not a so-called regime change war. But the regime sure did change. And the world is better off for it today."

—Defense Secretary Pete Hegseth, Pentagon press conference, March 2, 2026

"We are not at war with Iran. We're at war with Iran's nuclear program."

—Vice President JD Vance, Fox News interview, March 2, 2026

"We would not be heartbroken, and we hope that the Iranian people can overthrow this government and establish a new future for that country."

—Secretary Rubio, March 2, 2026

Three officials. Three different answers to the question on the same day.

On who started the war:

"We didn't start this war, but under President Trump, we are finishing it."

—Hegseth, March 2, 2026

This claim was stated as self-evident. No evidence was offered. Iran had not struck the United States in the hours or days before the Operation Epic Fury strikes began. The Pentagon's own briefings, as reported by multiple news organizations, confirmed there was no intelligence indicating Iran was planning a first strike on US forces. Rubio himself, in the same Capitol Hill appearance, acknowledged the precipitating factor was not an Iranian attack on America but anticipated Israeli military action: "We knew that there was going to be an Israeli action. We knew that that would precipitate an attack against American forces."

On the duration and endgame:

"There's just no way that Donald Trump is going to allow this country to get into a multiyear conflict with no clear end in sight."

—Vice President Vance, February 27, 2026, three days before strikes began

"Four weeks, two weeks, six weeks—it could move up, it could move back. The president has all the latitude in the world."

—Hegseth, on Trump's own four-to-five week estimate, March 2, 2026

"We will do this as long as it takes to achieve those objectives."

—Rubio, same briefing

There is something here that transcends ordinary inconsistency. General Dan Caine, Chairman of the Joint Chiefs of Staff, was the most honest voice in the room: "The military objective in Iran will be difficult to achieve and, in some cases, will be difficult and gritty work. We expect to take additional losses." He said this on the same day Hegseth said the mission was "clear, devastating, decisive."

On Iran's post-strike leadership and what comes next:

"I have three very good choices for who could lead Iran."

—Donald Trump, interview with The New York Times, *March 1, 2026*

"The attack was so successful that it knocked out most of the candidates. It's not going to be anybody that we were thinking of because they are all dead. Second or third place is dead."

—Trump, interview with Jonathan Karl of ABC News, *hours later, March 1, 2026*

In the span of a few hours, the president moved from "I have three very good choices" to "they are all dead." This is not a rhetorical inconsistency. It is a confession that the operation was conducted without a plan for what came after—and that the plan that existed was destroyed by its own success.

On whether Iran's nuclear program had already been destroyed:

"Iran's nuclear facilities have been completely and totally obliterated."

—Trump, after Operation Midnight Hammer, June 2025

"[Iran is] a week away from the bomb."

—US envoy Steve Witkoff, in the weeks before Operation Epic Fury, early 2026

The same program that was "completely and totally obliterated" seven months earlier was now, apparently, days from producing a weapon. The White House had, at the time of the June 2025 strikes, put out a memo saying any claims the facilities were obliterated were "fake news." The phrase had been the president's own.

An unclassified Defense Intelligence Agency assessment circulated in late 2025 estimated that Iran was still a decade away from being able to strike the US mainland with an intercontinental ballistic missile. This assessment, reported by CNN and others, contradicted the administration's public claims of imminent existential threat.

★★★

And then there is Netanyahu.

Israeli Prime Minister Benjamin Netanyahu, speaking from the roof of the Kirya defense headquarters in Tel Aviv on March 1, 2026, provided what may be the most honest statement of the entire operation's origins. He was addressing the nation about the joint US-Israeli strikes that had killed the Iranian Supreme Leader: "This coalition of forces allows us to do what I have yearned to do for forty years: smite the terror regime hip and thigh. This is what I promised—and this is what we shall do."

Forty years. Not forty days. Not a response to a specific threat that had recently emerged. Forty years of wanting to strike Iran, now made possible by the arrival of an American president who shared the appetite for the strike and did not require the legal justification that previous American presidents, of both parties, had.

On the same day, Netanyahu told his nation: "This coalition of forces allows us to do what I have yearned to do for forty years—bringing to this campaign the assistance of the United States, my friend, US President Donald Trump, and the US military."

Trump's tone when discussing the strike was similarly candid: "I got him before he got me. I got him first." This was his explanation for the killing of the Iranian Supreme Leader. The phrasing is that of a street confrontation, not a constitutional deliberation.

The record, read together, is one of a war launched without legal authorization, justified by a circular definition of "imminent threat" that would justify a preemptive strike on any country that any ally of ours might one day attack, predicated on the personal ambition of one leader and the impulsiveness of another, and carried out without a plan for what comes next.

PART TWO:
A CENTURY OF STRUGGLE
Iran's Democratic Tradition and Its Adversaries

To understand what was destroyed on February 28, 2026, one must understand what Iran built and what was built against it. A century of Iranian democratic aspirations had been thwarted by colonialism, by a CIA-backed coup in 1953, by a surveillance apparatus funded and trained by foreign powers, and by the impact of a devastating eight-year war that left a generation of young men in the ground.

Chapter 3: Understanding Iran – What Every Western Reader Needs to Know

Iran may fall silent, but it does not forget. —Persian proverb

Understanding what is happening to Iran today requires first understanding what Iran is. Before the politics, before the wars and the nuclear agreements and the sanctions and the regime changes, what we now call Iran is a civilization. That civilization is 2,700 years old. It produced Hafez and Rumi. It built Persepolis. It gave the world the first declaration of human rights, the Cyrus Cylinder, inscribed in 539 BCE, centuries before Athens was a democracy. In 539 BCE, Cyrus the Great entered Babylon and did something no conqueror in recorded history had done before. He freed the enslaved people. He declared that every person could worship their own gods. He sent the Jewish people home to Jerusalem, ending their captivity, and funded the rebuilding of their Temple. The Hebrew Bible honors him by name. Isaiah calls him the Lord's anointed one. The Jewish people carried the memory of what Persia did for them across twenty-five centuries. Many Israelis and members of the Jewish community still speak of this bond with genuine feeling. It is ancient, real, and documented in scripture as sacred to both peoples. That bond between Persian and Jewish civilization is not a footnote. It is foundational.

In the same vein, people across India and Pakistan respond viscerally to what they see as aggression against Iran. The reason is not geopolitics. It is memory.

For centuries before British colonization reshaped the subcontinent, Persian was not a foreign language in South Asia. It was the language of courts, scholarship, poetry, and administration across the region. This was not confined to Muslim elites. Hindu scholars studied it, taught it, and wrote in it. The Mughal emperors—whose rise was intertwined with Safavid Iran—presided over a civilization that was as much Persianate as it was Indian. Culture, architecture, music, and intellectual life flowed across borders that did not yet exist as we know them today.

These connections did not evaporate. They settled into families, names, and traditions. Lineages carrying names like Shirazi, Khorasani, and Mashhadi trace routes from Iran and Central Asia into the subcontinent across generations. Sayyed families—including my own—carry histories that move from Iraq through Iran and into South Asia, bearing intellectual and spiritual traditions that remain alive. Nowruz is still celebrated. The poetry of Hafez and Rumi is still recited. The roots did not die. They went underground and kept growing.

When the power grid of Iran is targeted, when its cities are struck, when its people are threatened, the response across South Asia is not simply solidarity with a neighboring state. It is something closer to watching a part of yourself being destroyed—a civilization that shaped your language, your family, your sense of beauty and meaning, reduced to a target.

What is being bombed is not simply a government. For hundreds of millions of people, it is a piece of their own inheritance.

Western audiences are not well served by the language used most often by the Western media: "the axis of evil," "state sponsor of terrorism," "rogue state." These labels flatten a complex civilization into a threat profile, and in doing so, obscure more than they illuminate. What follows is an attempt at the context such labels obscure.

Shia Islam: The Faith of a Minority

To understand Iran, it's necessary to first understand that Shia Muslims are a minority within Islam—roughly 15 percent of the world's 1.9 billion Muslims. Sunni Islam is the tradition of the overwhelming majority, dominant across the Arab world, South Asia, and sub-Saharan Africa. Shia Islam, which holds that legitimate authority after the Prophet Muhammad was passed onto his cousin and son-in-law Ali and his descendants, has always been a tradition defined in part by its members' experience of marginalization, persecution, and principled resistance to illegitimate power.

The founding traumatic event of Shia history is the Battle of Karbala in 680 CE—when Hussain ibn Ali, the Prophet's grandson, refused to pledge allegiance to the caliph Yazid, whom he considered corrupt and illegitimate. Hussain and his small band of followers were slaughtered on the plains of Karbala in what is now Iraq. That moment of choosing martyrdom over submission to unjust power became the central moral template of Shia identity. Every year, on Ashura, Shia Muslims around the world mourn Hussain's death—but more than mourning, they ask themselves the question Hussain asked: when faced with injustice, do you submit, or do you stand?

This theological inheritance matters enormously for how Iranians experience the current war. When bombs fall on Tehran, the Shia framework does not produce capitulation—it produces the memory of Karbala. The scholar Michael Fischer, who studied this tradition for decades, described it as a "paradigm" that activates whenever a minority community faces overwhelming force from an unjust power. You are not being defeated. You are being tested. And history, in the Shia reckoning, ultimately vindicates the righteous.

This is not, it should be emphasized, a theology of suicide or nihilism. It is a theology of endurance. The scholar Ghaleb Cachalia has noted that the Karbala Paradigm produces not suicidal behavior but resilience; it produces a people who are psychologically prepared for prolonged confrontation, who understand themselves to be on the right side of history even when they are on the losing side of a battle. This is something Western military planners consistently fail to incorporate into their assessments of "what it will take to win."

This past exploitation is real and has consequences for how ordinary Iranians relate to religious authority. But the theology underlying its political use is genuine, ancient, and not going away just because a particular government does.

A Secular Soul in a Clerical State

Here is something that surprises most Western audiences: Iran is not, at its cultural core, a particularly religious country. Survey data consistently show that Iranians are among the least religiously observant Muslim-majority populations in the world. A major survey conducted by the Group for Analyzing and Measuring Attitudes in Iran (GAMAAN) found that only 32 percent of respondents identified as Muslim when given the full range of options—a striking figure given that the state mandates Islamic practice and punishes deviation from it. Mosque attendance is low. Fasting during Ramadan is widely observed as a cultural practice but not universally as a religious duty.

What Iranians hold in high regard is not religious observance but something closer to a Persian moral code: education, intellectual refinement, hospitality, poetry, and a concept of dignity—or *sharm* (shame, in the positive sense of honor-consciousness)—that governs behavior more reliably than mosque attendance. The classical poets—Hafez, Sa'di, Ferdowsi, Rumi—are not museum pieces in Iran. They are living presences. Hafez is consulted for divination. Rumi's verses are read at weddings and funerals. Persian classical poetry contains more verses about wine, love, and clerical hypocrisy than about religious observance.

The government that rules Iran is therefore governing—and has always been governing—a population that is largely secular in its actual orientation, even if it uses Islamic vocabulary to frame moral life. The Woman, Life, Freedom movement that erupted after Mahsa Amini's death in 2022 was not anti-Islamic. It was anti-compulsion. Iranian women were not saying they rejected their faith. They were saying they rejected the state's right to enforce its rules on their bodies.

This matters for understanding what kind of Iran might emerge from the current crisis. The idea, sometimes floated in Western policy circles, that Iran needs to be "secularized" by outside force misunderstands the situation entirely. Iranian society is already largely secular in practice. What it needs is not a transformation of its values but an end to a government that criminalizes the values it already holds. That is a very different problem, and it requires a very different solution.

The Interior Civilization: What the State Could Not Reach

There is an Iran that does not appear in news reports, sanctions designations, or Western policy analysis, because it does not announce itself. It exists behind closed doors, in private homes, in the spaces the state cannot fully enter. To understand the people being bombed in March 2026, a Western reader must understand this interior civilization—not as sentiment, but as political fact.

The dinner party in Tehran, was a subversive act during any decade of the Islamic Republic. Behind closed doors, wine appeared. Banned music played. Women removed their headscarves. Conversations that could not be had in the street—about politics, about religion, about love, about the state's claims of owning your body—were had freely. This was not a mere social convention. It was a form of civil resistance, sustained across forty-seven years, that kept alive the values the state was trying to extinguish.

Literary culture went underground and flourished there. After 1979, the Islamic Republic banned thousands of books—Western novels, Persian poetry deemed insufficiently Islamic, anything that depicted the life Iranians actually lived. The response was not compliance. Iranians built an informal circulation network of samizdat quality: photocopied novels, passed-around cassette tapes of forbidden music, and hand-to-hand lending of books that could not be sold openly. In the 1990s, when Azar Nafisi—then a professor of English literature at the University of Tehran—was forced to leave her university post for refusing to wear the veil, she gathered seven of the most gifted female students in her home for two years and ran a secret literature seminar. They read Nabokov, Fitzgerald, Henry James, and Austen—books whose preoccupation with individual consciousness, with the interior life, with the right to feel, choose, and become made them, by definition, political texts in a state that denied all three. Her account of those sessions, published in English as *Reading Lolita in Tehran*, became one of the most widely read books about Iran in the Western world—not because it described the government, but because it described the people the government was trying to erase.

The مشاعره (Moshaereh)—a poetry recitation game—is one of the oldest and most specifically Persian social technologies. At a dinner party, someone quotes the opening line of a Hafez ghazal. Someone else must supply the next line from memory. The game can last hours. It is competitive, joyful, and deeply serious: to play it fluently is to have internalized a thousand years of Persian civilization. The Islamic Republic could not ban Hafez—he is too central to Persian identity, and the attempt would have been politically catastrophic. But the government could not fully control what Hafez meant either. When Iranians quoted the great fourteenth-century poet's lines about wine, hypocrisy, and the corruption of those who claim to speak for God, they were saying something about the present that they could not say directly. Persian classical literature is encoded with a vocabulary of political dissent, and every educated Iranian knows how to read it.

The university, even under the Islamic Republic, remained a site of intellectual life that periodically escaped the state's control. After 1999, when Ansar-e Hezbollah paramilitaries suppressed student protests at the University of Tehran, the student movement did not disappear—it reorganized, went into the spaces between permitted and prohibited, and produced the generation that filled the streets in 2009 and 2022. The professors who lost their positions for political reasons often continued teaching informally, in homes and in reading groups, in the same interior civilization that has always been Iran's deepest form of resistance.

This matters for the argument I am making. One of the central claims here is that the people of Iran are not the government of Iran—that the civilization being bombed is not the government that governed it. That claim is easy to state and easy to dismiss as sentimental. The interior civilization makes it concrete. The seventeen-year-old in Tehran who woke to bombs on March 1, 2026, was not an abstraction. She had memorized Hafez. She had passed novels to her friends in brown paper. She had sat in her family's living room and heard conversations about Mosaddegh, the Constitutional Revolution, and what Iran could be. She was the product of an interior civilization that the Islamic Republic spent forty-seven years trying to extinguish, and that survived, intact, into the war that was supposed to liberate her.

The distinction between government and people is not a rhetorical convenience. It is a historical and cultural fact. The bombs of February 2026 could not distinguish between them.

What Iranians Actually Want—and Why the Answer Is Complicated

The secularization I've described has a political dimension that outside analysis has consistently underestimated—not because it is hidden, but because it does not fit the frames most readily available to Western readers.

Survey research using encrypted platforms—most extensively by GAMAAN, a Netherlands-based research foundation that has surveyed between 38,000 and over 100,000 respondents inside Iran across multiple studies—consistently finds that approximately 70 percent of Iranians oppose continuation of the Islamic Republic, and roughly 89 percent express support for democracy in the abstract. These are significant findings. But what those numbers conceal is as important as what they reveal.

There is no consensus on what should replace the current order. A secular republic drew approximately 26 percent of the vote. A constitutional monarchy draws about 21 percent. A federal structure—concentrating support in regions with Kurdish, Azeri Turk, and Baloch populations, where the relationship to the central state is itself contested—draws 15 percent of the vote nationally. Roughly 22 percent say they lack enough information to choose, and 11 percent say the form does not matter as long as change occurs. No single opposition figure commands majority support. Among named figures, the former crown prince Reza Pahlavi polls highest at approximately 31 percent—but his support falls below 20 percent in Kurdish and Azeri regions, and roughly a third of respondents strongly oppose him. The picture is one of shared opposition and divergent aspirations: a society that knows what it no longer accepts, but is still working out what it wants to build.

Recent data has significantly revised the religious picture. Survey evidence indicates that approximately half of Iranian respondents now identify with categories such as atheist, agnostic, none, belief in God without formal religion, or spiritual—a shift that goes considerably beyond the anti-compulsion position. This is not the same as privately maintaining faith while opposing state enforcement. It reflects a broader change in how a substantial portion of Iranians relate to religious identity itself, occurring under a governing system that still requires public compliance with religious law—the Western portrait of Iran as uniformly and devoutly Islamic has been substantially revised by this evidence.

The political picture carries its own complexity. Alongside the strong demand for democratic governance, approximately 43 percent of survey respondents expressed openness to rule by a strong executive leader—a preference not confined to supporters of the current system but also evident among some who favor alternative political arrangements. This does not contradict the demand for change. It reflects the diversity of a society that has lived for decades under centralized authority and carries that experience into its political imagination.

★★★

A note on the evidence: GAMAAN's surveys are conducted using encrypted VPN platforms, in collaboration with Psiphon, to protect respondents in a country ranked 153rd on the Economist Intelligence Unit's Democracy Index (2024). Critics from within the Iranian opposition argue that survey research under such conditions cannot yield fully valid results, and that the surveys underrepresent certain constituencies. GAMAAN's researchers have responded to these critiques in peer-reviewed publications and subjected their methodology to academic review at Utrecht University. The data cited here represents the best available evidence with acknowledged limitations—the confidence level is "well-supported but contested," not "settled."

Taken together, what the evidence supports is this: Iranian society is politically and ideologically diverse in ways that outsiders frequently miss. The shared opposition to the current order is real. What a post-transition Iran might look like—its structure, its institutions, its relationship to religion and to its ethnic minorities—remains genuinely open. That openness is not weakness. It is what a society preparing to determine its own future actually looks like. It is the opposite of a closed and exhausted political culture.

★★★

These survey-level observations have geographic and ethnic dimensions that the aggregate numbers obscure. Kurdish cities—Mahabad, Sanandaj, and others—were among the first to erupt in protest during both the 2022 and 2025–26 uprisings and faced severe crackdowns; Balochistan's death tolls were among the highest recorded. Support for federalism is highest in Kurdistan, West Azerbaijan, and Sistan and Baluchestan—regions with distinct cultural and linguistic identities where historical grievances against the central state run deep. The current war has added another layer: airstrikes on military sites near Kurdish regions have damaged civilian infrastructure, and some minority communities question whether those who advocate most loudly for the bombing from abroad have weighed their losses. An inclusive post-transition Iran will need to address these tensions through dialogue, constitutional guarantees, and genuine power-sharing—not through narratives that treat the Persian center as synonymous with Iran as a whole.

Persian Time: A Civilization That Thinks in Millennia

Iran uses the Solar Hijri calendar. The year, as I write this, is 1404. Not 2026—though Iranians are fully aware of the Gregorian date—but 1404 in their own reckoning of time, a calendar that traces its new year back to the spring equinox and its epoch back to the migration of the Prophet. What this means is not merely a different date. It reflects a different relationship to time itself.

Iranians locate themselves in a civilizational narrative that stretches back twenty-seven centuries. Cyrus the Great's Achaemenid Empire, the Sasanian Empire, the poets of the Islamic Golden Age, the Safavid dynasty that consolidated Shia Islam as the state religion in the sixteenth century—these are not distant history. They are living reference points. When an Iranian says, "We are an ancient people," they are not being boastful. They are situating themselves in a temporal frame that makes the current crisis—however catastrophic—one chapter in a very long story.

That story includes three catastrophic conquests, each of which would have ended a less resilient civilization. Alexander the Great's Macedonian armies swept through Persia in 330 BCE, burning Persepolis—the ceremonial capital of the Achaemenid Empire and one of the architectural wonders of the ancient world—to the ground. The Arab armies of the seventh century CE brought Islam and a new language of power, threatening to dissolve Persian identity entirely into the Arab Islamic world. The Mongol invasions of the thirteenth century were among the most destructive events in human history: the Mongol sack of Baghdad in 1258 ended the Abbasid Caliphate, and cities across the Iranian plateau were reduced to rubble, their populations massacred.

Persian civilization survived all three. Not primarily through military resistance—it could not win those battles—but through the interior life: through language, poetry, and the stubborn persistence of a distinct cultural identity that proved impervious to conquest. After the Arab conquest, Persian did not disappear. It absorbed Arabic vocabulary and emerged as a literary language of extraordinary power—the medium of Rumi, Hafez, Sa'di, and Ferdowsi, poets whose work spread across the Islamic world and beyond. After the Mongol destruction, Persian civilization reconstituted itself so thoroughly that, within two generations, the Mongol rulers of Iran became patrons of Persian art, literature, and architecture. The conquerors were absorbed by what they had conquered.

This pattern—survival through cultural persistence rather than military victory—is not incidental to the current crisis. It is the template through which educated Iranians understand it. Western military planners, who measure success by targets destroyed and command structures eliminated, are operating within a framework that Persian history consistently rejects. You can burn Persepolis. The civilization that built it will still be there in three hundred years, writing poetry about your hubris.

Nowruz: The Year That Refuses to End

On the spring equinox—around March 20 or 21 of each year—Iranians celebrate Nowruz, the Persian New Year. The celebration predates Islam by more than a thousand years. It is the oldest continuously observed New Year's celebration in recorded human history. The government tried, in the years immediately after 1979, to replace it with an Islamic holiday that did not exist. The attempt failed. Nowruz was too old, too deep, and too loved. The authorities eventually gave up and declared the holiday officially recognized. However, the festival has always existed in some tension with a state with Zoroastrian roots, whose rituals are pre-Islamic, and whose central symbol—the Haft-sin table, spread with seven items whose names begin with the Persian letter *sin*—speaks of abundance, renewal, and the persistence of life without reference to any mosque.

The Haft-sin table holds, among its seven items: *sabzeh*, the green sprouts of wheat or lentil grown at home for two weeks before the new year, representing rebirth; *sib*, the apple, representing health and beauty; and *somāq*, the sumac spice, representing the color of sunrise. At the center of the table, many families place a mirror to reflect the light and a bowl of goldfish, swimming. The goldfish are released into a river or pond on the thirteenth day. The number thirteen is unlucky; you must be outdoors and in nature when it arrives. Then the fish are free.

The bombs of Operation Epic Fury fell on February 28, 2026—twenty days before Nowruz. The Iranian people were preparing for the New Year when the war began. In homes across Tehran, Isfahan, Tabriz, and Mashhad, the *sabzeh* were already growing in their bowls on windowsills. The green shoots had been planted by families who expected to welcome spring. In the rubble photographs that emerged in the days after the strikes, you could sometimes see them: the green sprouts, still growing, in homes that had been broken open.

Nowruz arrived on schedule. It always does. The year 1404 began on March 20, 2026, nineteen days into a war. In the cities and towns that had not been struck, families gathered. The Haft-sin tables were spread, if more quietly than usual. The fish were purchased at higher prices. The *sabzeh* had been grown from seeds planted in the weeks before the bombs, because families plant them weeks in advance and had not known not to. The new year came, as the new year comes, regardless of what governments decide.

That persistence is not sentiment. It is data about a civilization. People who have been observing the same new year for three thousand years are not going to be transformed by a military operation, however well-designed, into something they have never been. The green shoots on the windowsill in the rubble photograph are not a metaphor. They are an accurate description of what endures.

Ferdowsi's شاهنامه (*Shahnameh*)—the Book of Kings, the national epic of Iran—was written in the eleventh century CE specifically to preserve Persian language and identity after centuries of Arabic linguistic dominance. It is a sixty thousand verse assertion that Persian civilization would not be absorbed into the Arab-Islamic world. Ferdowsi spent thirty years writing it, and by the end, his patron had died, and the promised reward was never paid in full. He finished it anyway. The *Shahnameh* is not a literary curiosity. It is a text of civilizational resistance, and Iranians learn it as such.

Within this long story, the Arab conquest of the seventh century CE occupies a complicated place. Islam came to Persia through

Arab armies, and while Iranians adopted and profoundly shaped the Islamic tradition—Rumi, Avicenna, Al-Ghazali, and most of the great figures of the Islamic Golden Age were Persian—the Arab conquest is remembered as an invasion. The Persian word for it is *tazi*, which carries connotations of both Arab identity and the violence of conquest. This civilizational self-understanding means that Iranians do not identify as Arab, and deeply resent being categorized alongside Arab countries in Western discourse. When American politicians say "the Middle East," Iranians hear a category that groups them with societies they consider culturally distinct.

The tribal social structures that characterize some parts of the Arab world—and that have made democratic transition so difficult in Libya, Iraq, Yemen, and Syria—are largely absent in Iran. Iranian society is organized around a different set of institutions: the bazaar, the university, the extended family, the mosque (used more as a community center than as a site of tribal power), and the poetry recitation circle—the مشاعره (Moshaereh).

It also means that Iranians have a long memory for such interventions. The 1953 CIA-assisted coup that overthrew Prime Minister Mohammad Mosaddegh is not ancient history to the Iranians who lived it or who were shaped by those who did. It is taught in schools, discussed in families, and present in the political imagination as the foundational modern example of foreign powers deciding that Iranian democracy was less important than their own interests. Every subsequent intervention—every sanction, every threat, every bomb—is processed through the lens of that memory.

Iran's Thwarted Democracies

It is a fact little known in the West that Iran has attempted democracy three times, and three times those attempts were ended by external interference or an internal reaction to it. The first attempt was the Constitutional Revolution of 1905–1911—one of the first constitutional revolutions in Asia or the Middle East, in which Iranian merchants, clergy, intellectuals, and reformers forced the Qajar Shah to accept a constitution and an elected parliament (Majlis). The revolution was extraordinary: it produced a functioning constitutional system, a free press, and the beginnings of civic society. It was ended by a combination of Russian military intervention in the north, British imperial maneuvering in the south, and the reinstated Qajar monarchy's reassertion of autocratic control. Iran had tried, and the great powers had decided that Iranian democracy was inconvenient.

The second attempt came under Prime Minister Mohammad Mosaddegh, who was elected in 1951. He immediately moved to nationalize the Anglo-Iranian Oil Company. This British corporation had been extracting Iranian oil since 1913 while paying Iran a royalty that averaged roughly 16 percent of profits, far below what the company earned elsewhere. Mosaddegh's nationalization was overwhelmingly popular inside Iran. It was seen as the reclamation of a sovereign right: that a country's natural resources belong to its people. It was seen in London and Washington as a threat to Western energy interests and, in the Cold War framing of the time, as a potential opening for Soviet influence. In 1953, the CIA and British intelligence organized a coup—Operation Ajax—that removed Mosaddegh from power, reinstated Mohammad Reza Shah, and imprisoned Iran's democratically elected leader. The United States has officially acknowledged this operation. It is not contested history.

The consequences of 1953 cannot be overstated. They echo through every subsequent Iranian political development. The Shah, restored to power by foreign intervention, could never thereafter be seen as a legitimate nationalist leader—he was a foreign implant. His government's reliance on American support for its security apparatus deepened this perception. When Iranians rose against the Shah in 1979, they were rising up not merely against his government but against a system of foreign control that had been installed over their heads in 1953. The revolution produced the Islamic Republic—an outcome that most of the revolution's participants did not intend or want—precisely because the 1953 coup had discredited the secular nationalist and liberal democratic alternatives. Ayatollah Khomeini filled a vacuum that American and British policy had helped create.

The third attempt came with the reform movement of the late 1990s and early 2000s, under President Mohammad Khatami, who won a landslide in 1997 on a platform of civil society, rule of law, and dialogue between civilizations. Khatami's movement was ended not by foreign intervention but by the internal structure of the Islamic Republic itself—the Guardian Council's power to veto legislation and disqualify candidates, the Supreme Leader's authority over the judiciary and security services, and, eventually, the hard-line backlash against the suppression of the 2009 Green Movement. But the failure of the reform movement was also conditioned by American policy: the Bush administration's inclusion of Iran in the "axis of evil" in 2002—coming just months after Iran had quietly cooperated with American forces in Afghanistan—devastated Iranian reformers who had argued that engagement with the West was possible. It handed the hard-liners exactly the evidence they needed to claim that America could not be trusted.

Three attempts. Three times thwarted. Each one leaves Iran more defensive, more suspicious, and more convinced that the outside world does not want Iran to govern itself freely. That conviction, whatever one thinks of the Islamic Republic, has significant evidentiary support.

The Pahlavi Question: Why Reza Pahlavi's Return Is Not an Answer

In the weeks since Operation Epic Fury began, the name Reza Pahlavi—the son of the last Shah, who lives in the United States and has positioned himself as a potential leader of a post-Islamic Republic Iran—has frequently circulated in Western media as a possible figurehead for Iran's transition. This framing deserves careful examination because it raises questions that Iranians themselves have not resolved and that outside powers cannot resolve for them.

Mohammad Reza Shah, who ruled until 1979, is remembered by Iranians not as a modernizer who was unfairly deposed, but as a ruler whose legitimacy was fatally compromised by his dependence on American support, whose security service (SAVAK, trained by the CIA and Mossad) imprisoned and tortured thousands of political opponents, and whose White Revolution modernization program—however economically significant—was imposed from above without democratic consent. The population did not mourn his departure in 1979. It was celebrated.

Reza Pahlavi, his son, has a limited constituency inside Iran. NPR reported from Los Angeles in March 2026 that while some in the Iranian diaspora celebrated the strikes, waving the pre-revolutionary Pahlavi-era flag, other Iranian Americans were "very skeptical about Pahlavi," noting that "he's not inclusive of other voices in the opposition and that he stands to gain personally if the country chooses a constitutional monarchy." Iranian public opinion surveys conducted before the blackouts consistently showed monarchist restoration as a minority preference inside Iran. The question of his role, if any, in a post-transition Iran is one that Iranians inside Iran—not diaspora advocates and not foreign governments—are the appropriate people to answer.

The Brookings Institution noted in its assessment of the strikes that, just as the Shah's departure in 1979 failed to fulfill the aspirations of the millions who rallied in the streets, it is highly uncertain that the US-Israeli operation will successfully produce a real transition to a different government. History in Iran has a long record of external interventions producing the opposite of their intended effects. An Iran whose post-Islamic Republic government is seen as a product of American military force will face a legitimacy crisis from its first day—regardless of who leads it.

What Iranians who oppose the Islamic Republic want is not a different patron. They want what the Constitutional Revolution of

1905 wanted, what Mosaddegh wanted, what the Green Movement wanted, and what the Women, Life, Freedom movement wanted: the right to govern themselves. That is an aspiration that external military force cannot deliver, and that is undermined rather than advanced by foreign imposition.

The Invasion as Seen from Tehran: Illegality and Its Costs

The United States and Israel launched Operation Epic Fury on February 28, 2026, without a declaration of war from the United States Congress, without authorization under the War Powers Resolution, without a United Nations Security Council resolution, and—critically—while nuclear negotiations were actively underway. Oman's Foreign Minister Badr Al Busaidi, who had been serving as mediator between Washington and Tehran, stated publicly that Iran had agreed to zero stockpiling of nuclear enrichment just days before the strikes. Iranian Foreign Minister Abbas Araghchi confirmed that both sides had left Geneva expecting to seal a deal at their next meeting and characterized the strikes as bombing "the negotiating table."

Norway's Foreign Minister called the strikes a violation of international law, stating that preventive attacks require an immediately imminent threat, and that no such threat had been established. The United Nations Secretary-General Antonio Guterres condemned the use of force. China's Foreign Minister Wang Yi called the attack "unacceptable" and condemned the killing of a sovereign leader and the incitement of regime change. France, Germany, and the United Kingdom, while declining to condemn the strikes outright, made clear that they had neither participated in nor been consulted on them.

The legal case against the strikes is straightforward. The UN Charter prohibits the use of force against a sovereign state except in self-defense against an armed attack or with Security Council authorization. No armed attack on the United States or Israel had occurred. No Security Council authorization was sought. Secretary of State Rubio's public justification—that the United States struck Iran preemptively to prevent Iran from retaliating against a future Israeli strike that had not yet occurred—was not a legal argument. It was a description of a war of choice dressed up in the vocabulary of self-defense. The circularity was noted by legal scholars, former diplomats, and members of Congress within hours of his statement.

From inside Iran, the invasion looks different from how it looks from Washington or Tel Aviv. It looks like Karbala. It looks like 1953. It looks like a civilization that, once again, has had its political future decided by outside powers who believe they know better. Whatever Iranians think of their government—and many, if not most, carry deep grievances against it—the bombs falling on their cities belong to a different category of experience than the failures of their own government. Both things can be true simultaneously: that the Islamic Republic failed its people in fundamental ways, and that the American-Israeli strikes were illegal, reckless, and are likely to produce consequences worse than the problem they purported to solve.

The Human Cost: A Reckoning

Numbers are the beginning of understanding, not the end. They do not capture the texture of a family running for shelter, the silence of a classroom after the children who sat in it are gone, the particular emotional weight of a father identifying a child from a photograph because there is no other way. But the numbers must be stated, because they are the most accessible measure of what has been done.

Within the first three days of Operation Epic Fury, the Iranian Red Crescent Society reported at least 787 people killed across Iran. The Human Rights Activists News Agency (HRANA), a US-based organization with a verified track record of documenting Iranian casualties, estimated 742 civilian deaths in the same period. Strikes targeted at least 131 cities across 24 of Iran's 31 provinces. The Israel

Defense Forces stated that their initial strikes used more than 1,200 munitions in 24 hours.

The deadliest single incident, as of this writing, was the strike on the Shajareh Tayyebeh girls' elementary school in Minab, in southern Iran's Hormozgan province. Iranian authorities reported 180 young children killed; 96 others were wounded. *The Washington Post* and *The New York Times* verified footage taken immediately after the strike. The Israeli military said it was not aware of strikes in the area. The US military said it was looking into the reports. Video circulating on social media showed a man clutching the remains of a child he said was six or seven years old. A sports hall in Lamerd was struck during a girls' practice session, killing at least 18 civilians. Gandhi Hospital in Tehran was damaged, and patients, including children, were evacuated. Emergency medical facilities in Hamadan and Sarab were struck.

These numbers will grow. They are already, as of this writing, incomplete. Iran's retaliatory strikes have killed and wounded people across the region: in Israel, in Bahrain, in Kuwait, in Iraq. Six American service members have been killed; more have been wounded. Lebanese civilians have been killed in renewed Israeli strikes responding to Hezbollah's entry into the conflict. The Jordanian armed forces reported intercepting 49 drones and ballistic missiles. The Dubai International Airport closed. Airlines canceled flights across the region. Schools shifted to remote learning.

Iran is not Gaza, and it is not Iraq. It has a population of 90 million, a more educated and urbanized society, a more cohesive national identity, and a geography that makes occupation or sustained ground operations impossible to contemplate. The scale of what a prolonged air campaign would mean for Iranian civilian infrastructure—for hospitals, for water treatment, for food supply, for the ordinary fabric of 90 million lives—has not been adequately reckoned with in the Western public discourse that has accompanied this war.

President Trump, on March 2, told CNN: "We haven't even started hitting them hard. The big wave hasn't even happened. The big one is coming soon." A Reuters/Ipsos poll conducted that same week found 27 percent of American respondents approved of the strikes, 43 percent disapproved, and 29 percent were unsure. The American people have not been asked, by their elected representatives, whether they consent to what is being done in their name.

Chapter 4: The Constitutional Idea (1905–1911)

To understand Iran in 2026, you must begin in 1905, in the shops and mosques of Tehran, in the revolutionary ferment that produced the Constitutional Revolution—the first democratic uprising in Asia, a moment when ordinary Iranians, merchants, clerics, intellectuals, and peasants declared together that power must answer to the people.

The trigger was small: in December 1905, the governor of Tehran ordered the bastinado—the beating of the soles of the feet—to be applied to sugar merchants accused of price gouging. The merchants took sanctuary in a mosque. Within weeks, the sanctuary movement had grown into a mass uprising demanding a constitution, a parliament, and limits on the absolute power of the Qajar shahs. By August 1906, Mozaffar ad-Din Shah had signed a royal decree establishing a constitutional monarchy. The first Majles—Iran's parliament—convened in October of that year.

It is worth pausing to consider exactly what this meant. At a time when most of Asia and the Middle East were still ruled by the divine right of kings or the authority of colonial powers, Iranians were debating constitutional theory, writing a framework for limited government, and establishing a parliament that included merchants, religious scholars, landowners, and artisans. The ideas they were grappling with—sovereignty of the people, rule of law, separation of powers—were the same ideas that had animated the American and French revolutions, now being adapted to Persian soil, Persian culture, and Persian conditions.

The constitutional text itself was a serious document. It drew on the Belgian constitution, the French constitutional model, and the accumulated work of Iranian legal scholars who had been studying Western governance frameworks for decades. The Supplementary Fundamental Laws of 1907 established freedom of the press, freedom of assembly, equality before the law, and the inviolability of property. A Senate was created alongside the Majles. Judicial independence was articulated as a principle. These were not borrowed decorations. They were the product of genuine Iranian intellectual engagement with the question of how a modern state should be organized. The revolutionaries knew what they were building.

The coalition that built it was itself remarkable. Bazaar merchants provided funding and organizational infrastructure. Several Shia clerics lent religious legitimacy to the constitutional demand, arguing that Islamic principles of justice required limits on tyranny and protection for the governed. Secular intellectuals who had studied in Europe brought in legal and philosophical frameworks. The poet and journalist Ali-Akbar Dehkhoda wrote satirical columns that were circulated widely, translating political abstractions into language ordinary people understood. The women of Tehran contributed money sewn into their garments when men could not move freely. It was, for its moment, a genuine national coalition.

The Constitutional Revolution did not succeed, however. Mohammad Ali Shah, who came to power in 1907, never accepted constitutional limits on his authority. In June 1908, under the command of a Russian officer leading Iranian-Cossack forces, an artillery unit shelled the Majles building in Tehran. The constitutionalists who had gathered there were arrested, executed, or scattered. The parliament was dissolved. Sattar Khan, the folk hero of Tabriz who had led armed resistance against the royalist coup, was eventually wounded and confined. The reformers were hunted and imprisoned or killed.

The counterrevolution did not hold. Within fourteen months, constitutionalist forces from Tabriz and Gilan marched on Tehran, restored the constitution, and deposed Mohammad Ali Shah. The second Majles convened in 1909. The constitutional order was briefly and incompletely reinstated. Then Russian troops occupied northern Iran in 1911, ostensibly to protect their interests. When the brilliant American administrator Morgan Shuster—hired by the Iranian government to reorganize its finances and assert fiscal independence—tried to collect taxes from a Russian-connected Iranian noble, Russia issued an ultimatum demanding his dismissal. The Majles voted unanimously to refuse. Russia responded by advancing troops toward Tehran. Facing military occupation, the cabinet dismissed Shuster and dissolved the Majles. The constitutional period was over.

What survived was the idea itself. The idea that power is derived from the people. That law can bind rulers. That legitimacy is not inherited but earned. That an Iranian parliament—messy, factional, imperfect, alive—is preferable to a court that answers to no one. That idea would resurface in every subsequent generation: in the nationalist movement of the 1940s and 1950s, in the Green Movement of 2009, in the Woman, Life, Freedom uprising of 2022, and in the uprising that erupted in December 2025. The Constitutional Revolution did not succeed in 1911. But it planted something that no subsequent government—Qajar, Pahlavi, or Islamic Republic—has been able to fully extinguish.

Iran's Constitutional Revolution also established a pattern that would repeat throughout the twentieth century: domestic reformers, energized and organized, making genuine progress toward democratic governance, only to be undermined by foreign intervention. The British and Russians, who between them effectively controlled Iran's economy and territory through the Great Game, had no interest in a constitutional Iran that might assert control over its own resources. They preferred a weak, pliant monarchy to a strong, democratic parliament. Their intervention was the first payment of the recurring bill that Iran would pay for outside powers' interest in the country.

That bill is still being collected. When American and Israeli aircraft struck Iranian cities in February 2026, Iranians did not forget that event. They experienced it through 120 years of accumulated evidence about what outside powers do when Iranian democracy becomes inconvenient. The Constitutional Revolution is not ancient history in Iran. It is the opening of a case that has never been closed.

Chapter 5: The Bargain of Modernization (1921–1979)

In February 1921, a British-backed coup brought Reza Khan to power. Within four years, he had consolidated his hold on the military, the bureaucracy, and the political class. In 1925, the last Qajar shah was deposed, and Reza Khan crowned himself Reza Shah Pahlavi, founding the dynasty that would rule Iran for fifty-four years. The Pahlavi project was a classic twentieth-century bargain: modernization in exchange for authoritarianism. Reza Shah built railways, roads, and factories. He established modern universities and introduced secular education. He also dismantled political parties, imprisoned and executed opponents, crushed ethnic and tribal autonomy, and built the apparatus of a security state. Iran was modernized; Iranians were not liberated.

Reza Shah was forced to abdicate in 1941 when British and Soviet forces invaded Iran and occupied it during the Second World War. His twenty-two-year-old son, Mohammad Reza Shah, was then placed on the throne. In the late 1940s and early 1950s, Iran experienced a genuine democratic flourishing: political parties organized, a free press thrived, and a remarkable politician named

Mohammad Mossadegh rose to national prominence on a platform of nationalizing Iran's oil—the resource that British and American companies had been extracting for decades under arrangements that left Iran a minority partner in its own wealth. Mossadegh became prime minister in 1951. Two years later, he was gone. The CIA-backed coup toppled his government in August 1953 and restored the Shah to full power.

The US intelligence community now acknowledges the coup as an undemocratic act. But acknowledgment comes decades too late to undo the wound it opened in the Iranian political consciousness. The wound is not merely symbolic. It is structural. Because a foreign power had shown they could reverse elections and constitutionalism, the argument for radical alternatives gained force across ideological camps. The lesson that Iranian reformers drew from 1953—reasonably, given the evidence—was that peaceful change is not safe, because outside powers will not allow it. That lesson shaped the radicalism of 1979. It shapes Iranian political culture to this day.

Mohammad Mosaddegh was seventy-one years old in 1953 when American and British intelligence removed him from power. He was not a revolutionary. He was a constitutional lawyer and an aristocrat who had spent his career working within the legal structures of the Iranian state, serving as governor, minister, and member of parliament. He had become Prime Minister by the largest margin in Iranian parliamentary history. He wore a suit. He spoke French. He wept in the Iranian parliament when moved. Western journalists called him "the weeping prime minister." Iranians voted for him anyway.

What Mosaddegh wanted was a straightforward application of national sovereignty: that oil from Iranian soil should benefit the Iranian people. The Anglo-Iranian Oil Company had been extracting Iranian crude since 1913 under arrangements that gave Iran roughly sixteen percent of the profits. Workers at the Abadan refinery lived in segregated housing and were barred from eating in the same cafeteria as British employees. Mosaddegh nationalized the oil industry in

1951. The Iranian parliament voted for it unanimously. The Iranian people celebrated in the streets.

What followed was Operation Ajax. American and British intelligence organized a coup using royalist military officers and hired crowds paid to simulate popular unrest. The operation was run from the American embassy in Tehran. It lasted for three days in August 1953. Mosaddegh was arrested, tried for treason in a military court, and sentenced to three years in prison, followed by house arrest for the rest of his life. He died in Ahmadabad, tending his garden, in 1967. He had spent his last fourteen years a few hours from Tehran, forbidden to leave.

This is not history in the sense of something that has passed. It is the foundational grievance of modern Iranian political consciousness. Every Iranian leader who has cited foreign hostility since 1953 has been pointing at something documented. Every negotiation between Washington and Tehran conducted in the decades since has been shadowed by the memory of a democratically legitimate government removed from power, through American initiative, for the benefit of a foreign oil company. The JCPOA succeeded because both sides found a way to work around that shadow for a time. The shadow did not go away. The bombs of February 2026 landed on top of it.

Families like mine had committed to building a modern Iran—through education, medicine, science, and democratic governance. The 1953 coup did not destroy that commitment. It taught us the cost of idealism without power. That lesson was carried forward in everything that followed.

The Destruction of the Left

To understand why the 1979 revolution produced the Islamic Republic rather than the liberal democracy that most of its participants wanted, it's important to understand what happened to organized political alternatives in the quarter-century between the 1953 coup and the revolution.

The Tudeh Party—Iran's communist party, founded in 1941—was one of the most sophisticated political organizations in the country's history. At its peak in the early 1950s, it had tens of thousands of members, deep roots in the labor movement and the intelligentsia, and a coherent program for social transformation. It supported Mosaddegh's nationalization, though tensions between the party and the prime minister were real. After the 1953 coup, the Shah moved systematically to destroy the party: mass arrests, executions, show trials, and SAVAK infiltration reduced the Tudeh from a mass organization to a clandestine remnant. By the time of the revolution, its organizational capacity inside Iran had been effectively broken.

The secular nationalists who had rallied around Mosaddegh—the National Front and its successors—fared somewhat better, but not much. After 1953, they were denied any legitimate political space. Their leaders were periodically arrested. The institutions through which they might have built an organized alternative—a free press, independent political parties, open universities—were systematically closed. When the revolution came, they could mobilize people in the streets, but they could not govern. They had been denied the organizational experience that governing requires.

The left besides the Tudeh—Fedaian Marxist guerrilla organizations that had waged armed struggle against the Shah through the 1970s—was more visible but equally disorganized as a governing force. They had been forged in clandestine resistance, not by democratic institution-building. When the Shah fell, they had guns and courage and no workable theory for political transition.

What remained, with its institutional depth and organizational coherence, was the clerical network. The mosque system had survived the Shah's repression because the Shah, for reasons of both political calculation and genuine belief, had not systematically attacked religious institutions. The clerics had Friday sermons, seminary networks, charitable organizations, and the *basij* of popular trust that comes from being present at births, marriages, and deaths in a way that secular political parties cannot replicate. Ayatollah Khomeini had spent years in exile—in Turkey, in Iraq, and finally in France—building his theory of clerical governance, the Velayat-e Faqih, and his network of followers inside Iran. When the Shah fell, the clerics had the organizational infrastructure that everyone else lacked.

This is the crucial point that Western observers, and some Iranian exile communities, have consistently missed: the Islamic Republic was not imposed on Iran against the will of a secular population. It was the outcome that filled the organizational vacuum that foreign intervention, systematic repression, and the destruction of alternative political formations had created. The millions who marched against the Shah did not march for theocracy. But they could not march for a viable alternative, because every viable alternative had been systematically destroyed over twenty-six years. Ayatollah Khomeini's genius was to move faster than the confusion, to consolidate power before the coalition that had overthrown the Shah could cohere around anything else.

Understanding this history is essential for understanding the current crisis. When external actors argue that removing the Islamic Republic will produce democracy in Iran, they are not accounting for what democracy really requires: organized political formations, civic institutions, and the experience of legitimate governance. The Islamic Republic itself destroyed most of what existed inside Iran. The forty-five years since 1979 have produced a new generation of Iranians with the education and the values that have created a desire for democratic governance—but the organizational infrastructure needed to translate those values into durable institutions has yet to be rebuilt. It cannot be built from the outside. It cannot be built under bombs.

The Revolutionary Coalition and Its Betrayal

By the late 1970s, Iran held the elements of a revolution waiting to ignite: rapid socioeconomic change, rising expectations, and a legitimacy crisis sharpened by both the costs of political closure and deep foreign entanglement. In 1979, the monarchy fell. The revolution was not Ayatollah Khomeini's alone. It was a coalition: secular nationalists, leftists, Islamist modernizers, *bazaari* merchants, workers, students, and women—who were united by their opposition to the Shah and, though they did not yet fully realize it, divided about everything else.

Ayatollah Khomeini moved to consolidate power with a tactical sophistication that his coalition partners underestimated. The liberals and secular nationalists who had joined the first post-revolutionary government found themselves progressively sidelined, then expelled, and finally imprisoned. The Tudeh Party, which had cautiously supported the new government as an anti-imperialist force, was dissolved in 1983—its leaders arrested and, according to documented accounts, forced to make public recantations before being executed. The Fedaian and the Mojahedin-e-Khalq were first marginalized and then driven into exile or underground. The vision of an Islamic Republic that respected democratic rights—articulated by figures like Mehdi Bazargan, Iran's first post-revolutionary prime minister, who resigned in 1979 in protest at the direction events were taking—was not realized in the years that followed.

What emerged from the revolution and the eight-year war was a specific economic architecture: the IRGC's military-industrial complex, built to fight a war and never fully demobilized; the bonyad foundations, accumulating economic power through the chaos of post-revolutionary property reallocation; and a patronage economy in which proximity to revolutionary institutions determined economic survival. This architecture was not designed in isolation—it was continuously shaped by external pressures, particularly the sanctions regime, which reduced the size of the formal economy while leaving informal networks intact and, in many cases, strengthening them.

The consequences of that failure run through every subsequent chapter of Iranian political history. The diaspora's inability to unite around a coherent alternative to the Islamic Republic—visible today in the fractious exile politics of Los Angeles and London—is not a character flaw. It is the structural consequence of a revolution that destroyed every organized alternative and then spent forty-five years preventing new ones from forming. Thc fragmentation is not incidental. It was designed.

Chapter 6: The Fear Infrastructure – SAVAK and Its Successors

Authoritarian consolidation requires institutional muscle. The muscle Iran built in the mid-twentieth century was SAVAK—its national intelligence and security organization—and its successors. To understand why Iran in 2026 looks the way it does, why a society of enormous creativity and intelligence has spent decades navigating the distance between what it thinks and what it says, it's important to understand what this infrastructure was designed to produce. It was not designed to catch criminals. It was designed to make dissent unthinkable.

SAVAK: Structure and Design

SAVAK was established in 1957 with direct assistance from the CIA and Israel's Mossad, at the instigation of Mohammad Reza Shah, who had been returned to power four years earlier by the coup that removed Prime Minister Mosaddegh. The Shah understood the lesson of 1953: that his throne rested on foreign support and that domestic opposition, if allowed to organize, would threaten it. SAVAK was the institutional answer to that vulnerability. Its formal mandate was counterintelligence and the suppression of communism. Its operational reality was the systematic monitoring and suppression of any organized political life.

At its peak, SAVAK employed between 4,000 and 6,000 full-time agents, supplemented by a far larger network of informants whose precise numbers are difficult to establish precisely because the system was designed that way. SAVAK maintained files on approximately three million Iranians in a country of thirty-three million. Every university professor, every journalist, every civil servant, and everyone who wanted a government contract knew a file existed with their name on it. The result was not merely that opposition was suppressed. The interior life of an entire society became self-censoring. People stopped saying what they thought, even to people they trusted, because trust was the first casualty of a surveillance state. A man could be arrested for a conversation he had in his own kitchen if one of his dinner guests was reporting to SAVAK. Many were.

The organizational structure reinforced this effect. SAVAK operated eight departments covering internal security, counterintelligence, external intelligence, and administrative functions. Still, the most feared was its interrogation and detention apparatus centered at Evin Prison in northern Tehran, where political prisoners were held in conditions that were documented extensively by Amnesty International, the International Commission of Jurists, and the Red Cross in the 1970s. Evin became, across decades and two regimes, the most feared address in Iran—not because of what was known about it but because of what was not. Families of detainees often received no information. The uncertainty was part of the mechanism.

The American Relationship

Amnesty International documented SAVAK's interrogation practices in its 1976 report, finding methods that violated international human rights standards. These practices were documented while President Carter toasted the Shah at a New Year's dinner in Tehran on December 31, 1977, calling Iran "an island of stability in one of the more troubled areas of the world." Carter was not uninformed. The documentation was public. Multiple human rights organizations had reported on SAVAK's methods. He chose stability over what was happening in the cells behind closed doors.

The United States created, trained, funded, and politically protected this apparatus for more than two decades. This is not a contested claim—it is in declassified records, in the CIA's own subsequent assessments, and in the congressional hearings of the 1970s. And then American officials expressed surprise when Iranians concluded that the American-backed government was synonymous with oppression. The memory of the events that produced that conclusion did not dissolve when the Shah fled in January 1979. It became one of the foundational facts of Iranian political culture—the experiential basis for a deep, justified suspicion of governments that arrive with foreign credentials.

The Successor's Architecture

The Islamic Republic that replaced the Shah did not dismantle the surveillance state. It inherited it, rechristened it, and expanded it with its own institutional elaborations. SAVAK was formally dissolved in 1979. Within two years, SAVAMA—the Organization for Intelligence and National Security—had been established in its place. By 1984, the Ministry of Intelligence and National Security (known by its Persian acronym VEVAK) had been created as the primary intelligence and internal security organ of the new state. Evin Prison, which SAVAK had built and filled, became the Islamic Republic's Evin Prison: with different prisoners, and different ideological justifications but continuous architecture.

The Islamic Revolutionary Guard Corps added another layer. Founded in 1979 as a revolutionary militia answerable to Ayatollah

Khomeini rather than to the regular military, the IRGC developed its own intelligence apparatus—the IRGC Intelligence Organization—that operated parallel to and often in tension with MOIS. The result was not a single surveillance state but competing surveillance states, which produced their own dynamics: interagency rivalry, overlapping jurisdictions, and, for ordinary Iranians, the experience of facing multiple layers of potential scrutiny with no clear recourse against any of them.

What the Infrastructure Produced

The psychological legacy of seven decades of this infrastructure is not theoretical. It is present in the way Iranians speak, in the language they use in public versus private, and in the precision with which educated Iranians navigate the distance between what they believe and what they will say in a room whose allegiances are uncertain. The interior civilization described in Chapter 3—the dinner parties, the poetry circles, the underground reading groups—is not merely a cultural preference. It is a rational adaptation to an environment in which public expression has historically carried lethal risk.

That adaptation does not disappear when the political environment shifts. It becomes structural. Children who grew up watching their parents measure words in public carry that measurement forward even when the immediate threat is reduced. The Green Movement protesters of 2009, who chose green ribbons and constitutional demands instead of explicit anti-regime language, were not being timid. They were being precise—using the strongest words they judged they could say at the cost they were willing to pay. The Woman, Life, Freedom protesters of 2022 made a different calculation at a higher cost. Both calculations were made by people shaped by the institutional reality described in this chapter.

When people ask why Iranians who despise their government react with ambivalence to foreign-backed regime change, part of the answer lies here. They remember what the foreign-backed government looked like the last time. They remember the files. They remember Evin. The Islamic Republic that replaced the Shah did not dismantle the fear infrastructure. It proved the fear infrastructure was not the Shah's invention—it was the apparatus that any authoritarian state builds when it chooses subjects over citizens. Different rulers. The same architecture of control. That knowledge, earned over generations, does not produce passivity. It produces calculation.

Chapter 7: The Postwar Economic Architecture – How Sanctions and War Shaped Iran's Political Economy

The post-1979 order fused republican forms—elections, parliament—with clerical supremacy. The Office of the Supreme Leader became the apex of command. Article 110 of Iran's constitution enumerates sweeping leadership powers: the power to declare war and peace, appoint commanders, and set broad policy direction. The specific circumstances of its creation shaped the constitutional architecture: a revolution that had defeated one form of externally backed authoritarianism and now faced immediate external threats. Within a year, Iraq invaded—with American backing. The constitutional choices made under siege reflect those conditions. Understanding the system requires understanding what it was built against.

The War That Built the IRGC

To understand how the Islamic Revolutionary Guards Corps became a state within a state—commanding an economic empire estimated at 20 to 40 percent of Iran's GDP, running its own intelligence networks, fielding allied regional forces from Lebanon to Yemen—we must begin not with ideology but with war.

In September 1980, Saddam Hussein's Iraqi army invaded Iran along a 1,200-kilometer front. The invasion was calculated to exploit the chaos of Iran's revolution: the regular military had been purged and demoralized, the new government was unstable, and Iraq's backers in Washington and Riyadh believed Iran was ripe for a humiliating defeat that would end the Islamic Republic's first years in power. They were wrong. The Iran-Iraq War lasted eight years—from 1980 to 1988—and became one of the most destructive conflicts of the twentieth century. Total casualties on both sides reached somewhere between one million and two million; Iran alone suffered between 300,000 and 500,000 dead, with hundreds of thousands more seriously wounded.

I lost nineteen friends and classmates in that war. They died in conditions that Western audiences do not associate with the late twentieth century: human wave assaults across minefields, trench warfare reminiscent of the First World War, and—this is not a contested historical point—chemical weapons attacks by Iraqi forces using agents that the United States knew about and did not stop. The Reagan administration, determined to prevent an Iranian victory, provided Iraq with satellite intelligence, dual-use materials, and diplomatic cover even as the casualty figures mounted. The Iranian soldiers who died in those gas attacks were dying in a war that American policy was enabling.

The scale of the loss is difficult to hold in one's mind as a single number. Iran mobilized more than two million soldiers over the eight years of the war. According to the *Encyclopedia Iranica*, approximately 500,000 Iranians died, with many more permanently disabled. A generation of young men was gone. In cities and villages across the country, families lost fathers and brothers and sons. The war ended in August 1988 with no territory gained, no objectives achieved, and no meaningful change in the border between the two countries. It ended exactly where it started, with the same line on the map.

What the war produced in Iranian consciousness is something that cannot be captured by casualty statistics alone. It produced a generation for whom sacrifice was not abstract, for whom the cost of conflict was not something that happened somewhere else to other people. It produced a specific, bone-deep suspicion of leaders who speak easily about war. And it produced something else that Western analysts consistently underestimate: a fierce, justified pride in having endured. Iran fought the longest conventional war of the twentieth century, against an enemy supported by the United States, the Soviet Union, France, and most of the Arab world. It survived. Survival is a defining fact of modern Iranian national identity, as central to how Iranians understand themselves as any religious tradition or classical heritage.

The use of chemical weapons against Iranian soldiers is part of this memory and must be named here. Iraq deployed mustard gas and nerve agents against Iranian forces repeatedly during the war, killing and permanently injuring tens of thousands. The United States, which was providing Iraq with battlefield intelligence during this period, knew about the use of chemical weapons. American officials have acknowledged, in declassified documents and subsequent interviews, that the provision of intelligence continued even after the chemical weapons use was known. The survivors of those attacks are still alive. Some are still in Iranian hospitals. Their families are still in Iran. When Iranians speak of why they do not trust American assurances, this is part of what they mean.

The IRGC was born in this war and shaped entirely by it. Founded in 1979 as a revolutionary counterweight to the regular military—which the new government did not fully trust—the guards had been a political militia. The eight-year war transformed them into a serious military force with battle experience, organizational depth, and a moral authority of sacrifice. More than a hundred thousand IRGC fighters died. The survivors emerged from the war with an institutional identity built on three foundations that have never weakened: the belief that they had saved the Islamic Republic when no one else would; the conviction that they could trust no outside power; and the organizational infrastructure—supply chains, construction capabilities, intelligence networks, foreign relationships—that the war had forced them to build.

The war also produced the economic architecture that defined the postwar period. The IRGC's engineering arm, called Khatam al-Anbiya—established during the war to build military infrastructure—was not disbanded when the war ended. It was repurposed. It began taking on civilian construction contracts: roads, dams, pipelines, ports. Within a decade, it had become one of the largest construction conglomerates in the Middle East, operating largely outside the normal procurement process and securing contracts through political connections rather than competitive bidding. The war had given the IRGC the institutional infrastructure. Peace gave it the economic opportunity to use it.

Reconstruction and the Postwar Political Economy: The Rafsanjani Years

Ayatollah Khomeini died in June 1989, one year after the war ended with a ceasefire. Ali Khamenei, who had served as president, was elevated to the post of Supreme Leader. And Akbar Hashemi Rafsanjani—the canniest political operator of the revolutionary generation, a man who had survived every purge and faction fight since 1979—became president with a mandate to rebuild the country.

Rafsanjani's reconstruction period, from 1989 to 1997, is the missing chapter in most Western accounts of Iran. It is missing because it is not dramatic—there was no revolution, no war, no mass protest. What there was instead was the systematic conversion of revolutionary ideology into economic empire. Understanding it is essential for understanding what the postwar economic architecture actually was and how it came to control so much of Iran's economic life.

Rafsanjani was a pragmatist who understood that the Islamic Republic could not survive on ideology alone. The war had devastated the economy: oil infrastructure had been bombed, foreign debt had accumulated, inflation was running at catastrophic levels, and a generation of young men had returned from the front to a country with no jobs and no clear future. His solution was economic liberalization—but liberalization of a very particular kind. State assets were privatized, but to IRGC-connected foundations and revolutionary organizations rather than the private market. The bonyads—tax-exempt religious foundations that had been endowed with property confiscated from the Shah's supporters and wealthy Iranians who fled after 1979—were given expanded mandates and required minimal accountability. The IRGC's economic arm was handed major infrastructure contracts as part of the reconstruction program.

What Rafsanjani built was not a market economy. It was a patronage economy in which access to economic opportunity was mediated by proximity to revolutionary institutions. This had a perverse but entirely predictable effect: it created a set of organizations—the IRGC, the bonyads, the foundations controlled by the Supreme Leader's Office—whose economic interests were now directly tied to the maintenance of the political system that had created them. They were not merely ideological defenders of the Islamic Republic. They were its shareholders. The reform that threatened the political system threatened their economic empire. The structural incentives to resist change became overwhelming during the Rafsanjani years.

Setad—the organization controlled by the Supreme Leader that originated from properties confiscated from citizens who fled or were expelled after 1979—grew during this period into a sprawling economic empire with holdings in telecommunications, real estate, financial services, and pharmaceuticals. Astan Quds Razavi, the foundation that controls the Imam Reza Shrine in Mashhad, became one of the wealthiest organizations in the Middle East. These were not charities in any meaningful sense. They were instruments of political control that were also enormously profitable, and their profitability depended entirely on their political connections.

By the time Mohammad Khatami won the presidency in 1997 on a reform platform, the postwar economic architecture was fully in place. Khatami could change his rhetoric. He could release some political prisoners. He could open some civic space. But he could not touch the IRGC's economic empire, the bonyads' tax exemptions, or the foundations' control of major sectors of the economy—because those institutions had the political power to block him, and because the Supreme Leader, who had his own economic interests in the system, would not permit it. The reformists failed not only because of political repression but also because the state's economic structure, designed during the Rafsanjani reconstruction, made fundamental reform impossible without dismantling the entire system.

The Iran-Iraq War's Long Shadow

The Iran-Iraq War militarized Iranian society and expanded coercive institutions in ways that outlasted the conflict by decades. Total casualties ranged from one million to two million—numbers that reshaped demographics, economics, and the narrative of legitimacy around sacrifice. The war's political afterlife was a permanent "national security" frame—useful for repressing dissent and justifying extraordinary control over resources and information.

That frame persists today. When the Islamic Republic arrests a journalist, it invokes national security. When it restricts public assembly, it invokes national security. When it denies information to its own citizens, it invokes national security. This is not a coincidence. It is the institutional logic of a state forged during an eight-year war for survival, one that has never stopped governing as if the war were still ongoing. The IRGC, which runs the national security state, has a structural interest in perpetuating a threat environment—because a threat justifies its budget, autonomy, economic empire, and political power. A genuinely peaceful Iran, at peace with its neighbors and fully integrated into the international economy, would have no institutional need for an IRGC of the current size and power. The IRGC understands this better than anyone.

The Iranian civilians who lived through that war know the history of external interference; internal political and economic consolidation of control; but most of all human loss personally. They know it the way you know something that happened to your family—not as an abstraction, not as a lesson in a textbook, but as a fact about a specific person who did not come home, or who came home changed, or who came home carrying something in their lungs that would kill them twenty years later. The political scientist Vali Nasr, writing about the legacy of the Iran-Iraq War, observed that it produced in Iranian society a form of siege mentality that no subsequent government—including a democratic one—would be able to dissolve. The war is over. The memory of it is not.

Understanding this matters for what follows. When Iranians in 2026 look at American military action and ask why they should trust the government that provided intelligence to Saddam Hussein when it was documented that Iraq was using chemical weapons against Iranian forces, they are asking a historically grounded question. The United States's record in the Iran-Iraq War is not a grievance manufactured by ideologues. It is a documented fact. The bombs of Operation Epic Fury fell on people who know that fact intimately.

The Postwar Economic Architecture: How External Pressure and Internal War Created the Current System

Structural Actors

- Supreme Leader (apex authority; formal veto over all state functions)
- IRGC (military + economic arm; controls ~20–40% of GDP through subsidiaries)
- Bonyads (tax-exempt religious foundations controlling major industries)
- Parallel security and intelligence institutions
- Sanctioned economy intermediaries (front companies, cryptocurrency networks, third-country banks)

The Key Mechanisms — And What Produced Them

Every mechanism that analysts describe as enabling economic dysfunction in Iran has a documented external cause. Broad sanctions reduce the size of the formal economy while leaving informal networks—controlled by institutions with political connections—intact and, in fact, more powerful. This is not a theoretical claim. It is what sanctions scholars, including Elizabeth Economy, Gary Clyde Hufbauer, and the RAND Corporation, have documented across multiple cases: broad economic sanctions typically strengthen the institutions they are designed to weaken, because those institutions control the parallel economy that emerges when the formal economy is destroyed. The Trump administration's Secretary of the Treasury described this outcome with pride. He did not describe it as a side effect. He described it as the point.

Sanctions eliminate formal access to dollars, forcing monetary policy choices that benefit those who hold hard currency—typically institutions with political connections rather than ordinary citizens. The rial's collapse to 1.38 million per dollar in December 2025 was the direct result of this maximum pressure policy.

When legal imports are sanctioned, illegal imports fill the gap—at premium prices, through channels controlled by whoever has the political connections and enforcement capacity to run them. Sanctions create this dynamic. They do not eliminate it.

The sanctions architecture itself creates smuggling networks and other illicit channels. This has been documented in Iraq, Cuba, North Korea, and Iran. The RAND Corporation's 2019 assessment found that broad sanctions on Iran were strengthening the very institutions they were designed to weaken.

Patronage economies emerge when formal market mechanisms are disrupted. American sanctions disrupted Iran's formal economy for four decades. The resulting economic distortions were a predictable consequence of that policy, as noted by economists on both the left and the right.

Political constraints on organizing and opposition—which exist in different forms across many countries in the region—are reinforced when external threats are real and perceived. The 2002 "axis of evil" designation and the forty-six-year sanctions campaign provided a continuous supply of external threat that could be invoked to justify continued political constraints. American policy manufactured the external pressure that made those justifications possible.

The Failure Modes of Maximum Pressure Policy

Surveillance and security infrastructure—present in various forms across the region, including in US-backed states like Saudi Arabia and the UAE—were built in Iran with specific reference to external threat. The Shah's SAVAK was built with American and Israeli technical assistance. Its successor institutions inherited that architecture.

Religious governance systems—present across the region in various forms—emerged specifically in Iran's case from a revolution whose democratic reformers were defeated by the combined effect of internal power struggles and external interference. The secular democratic forces that might have produced a different outcome were the same forces that 1953 had destroyed.

Information restrictions in Iran—also present in US-allied Egypt, Saudi Arabia, and the UAE—are intensified by the external threat environment that forty-six years of sanctions and military pressure have sustained.

Patronage economies are the predictable result of sanctions-distorted markets. When external sanctions block legal pathways to economic participation, political connections become the only reliable route to economic survival. Sanctions create the patronage incentive.

Why Maximum Pressure Failed to Produce What its Architects Claimed

Economic collapse reaches the population before it reaches the institutions that sanctions were meant to target. This is documented in every major sanctions case. US Secretary Bessent described these latest US sanctions as a success. What he described was the population running out of money before the political institutions ran out of power.

When an economy collapses, the government that presided over it loses credibility—but the collapse also produces conditions of crisis in which political change becomes difficult to direct. The Trump administration caused such a collapse and had no plan for what came next. Their own members admitted this.

Decapitation strikes—targeting leadership rather than capabilities—have a documented record in political science and military history of producing fragmentation rather than democratic transition. Iraq in 2003, Libya in 2011, and Somalia all produced this outcome. The Trump-Netanyahu operation targeted Iranian leadership directly, without a transition plan, against the advice of career officials who could read the historical record.

Operation Epic Fury removed Iranian leadership without having established any alternative framework for Iranian governance. The civil society voices that had been demanding free elections and people-based institutions—the Iranians who had the legitimacy to speak about Iran's future—were not consulted. They were not even present in the room.

Broad sanctions in Iran reduce the legal economy's size while leaving the illegal/parallel economy—controlled by IRGC and bonyads—intact. The government becomes the sole provider of access to sanctioned goods, increasing its monopoly power. The population bears the economic pain; the IRGC earns the smuggling premium. Targeted sanctions—freezing specific assets and barring specific individuals from international financial systems—disrupt extraction channels without strengthening stabilizers. The distinction is not technical. It is the difference between punishing a population for its government's choices and punishing the government itself.

The Ecological Consequences

The failure modes of this economic architecture are not only political. They are physical. Lake Urmia, once one of the largest saltwater lakes in the world and a UNESCO Biosphere Reserve, has shrunk to approximately ten percent of its historical size. The primary drivers, according to NASA satellite imagery analysis and Iranian environmental researchers, were dam construction and irrigation projects that reduced inflow to the lake, combined with decades of groundwater overuse and agricultural policy decisions that failed to account for long-term hydrological consequences. Tehran itself faced acute water shortages in late 2025.

Infrastructure that should have been maintained and expanded has instead been ignored which has produced exactly the cascading failure that a systems scientist recognizes: not a single catastrophic event, but the slow accumulation of neglected signals until the threshold is crossed. The IRGC's construction empire built infrastructure for political and economic reasons, not engineering ones. The results are visible in crumbling roads, unreliable power grids, and a water crisis that the government was still publicly denying when the bombs began to fall.

Chapter 8: Women, Bodies, and Statecraft

To understand what the Women, Life, Freedom uprising meant, it's important to understand what existed before, and what was taken away.

In the decades before 1979, Iranian women occupied a place in public life that was, by the region's standards, relatively expansive. Women had held the right to vote since 1963, granted under the White Revolution. Women attended universities and composed a significant share of the student population. Women worked as lawyers, physicians, journalists, professors, government officials, and engineers. They appeared without covering requirements in public spaces, offices, cinemas, and restaurants. The image of Tehran in the 1960s and 1970s that survives in photographs is of a cosmopolitan city where women moved freely in the full range of modern professional and social life.

This is not a portrait of paradise. Significant inequalities persisted under the Shah, and many educated women were among the most committed opponents of his government, marching in the 1979 revolution alongside their male counterparts. They marched for the full range of reasons that Iranians marched: opposition to authoritarianism, to the secret police, to economic corruption, to political imprisonment.

They did not march to lose rights they had. The compulsory hijab, introduced in 1981, was among the first shocks of what the revolution had actually produced. Tens of thousands of women marched in Tehran in March 1979, weeks after Ayatollah Khomeini announced the policy, in what became one of the largest feminist demonstrations in Iranian history. That protest was not successful. But it was immediate and vast, and it tells you something essential about what Iranian women understood themselves to have lost.

Four decades of compulsory covering did not eliminate the memory of what came before. It preserved it, in family albums, in the testimonies of grandmothers and mothers, in the comparative consciousness of every Iranian woman who knew that her counterparts in Paris and New York were not asked to prove their virtue with their clothing. The Woman, Life, Freedom uprising of 2022 was not a novelty. It was the return of a claim that had been waiting for forty years to be made again at the scale of the street.

In September 2022, a twenty-two-year-old Kurdish-Iranian woman named Mahsa Amini was arrested in Tehran by the morality police for allegedly wearing her hijab improperly. Three days later, she was dead. Her death triggered the Women, Life, Freedom uprising—the most sustained and geographically widespread protest movement in Iran in decades.

What followed was the Women, Life, Freedom uprising: the most sustained and geographically widespread protest movement in Iran since the revolution, driven primarily by women but supported across gender, class, ethnic, and religious lines. Women removed their headscarves in public. They burned them. They cut their hair in the streets. They chanted slogans that made explicit what the uprising understood itself to be: not a protest about a dress code, but a rebellion against the fundamental claim of the Islamic Republic to own Iranian women's bodies.

The Women, Life, Freedom uprising understood something that Western analysts frequently missed: the fight over women's appearance in public was not peripheral to Iranian political life. It was central to it. A state that legislates what you wear in public has demonstrated its willingness to reach into the most intimate aspects of daily life. The women who removed their headscarves in public and cut their hair in the streets were not making a fashion statement. They were making a constitutional claim: that their bodies belonged to themselves. That claim—made at enormous personal cost, without foreign bombs, without foreign funding—was the most serious democratic act in the region in 2022. It was made by Iranians, for Iran, on Iranian terms.

The Women, Life, Freedom uprising was eventually suppressed. Amnesty International and Human Rights Watch documented a sharp rise in judicial executions in 2024, with figures they described as alarming. The movement faced severe repression. The international response fell short of what events demanded. But the uprising established a cultural and political baseline that would not be walked back: a generation of Iranians had clearly seen that the women of Iran were articulating, in the streets, courts, and daily lives, a vision of dignity and self-determination that went beyond what the existing system offered.[3]

The Eight-Year War—How the Iran-Iraq Conflict Shaped Everything That Followed

The Iran-Iraq War lasted from September 1980 to August 1988. It left a generation of young Iranian men buried. It left the generation that survived them—the parents and older siblings of the people who would fill the streets in 2022—shaped by an experience of total war that Westerners have not had since 1945. Understanding this war is not background. It is the key.

Iraq invaded Iran on September 22, 1980, eight days after Saddam Hussein unilaterally abrogated the 1975 Algiers Agreement that had governed the shared Shatt al-Arab waterway. The United

3 See Appendix: Poems of Witness, "The Fire-Crowned Woman"

States, which had publicly declared neutrality, was providing Iraq with satellite intelligence, agricultural credits that freed up cash for weapons purchases, and precursors for the chemical weapons that Iraq deployed against Iranian forces and Kurdish civilians. The chemical weapons included mustard gas, tabun, and sarin.

The war produced three structural consequences that directly influence the present. First, it created the IRGC as a serious military institution.

Second, the war created the economic architecture that sanctions would later exploit and distort. Rafsanjani's postwar reconstruction and subsequent patronage system was not corruption in the simple sense—it was the rational response of a government that had just fought an eight-year war without reliable external allies and needed institutions it could trust. The problem is that what begins as emergency rationality calcifies into structural inequality. By the time international sanctions took effect, the IRGC's economic empire was already the backbone of the parallel economy that sanctions could not reach.

Third, the war created a deep, structural suspicion of Western intentions that is not paranoia but historical inference. Iran asked the United Nations Security Council to condemn Iraq's use of chemical weapons. The Security Council passed a weak resolution that mentioned "chemical weapons" without naming Iraq. The United States blocked a stronger resolution. Iran drew the only conclusion the evidence supported: the international community's rules applied selectively, and Iran was not among the protected. When Western officials, four decades later, expressed shock at Iranian resistance to international inspection regimes and verification frameworks, they were encountering the institutional memory of a country that had watched the international community stand by while its soldiers were gassed.

The war ended on August 20, 1988, with a UN-brokered ceasefire that Ayatollah Khomeini described as "more lethal for me than drinking poison." He died eleven months later. The line is famous because it is honest: the man who had said Iran would fight until final victory, who had rejected every ceasefire offer for years as the body count mounted, finally accepted what the ground had been saying all along. The ceasefire resolved nothing. The borders returned to where they had been. The Shatt al-Arab River remained contested. The families who had buried their sons, brothers, and fathers buried them, having gained nothing except the end of the dying. The moral accounts with their subsequent debts have never been formally closed. It lives on in the political culture of a country that still holds ceremonies for its war martyrs forty years later—and in the political calculations of a leadership that watched what happened to the governments of Iraq and Libya after they disarmed or weakened their military forces.

The Green Movement (2009)—The Precursor Generation

Between the Constitutional Revolution of 1905 and the Women, Life, Freedom uprising of 2022, there is a moment that Western attention largely moved past and that Iranians carried forward into every subsequent year: the Green Movement of 2009. To understand why the Woman, Life, Freedom generation fought the way it did, it's vital to understand what the Green generation learned, and what it cost them.

On June 12, 2009, Iranians went to the polls in a presidential election that millions of them believed was stolen. The official count gave incumbent Mahmoud Ahmadinejad a landslide victory over reformist challenger Mir-Hossein Mousavi. The result was announced with implausible speed, before a meaningful count could have been achieved. Mousavi and fellow candidate Mehdi Karroubi, who had both run as part of the Islamic Republic's approved candidate list, rejected the results. Within hours, millions of Iranians had reached the same conclusion. What followed was the largest popular mobilization in Iran since the 1979 revolution.

An estimated three million people marched silently through Tehran on June 15, 2009, stretching from Enqelab Square to Azadi Square—an enormous river of people wearing green, making no sound. The march required no foreign organizer, no outside funding, no amplification. It required only the shared understanding that something had been taken, and the shared decision was to say so. "Where is my vote?" appeared on handwritten signs, on green ribbons worn around wrists, words voiced by millions across the country. It was a constitutional demand, not a revolutionary one. The movement was an appeal to the system's own legitimacy, not a rejection of it. That distinction matters, and its failure would matter even more.

The suppression was systematic. Security forces and Basij paramilitaries attacked protesters with batons, tear gas, and live ammunition. The Kahrizak Detention Center became notorious for the torture, sexual assault, and deaths of protesters held there. At least seventy-two people were killed, though independent estimates range considerably higher under the information blackout. Thousands were arrested; many were subjected to forced confessions in show trials that the movement's leaders refused to legitimize. Neda Agha-Soltan, shot on June 20 by a sniper as she stood watching a protest, was filmed dying on a phone camera and became, within hours, a global symbol. Her name means "voice" in Persian. She was twenty-six years old.

Mousavi and Karroubi were placed under house arrest in February 2011, where they remained for years—their health deteriorating, their phones monitored, their visitors restricted, their silence enforced. The movement did not produce the change it sought. The international community noticed, expressed concern, and moved on. The Iranian people endured, as they have always endured.

★★★

What the Green Movement produced, instead of the change it sought, was the political education of the generation that would fill the streets again thirteen years later. The woman who cut her hair in the street in Tehran in October 2022 was not making an impulsive gesture. She was making a considered one, by someone who understood the full weight of what she was doing—someone formed in part by watching what happened in 2009 and drawing her own conclusions.

The lesson the Woman, Life, Freedom generation took away from the events of 2009 was not cynicism. It was precision. The Green Movement had appealed to the system's own legitimacy and discovered that the system's legitimacy was not something it would allow to be questioned by an internal force, no matter how large or peaceful. That lesson had to be learned. The 2022 generation, having learned it, did not make a constitutional demand. They made an existential one: that their bodies, their lives, and their choices belonged to themselves. Woman, Life, Freedom was not born in 2022. It was born out of the lesson of what happened in 2009—carried forward with the precision of people who cannot afford to repeat their failures.

Every chapter of Iranian history since 1953 has followed the same structure: a generation mobilizes, is suppressed, and passes on what it has learned to the next generation as a harder, more honest reckoning with what is possible. The Green generation did not fail. They prepared a path, a path for those who would take the streets again in 2022, and again when the bombs fell in 2026, and who will take the streets again after that—the world notices. The Iranian people endure.

The JCPOA and Its Destruction—What Diplomacy Built, and What Abandonment Cost

On July 14, 2015, after twenty months of negotiations involving Iran, the United States, the United Kingdom, France, Germany, Russia, and China, the Joint Comprehensive Plan of Action (JCPOA) was signed in Vienna. It was, by the technical standards of arms control, an extraordinary achievement. Iran agreed to cap its uranium enrichment at 3.67 percent purity (far below the 90 percent needed for weapons), reduce its enriched stockpile by 98 percent, dismantle two-thirds of its centrifuges, redesign its Arak reactor to produce less plutonium, and accept the most intrusive inspection regime in the history of arms control; it allowed International Atomic Energy Agency (IAEA) inspectors with access to cameras at every enrichment facility, and the ability to request access to any site within twenty-four days. In exchange, international sanctions were lifted. Iran received access to frozen assets and could return to the global oil market.

The IAEA certified Iranian compliance eight consecutive times between 2016 and 2018. The US intelligence community and European allies continuously assessed Iran's compliance. The deal was working by every available technical measure. On May 8, 2018, President Trump withdrew the United States from the agreement over the objections of all of these institutions, plus other US European allies and other parties to the deal. His stated rationale was that the deal was "defective at its core." His actual reasons, spelled out more candidly in other statements, were that his predecessor had negotiated it, that it did not address Iran's ballistic missile program or regional activities, and that he had promised during his campaign to undo it. None of these reasons changed the fact that the nuclear program it constrained had remained constrained, and that withdrawing from it unconstrained it.

Immanuel Kant, in his 1795 essay on perpetual peace, identified that a precondition of any durable settlement was the prohibition against the secret reservation for future war—the principle that a negotiated agreement that either party intends to abandon when convenient is not an agreement but a pause between rounds. The JCPOA, whatever its limitations, was a genuine preliminary article in Kant's sense: a verified framework which, once removed, allowed the structural conditions that made the next war more likely. Its abandonment in 2018 reintroduced the reservation for future war. Every kilogram of uranium Iran enriched beyond civilian requirements after May 2018 is the direct and documented consequence of that reintroduction. The strikes of June 2025 were the consequence of the enrichment. The strikes of February 28, 2026, were the consequence of June 2025. A decision framed as leverage produced, step by documented step, the war it claimed to prevent.

The trajectory from 2018 to 2026 runs in a straight line. When the United States withdrew, Iran had 300 kilograms of uranium enriched to 3.67 percent. European powers tried to keep the deal alive through a financial mechanism (INSTEX) designed to enable trade despite US sanctions, but its results were negligible. Iran, observing that it was absorbing the economic costs of the deal while the United States was absorbing none of the diplomatic costs of violating it, began stepping back from its commitments: enrichment to 20 percent in 2021, 60 percent by 2022, 83.7 percent at Fordow by early 2023. The inspection cameras were disconnected. By 2026, the IAEA had lost its continuous monitoring access entirely. The program that had been under the most rigorous inspection in arms control history was now the least visible it had been since 2003. Every step in that deterioration can be traced to the decision of May 8, 2018. The cost of abandoning diplomacy is now legible in the school's rubble in Minab.

The JCPOA was not a perfect agreement. It did not address ballistic missiles, regional proxies, or human rights. Its critics, who noted those omissions, were correct. But a perfect agreement that does not exist cannot constrain a nuclear program. An imperfect agreement that exists and is being complied with can. The lesson of 2018 is not that imperfect agreements should be accepted forever. It is that walking away from a working agreement, without a viable alternative, does not produce a better agreement. It produces no agreement and an unconstrained program. The alternative to the JCPOA was not a better deal. It was what happened next.

PART THREE: THE RECKONING

From Amini to Epic Fury

Between December 2025 and March 2026, a series of events unfolded that were not inevitable. The economic conditions that produced the protests were deliberately manufactured, as admitted by the United States Secretary of the Treasury under oath. The diplomatic breakthrough in Geneva was real and was actively working. The decision to bomb Iran while negotiations were producing results is the central event this part examines.

Chapter 9: When the Currency Becomes a Referendum – December 2025

Witness Voice

Tehran, December 28, 2025, Identity withheld.

> "My cousin called from Tehran. She said: 'I went to three banks today. The first told me the system was down. The second told me there was a limit—I could only withdraw one million toman. One million toman is worth about thirty dollars. The third said come back tomorrow. I came back the next day. They said to come back next week. My salary is four million toman a month.' She laughed when she told me this. Not because it was funny. She laughed because she had already made the calculation that the government made sure she could see: the currency is worthless, the banks are paralyzed, and the government is watching to see what you do with that information."

What this voice complicates: the Western framing of an "economic crisis" as a technocratic problem. This is not a failed monetary policy. It is a tool.

What Was Lost Before the Bombs: The Economic Biography of the Iranian Middle Class

To understand what the currency collapse of December 2025 meant to ordinary Iranians, it's necessary to first understand what ordinary Iranians had, and what they had watched disappear during the preceding decades.

In the 1970s, Iran had one of the fastest-growing economies in the developing world. Oil revenues funded an ambitious modernization program—universities, hospitals, roads, and industrial infrastructure. The middle class that emerged from that period—engineers, doctors, professors, architects, civil servants—was not wealthy by Western standards, but it was educated, aspirational, and growing. Tehran in the early 1970s had a cultural life that rivaled that of other major cities in the region: film festivals, literary magazines, modern architecture, and a university system that sent graduates to the best institutions in Europe and America.

The 1979 revolution promised them a better future. What they got instead was eight years of devastating war, followed by the systematic conversion of the economy into a state-designed postwar economic architecture. The middle class did not disappear immediately. Through the 1990s and early 2000s, it adapted, found the spaces the state had not yet captured, and built the interior civilization described earlier. But the structural forces were relentless.

The rial, which stood at approximately 70 to the dollar when I left Iran in 1978, had fallen to 150,000 to the dollar by 2019, when the reimposition of American sanctions following the JCPOA withdrawal accelerated the collapse. By late 2025, it had reached approximately 1.38 million to the dollar. This is not an abstraction. It means that a physician who had spent thirty years building a practice—who had saved carefully, invested prudently, and paid into a pension system—watched the real value of everything they had accumulated evaporate in a decade. It means that a university professor's monthly salary, which might have supported a comfortable middle-class life in 2005, could not, by 2025, cover the rent for a modest apartment in Tehran.

The resulting brain drain was staggering in scale. Iran has one of the highest rates of emigration of college-educated citizens in the world. The Islamic Republic Medical Association estimated in 2023 that tens of thousands of Iranian physicians had emigrated in the preceding decade. University faculties were hollowed out as professors left for positions in Turkey, Canada, Germany, and the Gulf states. Engineers who built Iran's industrial infrastructure retired or emigrated, and were not replaced at anything close to the same rate. A country that had invested enormous resources in producing an educated, skilled population was watching that investment leave because the political and economic system made staying an act of financial self-destruction.

Those who stayed faced a daily financial reckoning that the currency figures do not fully capture. A family that had owned a modest apartment in Tehran in 2000 was, by 2025, asset-rich on paper and cash-poor in practice: the apartment's nominal value had risen, but its real value was unmeasurable in a currency that was losing purchasing power faster than inflation statistics acknowledged. Savings held in rials evaporated. Savings held in dollars were illegal—the government criminalized dollar-denominated transactions precisely because dollarization would have revealed the rial's true weakness. A family trying to pay for their child's medical treatment was navigating a black market for hard currency. At the same time, the official rate bore no relationship to the price at which any actual transaction could occur.

The people in the streets in December 2025 were not, primarily, the desperately poor—though they were there too. They were the remnant of the middle class: people who had spent their entire professional lives trying to build something within the constraints of the postwar economy, who had watched the rules change every few years to ensure that whatever they built could be captured by the system, and who had finally, in December 2025, run out of patience at the pretense that the system was capable of governing them.

The woman in the voice capsule above—withdrawing thirty dollars from a bank that owed her a month's salary—was not experiencing an economic event. She was experiencing the final settling of accounts of forty-seven years of systematic extraction. She laughed. She had already made the calculation.

The Referendum

By late December 2025, the Grand Bazaar in Tehran—the commercial heart of the city that had been, in 1979, one of the engines of revolutionary mobilization—closed for several days in protest. The central bank governor resigned. Inflation was running at forty percent or higher by most estimates. The authorities' own notoriously unreliable statistical releases showed numbers lower than those Iranians experienced at their grocery stores and pharmacies. The gap between the official reality and lived reality was itself an act of the postwar economic architecture: a state that lies about price levels expects its citizens to accept the lie. They did not.

On December 28, protests began in the Grand Bazaar area and spread within days to all thirty-one provinces. Slogans that had appeared in 2019 and 2022 returned, sharpened by accumulated grievances. Protesters chanted: "Woman, Life, Freedom," and "Independence, Freedom, Iranian Republic." Some crowds gave voice to older chants that reflected the depth of their frustration; but what mattered most was the breadth: the Grand Bazaar merchants, the factory workers, the students, the teachers—all explicitly rejecting both the monarchist past and the theocratic present.

The IRGC and the Basij mobilized quickly. Security forces were deployed across affected cities. Iranian human rights organizations noted the presence of non-Persian-speaking personnel among those present during the most intense confrontations. However, the full composition of the forces deployed remains under investigation.

In Washington and elsewhere, the debate about Iran has long reduced the country to two poles: the government on one side, and the exiles who argue that external pressure or military intervention will deliver liberation on the other. That binary is politically convenient. It is also wrong. It erases a third current—one that exists not in think tanks or diaspora conference rooms but inside Iran itself: the doctors, teachers, journalists, factory workers, students, and engineers who oppose both current domestic conditions and foreign military intervention. They seek self-determination through civic action, labor organizing, student movements, and nonviolent resistance. They understand something that advocates of war, safely located in Los Angeles, D.C., or London, do not: that external bombs do not liberate a people—they bury them deeper under the rubble of both physical destruction and nationalist grievance.

This third current is the most politically sophisticated force in Iranian society. It is also the most endangered, because it is caught between a state that imprisons it and a diaspora that sometimes ignores it when calling for intervention.

One account from this period, circulating among Iranian diaspora communities and verified by multiple sources, captures what the people inside the country were saying to those calling for war from outside: "This is a message to those abroad who argue that war against Iran is justified and necessary. If war is painless and liberating, stand here and live under it. Families sleep together in living rooms because homes shake from explosions. Parents hold their children while missiles fall. Journalists attend funerals and visit morgues. Hospitals are full. People are grieving. Those inside the country face difficult conditions from the state and, at the same time, condemnation from some abroad who say war will bring democracy. From inside, the response is direct: war is not a slogan. It is fear, funerals, and economic collapse. If you call for war from safety, be willing to share its consequences. Otherwise, do not romanticize it."

That danger is itself an argument against the easy romanticism of war called for from a safe distance.

The human cost that Iranians have borne across decades—the imprisoned, the exiled, the families separated by politics and by borders—is one reason for writing this book. The question it addresses is not whether that suffering is real. It is whether external military bombardment is a remedy for it. Iraq and Libya demonstrate, with terrible clarity, that removing a government by force is not the same as building a viable alternative. A durable transition requires internal legitimacy, organized leadership, and functioning institutions. Bombardment does not create them. It destroys the preconditions for them.

Under the 1906 Constitution, the Shah had the authority to appoint and dismiss ministers; the historical dispute concerns how that authority was exercised in 1953, as well as the documented role of foreign intelligence services in subverting an elected government. That history—the CIA-backed coup, the restoration of a weakened monarchy, the promise that foreign intervention would stabilize what it ultimately destabilized—is not an ancient grievance. It is a lesson that's alive, absorbed into the political consciousness of every Iranian who has studied their own country's history.

Chapter 10: January 8, 2026 – Iran's Darkest Hour

Witness Voice

> Rasht, January 9, 2026, Identity withheld
>
> "My neighbor's son was seventeen. He went out on January 8 with his friends. He did not come back that night. She waited. On January 10, a man called her phone—she does not know who—and told her to go to a specific hospital. She went. She identified her son from a photograph they showed her on a phone. He had been shot in the back. They told her she could have the body if she signed a paper saying he died in an accident. She signed it. She had no choice. She told me, 'I signed it. Now they can say he fell.'"

What this voice complicates: casualty statistics. The range of 3,000-36,000 dead is not a failure of accurate counting. It is the record of an authority that made accurate counting impossible, then required families to certify the falsification.

★★★

On January 8, 2026, communications across Iran were severely disrupted in a blackout that Amnesty International documented as part of a pattern of information suppression during protest movements. UN human rights monitors and independent journalists attempted to document events in cities across Iran. The blackout made comprehensive documentation impossible, which is why death toll estimates range so widely, from the Iranian government's figure of 3,117 to the Human Rights Activists in Iran's estimate of over 7,000 to the Trump administration's cited figure of approximately 32,000. The uncertainty about the numbers is itself a statement. It is what a blackout is designed to produce.

The death toll is disputed and will remain disputed because the communications blackout also severely limited documentation efforts. The Iranian government later acknowledged 3,117 dead. Human Rights Activists in Iran (HRANA) noted a higher number and warned of significant undercounting. Some estimates, based on hospital sources, family testimony, and analysis of morgue capacity, suggested the number could be as high as 36,500—a number that, if accurate, would constitute one of the worst massacres of civilians in the twenty-first century.

Human rights investigators recorded cases in which families reported difficulty obtaining information about detained loved ones or received bodies with injuries inconsistent with official accounts. Amnesty International and the UN Human Rights Council called for independent investigations and the preservation of evidence.

Taha Safari, sixteen years old, was identified from photographs his family had been shown. He was among the youngest of the dead. He went into the street because the price of bread had tripled. He did not go into the street to serve any foreign government's strategic agenda. He went because he was sixteen and the country he was going to inherit had been economically destroyed—on purpose, by a foreign power, which then congratulated itself under oath for the results.

On January 23, 2026, the UN Human Rights Council held a special session on Iran. A resolution passed 25-7-14—with Russia and China among those voting against. The resolution condemned the killings and called for accountability. It did not stop them.

While institutions deliberated, a woman in Tehran was writing a letter she did not intend to publish. Her name is Shahrzad Hemati. She is the social affairs editor of *Sharq* newspaper in Tehran and a member of the Iranian Women's Association. She wrote the letter during the bombing, while her small daughter Afra slept between her and her husband Nader on the living room floor—the floor where they had slept during another war, now the only shelter available to a family that had nowhere safer to go. A colleague shared it. It traveled. I read it with trembling hands.

I reproduce it here in full—first in the original Persian, then in my own translation—because no paraphrase can fully communicate what it carries. It is a document of the human cost of war, written from inside that cost, addressed to those outside it who have been calling for it.

کانون زنان ایران

اگر جنگ درد ندارد؛ لطفاً بیایید کنار ما

هفته‌ای یک شب قرار است هر سه نفر کنار هم بخوابیم. من و نادر و افرا. امروز جایمان را همان‌جایی پهن کرده‌ایم که روزهای جنگ می‌انداختیم؛ اتاق پذیرایی اصلی. افرا وسط من و نادر می‌خوابد و قصه گوش می‌دهد و می‌خوابد. خوابش سنگین است. برای همین کلاً نفهمید جنگی در کار است.

لحظاتی که خانه مثل گهواره می‌لرزید، افرا در آغوش من خواب .بود. درها محکم به هم می‌خوردند و من گوش‌هایش را گرفته بودم امشب آن‌جا خوابیدیم، همان‌طور تنگ هم. بچه سرماخوردگی دارد و ناراحتی می‌کند اما زود خوابش می‌برد. ما چه‌کار می‌کنیم؟; من خبرهای جنگ را برای سحر می‌فرستم، عکس کشته‌ها را برای نادر، و بعد یک‌دفعه می‌زنیم زیر گریه.

من به پزشکی قانونی رفته‌ام، در بیشتر تشییع‌پیکرها حضور
داشتم و همین باعث می‌شود در برابر هر اظهارنظری سکوت کنم. ما
روایت کردیم. از بیمارستان‌های پر از بیمار، از خانواده‌های کشتگان
همین از دستمان برمی‌آمد، خاک بر سرمان.

بگذارید یک اعتراف تلخ بکنم. رفتار شما با ما از جمهوری اسلامی
هم ترسناک‌تر است. خیلی از فعالان مدنی حاضرند زندان ج.ا. را تحمل
کنند اما هدف حمله سایبری هتاکانی قرار نگیرند که روزهای شکنجه
دموکراسی‌خواهان را فراموش کرده بودند.

حالا وقت جنگ است که عزیزانی می‌فرمایند درد ندارد. زود
می‌آید و یک جراحی خیلی تر و تمیز می‌شود و باید از آن استقبال کرد.
خب چرا در تمام این لحظات حساس کنونی ما این‌جا باشیم و شما دور
از ما؟; بیایید این لحظات شیرین و قشنگ را که عزیزانمان در زندان
هستند با هم تجربه کنیم.

و اما خودم: من تماشاگر این روزهای سردم و امیدوارم بمبی
که می‌آید اگر به خانه ما خورد، همه‌مان را ببرد؛ من و افرا و نادر را
وقتی یکدیگر را در آغوش کشیده‌ایم...

Iran Women's Association

Once a week, we agree to sleep together, all three of us: Nader, Afra, and me. Tonight we laid our bedding in the same place we laid it during the last war—the main living room. Afra sleeps between Nader and me, listening to a story until she drifts off. Her sleep is deep. So deep she never knew there was a war at all.

During the moments when the house shook like a cradle, Afra was asleep in my arms. The doors slammed hard, and I had my hands over her ears. Tonight we slept there again, pressed close together. The child has a cold and fusses, but she falls asleep quickly. What do we do? I sent the war news to Sahar. I send photos of the dead to Nader. And then we suddenly break into tears. Then I see something that makes me angry, and someone says, "Shahrzad, be quiet!" This is not the moment to speak.

I have been to the forensic medicine office. I was present at most of the funeral processions. And this is exactly why I fall silent before every opinion. I leave the final word to the grieving families, and I do my work—the same work we did through all these days and all these pressures. We bore witness from hospitals overflowing with the wounded, from the families of the dead. We wrote as much as our capacity allowed. We published photographs of people's loved ones. This was all we could do. God forgive us.

One tactic of security forces, when they are displeased with a post of yours, is to pressure you into taking it down. Their threats are security-based. What do I do? Like a citizen who knows her primary duty is her journalism, I grit my teeth and take the post down. But this act of taking down, this fear of writing, now has another face—one that may wound civil activists, writers, and journalists more than security threats themselves. Social pressure, online threats, being bullied, being branded a traitor to the homeland: here, too, you are censored.

We have been censored all these years. They said war must come because those of you inside Iran don't understand clearly, you are sellouts, and war brings democracy—so we went silent. They said a red carpet woven from the blood of our loved ones has been laid out for migrants abroad and their chosen leader—and we stared with wide eyes, tears running down, and went silent. During the protests, they shouted a slogan mocking the women's movement—and we went silent. They called the only movement that managed to crack the walls of dictatorship an "expired" movement—and again, we went silent.

From the other side, the story was told differently. They said: terrorists killed. We watched the footage and went silent. They said: terrorists struck, and held forty-day mourning ceremonies for them, and we went to Behesht-e Zahra cemetery and beat our chests and struck our heads and said nothing. Someone kept coming up behind us and saying, "Hush! Don't speak. Now is not the time."

Allow me a bitter confession. Your behavior toward us is

more terrifying than the Islamic Republic's. Many civil activists are willing to endure IRI prisons rather than become targets of abusive cyberattacks by people who have forgotten the days of torture inflicted on those who sought democracy.

Now it is the moment of war, and our dearest ones say it brings no pain. That it will come quickly, a very clean and tidy surgery, and we should welcome it. So why, in all these sensitive moments, are we here while you are far from us? Why should we wait—with the dollar at 165,000 tomans—for America to come and strike and leave and kill, and for the carpet of blood to grow more beautiful? Why don't we enjoy these "blessed moments of freedom" together? Come, let us experience these sweet, "nice" moments together while our loved ones are in prison. Let's go on a tour of Kahrizak together, visit the graves of our loved ones until Trump comes and strikes, and all of us can enjoy this bloodless surgery together.

The truth is, I wrote this text not to publish it, not because years ago on Twitter you promised to hang me from a tree in Haft-e Tir Square on the day after the protests; I will face that day one way or another, at the hands of one side or the other. I am keeping a fast of silence out of respect for the eternally-named of the homeland—for all those who have lost a loved one and who are the true owners of this grief. I keep silent to submit to their decision.

But I will not forget that on the days when the smell of blood was here, you marched in Munich for the Prince and said: "We have spread a red carpet of blood." I will carry this cruel metaphor of yours for as long as I live…

And as for me: I am a spectator on these cold days, and I hope that if the bomb that is coming hits our house, it takes all of us—me and Afra and Nader—while we are holding each other in our arms…[4]

—Shahrzad Hemati, Social Affairs editor, *Sharq* newspaper,
Tehran Member, Iran Women's Association, February 2026

4 Emphasis mine

I have read this letter many times. I still cannot read the final sentence without my hands shaking. Shahrzad Hemati is not asking to be saved. She is not asking for democracy to arrive by missile. She is telling those who live safely abroad and cheer for war that they do not know what they are cheering for—that the bomb does not distinguish between the government and the mother, between the geopolitical target and the child sleeping between her parents on the living room floor, between the clean surgery of abstraction and the specific, irreplaceable body of a small girl named Afra who never knew there was a war at all.

Hemati's letter belongs alongside other voices from this same season of pain. The Palestinian mother trying to explain to her child why they had to leave again, why there was no safe place to go. The Israeli family in a shelter with sirens overhead. The hostage families holding vigils in public squares, refusing to let the world forget. The Gaza medic working by torchlight in a hospital without power. The Israeli children who grew up in the shadow of October 7. All of them are inside the same moral reality: human beings in the path of forces set in motion by people who will never personally feel the house shake, who will never press their hands over a child's ears in the dark, who will never lie awake on a cold floor writing a letter they did not intend to publish because the weight of what they were living through had become too heavy to carry alone.

Human dignity is not a value that can be applied selectively—the child in Minab whose name I cannot find. The sixteen-year-old Taha Safari who was identified from a photograph at a police station. The children in Gaza whose names the world learned to scroll past. The hostages in tunnels. The Israeli children who survived October 7. All of them—every single one—are bearers of the same inviolable human worth that every declaration of rights, every serious moral tradition, every philosophy worth its name has insisted cannot be stripped away. This is not a political statement. It is the bedrock on which all other moral claims rest. And when we fail to hold it—

when we apply it selectively, when we mourn some children and not others—we do not merely fail those we exclude. We undermine the very principle that protects everyone, including ourselves.

Chapter 11:
Who Was in the Room? – External Interference in the January 2026 Protests

The Economic Engineering: What is Not Under Dispute

The clearest form of external interference in the January 2026 protests is the one admitted under oath by Scott Bessent, the official responsible on February 5, 2026, he confirmed the US had deliberately engineered the economic conditions that produced the protests. He spoke proudly of Iranian people in the streets. He said it was a success story. He did not describe it as a side effect.

What Bessent described is a form of economic warfare designed to produce civilian suffering severe enough to generate civil unrest. USInflation was running high. The banking system was in crisis. These conditions did not emerge from Iranian domestic policy alone—they were the result of the most aggressive sanctions campaign in modern history. The protests that followed were the American government's intended outcome. The Iranians who went into the streets were, by Bessent's own account, fulfilling a plan made in Washington.

The Mossad Communications Channel: What is Credibly Reported

An Israeli Channel 13 investigation published in January 2026 reported that Israeli intelligence—specifically Mossad—had transitioned from "passive observation to active technical facilitation" of the Iranian protest movement. The specific claim: Mossad provided cyber support to help protesters communicate through the Iranian government's digital blackout. A secondary report in *Haaretz*, citing unnamed security officials, said the support included encrypted communication tools distributed through overseas networks and technical assistance with VPN infrastructure. The Israeli government has not officially confirmed these reports, nor have they been officially denied. The Israeli government declined to comment. Channel 13 and *Haaretz* are credible Israeli media institutions with established national security reporting.

What the Channel 13 and *Haaretz* reporting describes, if accurate, is covert technical facilitation—not leadership, direction, or creation of the protests. The protesters themselves had entirely genuine motivations. Providing communications tools to people who are already protesting is different from directing them. The moral and political weight of that distinction is real. It does not change the underlying question: whether a foreign intelligence service was operating within a protest movement without the protesters' knowledge or consent. If the reporting is accurate, the answer is yes.

The CIA-Kurdish Arms Program: What CNN Reported

On March 3, 2026, CNN, citing three intelligence officials, reported that the CIA had been running a program through Kurdish intermediaries to facilitate the movement of arms and communications equipment into Iran in the months before the protests. The report described the program as "pre-positioned" infrastructure—assets placed ahead of anticipated unrest rather than in response to it. This is a significant distinction: it suggests prior planning for the contingency of protests, not merely opportunistic support once protests began. The CIA has not denied or confirmed these reports. The CIA has declined to comment on intelligence matters.

The Kurdish dimension of this reporting has received less attention than it deserves. The Trump administration, concurrent with the strikes, was running direct calls with Kurdish regional leaders—including Nechirvan Barzani in Iraq and the Talabani family network. The CIA-Kurdish program, if accurately reported, suggests that the external infrastructure being built around the protest movement was coordinated at the presidential level, not conducted as a rogue intelligence operation. The question of who authorized it and when remains unanswered by CNN's reporting. It is the question that congressional oversight would need to answer—oversight that the Senate declined to exercise when it voted 47-53 against a war powers resolution on March 4, 2026.

Trump's January 2 Threat: On the Record

On January 2, 2026, President Trump posted on Truth Social: "To the leadership of Iran: DO NOT KILL YOUR PROTESTERS. If you do, you will face consequences unlike anything you have ever faced before. THE USA IS LOCKED AND LOADED. BE CAREFUL!" This statement is not disputed. It is part of the public record. It was a direct, public communication from the President of the United States to an ongoing Iranian protest movement, issued while the CIA and Mossad were—according to credible reporting—operating inside that movement. The statement was understood by anyone watching as a signal that American military force was available on behalf of the protesters. Whether that signal was intended to protect the protesters or to encourage the protests to continue is not clear from the text alone. Both interpretations are consistent with the public evidence.

What the Evidence Supports and What it Does Not

The evidence supports the following conclusions, stated with the confidence appropriate to each level of sourcing: First, with certainty (on record, under oath): the United States Department of the Treasury deliberately manufactured the economic collapse that produced the December 2025 protests. Second, with high confidence (credible multisource journalism, not officially denied): Israeli intelligence provided technical communication support to the protest movement. Third, with moderate confidence (three-source CIA reporting, not confirmed or denied): a CIA-Kurdish arms and communications program positioned assets ahead of the protests. Fourth, on the record: the President of the United States publicly threatened military consequences during the protests, signaling American involvement to everyone watching.

The evidence does not support the conclusion that the protests were invented, directed, or primarily driven by external actors. The economic conditions were real. The political frustrations were real. The Woman, Life, Freedom generation had been building toward this moment since 2022. Taha Safari did not go into the street because the CIA told him to. He went because the price of bread had tripled. The distinction between manufactured grievances and genuine grievances that external actors exploit is real, and it matters for how Iran's future is understood and built. Iranians on those streets were not puppets of Washington or Tel Aviv. They were human beings, acting on their own behalf, in conditions that external powers had deliberately made worse.

The Unanswered Questions

What the public record has not yet answered: whether the CIA-Kurdish program involved weapons that were used during the protests;

whether the Mossad communications support was coordinated with Trump administration actions; whether the January 2 Trump threat was coordinated with Israeli operational planning; and whether any American or Israeli official had prior knowledge of the specific timeline of the strikes and deliberately accelerated the protest environment to create the political conditions for military action. The available evidence does not answer these questions. These are the questions that a functioning congressional oversight system would investigate. That system declined to exercise its authority on March 4, 2026, when fifty-three senators voted to allow the war to continue without authorization. The record is incomplete, not because the evidence is hidden. It is incomplete because the institutions that would compel its completion chose not to.

Chapter 12: The Nuclear Dimension—What the Bombs Were Really About

Witness Voice

Vienna, February 24, 2026, Identity withheld; account consistent with IAEA February 2026 quarterly report.

"We had not had continuous monitoring at Fordow since October 2025. The cameras were disconnected. We knew enrichment was continuing based on our inferences from truck traffic patterns, procurement signals, and the rate at which Iran was consuming certain materials. But 'continuous monitoring' means something specific in verification language: it means you know, in real time, that nothing is being diverted. We did not have that. What we had was a picture with significant dark areas. And we had—as of February 24—an agreement being brokered by Oman to restore monitoring. Two days later, the bombs fell on the monitoring problem and the solution simultaneously."

What this voice complicates: the binary of "Iran was hiding something" vs "Iran was cooperating." Both were simultaneously true, in different proportions, until the strikes made the question moot.

This section argues that the nuclear case for the strikes was real but not sufficient: Iran was enriching to 60 percent and the IAEA had lost monitoring continuity, but Iran was simultaneously negotiating to zero stockpiling. The evidence is from IAEA quarterly reports, Omani mediator statements, Araghchi's post-strike account, and the Geneva timeline. After reading, the stated nuclear justification and the documented diplomatic reality cannot both be fully true; the record favors the diplomatic account.

★★★

By late 2025, Iran had accumulated approximately 440.9 kilograms (972 pounds) of uranium enriched to 60 percent—a short technical step from weapons-grade enrichment at 90 percent. As of May 17, 2025, the stockpile of 60 percent enriched uranium in the form of uranium hexafluoride was 408.6 kg of uranium, superseded by the June 13 figure of 440.9 kg, the last verified IAEA measurement before the strikes. The IAEA calculated this in its September 2025 verification and monitoring report as the figure on the eve of the June 2025 attacks.

The weapons implications—nine to eleven nuclear weapons—are consistent with the 440.9 kg figure. Iran's supply of 60 percent enriched uranium, when processed to weapons-grade 90 percent enrichment, would provide the fuel for nine nuclear weapons, with a single cascade of 175 IR-6 centrifuges able to produce weapons-grade material for one weapon every twenty-five days.

The IAEA had lost continuous oversight of Iran's enrichment activities after the Twelve-Day War of June 2025. Intelligence assessments varied on the precise timeline, but most agreed that Iran was within weeks to months of being able to produce enough material for a nuclear device if it chose to.

On February 6, 2026, diplomatic talks were held in Muscat, Oman. On February 27, Oman's Foreign Minister announced a "breakthrough": Iran had reportedly agreed to a verification regime. The next day, Operation Epic Fury began.

I want to dwell on that sequence. A diplomatic breakthrough was announced. Twenty-four hours later, bombs fell. Either the breakthrough was a lie—a Potemkin negotiation designed to provide cover for a predetermined strike—or the decision to strike had already been made, and the diplomacy was irrelevant. Either way, the conclusion is the same: the United States and Israel had decided that Iran's nuclear program could not be allowed to exist, and they were prepared to use military force to eliminate it regardless of what the diplomats were saying.

This matters because the stated justification for Epic Fury was anticipatory self-defense: the claim that Iran's nuclear program posed an imminent threat that required immediate military action. But a threat cannot be both imminent and solvable by diplomacy. If diplomacy was working on February 27, then the threat was not imminent on February 28. And if the threat was imminent on February 28, then the diplomacy of February 27 was theater.

The nuclear question is genuinely difficult. A nuclear-armed Iran would change the security calculus of the entire Middle East, accelerate proliferation pressures, and create dangers that are real and serious. I do not dismiss those dangers. But the solution to the development of a nuclear program is not always bombing. The JCPOA—the nuclear deal that the United States negotiated in 2015 and abandoned in 2018—had worked. It had put Iran's nuclear program under the most rigorous inspection regime in the history of arms control. When the United States withdrew from the deal, Iran had roughly 300 kilograms of low-enriched uranium. When Operation Epic Fury was launched, it had 440.9 kilograms enriched to sixty percent. Every kilogram of that increase is the direct consequence of the decision to abandon diplomacy in 2018.

The misreading of Iran that produced this outcome was not new in 2026. It had been documented forty-seven years earlier, and the documentation is worth examining precisely because it names the structural error before the error repeated.

In February 1979, as the Shah was leaving Iran and Ayatollah Khomeini was returning from exile in Paris, a Pakistani political scientist named Eqbal Ahmad published an analysis in *Mother Jones* titled "The Iranian Hundred Years' War." Ahmad held a doctorate in political science and Middle Eastern history from Princeton. He had interviewed Ayatollah Khomeini directly. He was writing for an American audience that had been told, by the *New York Times* among others, that the Shah had a broad base of popular support.

Ahmad identified three things with documented precision. First, that the American media had systematically misrepresented a broad coalition—workers, lawyers, liberals, clerics, bazaar merchants, and students—as a reactionary religious movement hostile to modernization; this was not an emphasis but a foundational error that made rational policy formation structurally impossible from the start. Second, that Ayatollah Khomeini emerged from the same nationalist tradition as Mohammad Mossadegh—that of resistance to foreign domination of Iranian resources, not from Saudi Wahhabism or Ottoman theocracy. Ahmad's comparison of Shia Islam to the Quaker tradition within Christianity—a minority faith built on resistance to established authority rather than the exercise of state power—remains one of the most precise descriptions of Iranian political theology written in English in the twentieth century. Third, that American support for the Shah continued through its sending of riot-control equipment, advisers, trainers, and at least $2.5 billion in weapons during 1978 alone, even as the Shah's security forces were killing Iranians in the streets.

All three of those structural conditions recur in 2026. The coalition that rose in January 2026 was again described in terms of its most radical elements rather than its breadth. The religious and nationalist dimensions of Iranian resistance were again treated as interchangeable. American material support for a government suppressing its population continued until the government itself became the target.

The systems science framework this book applies to infrastructure has a precise name for what Ahmad identified: a failure of observability—a decision-making system so unable to see what is actually happening inside the system it is attempting to influence, that it consistently produces outcomes that are the opposite of its stated objectives. Ahmad saw it in 1979. The pattern continued through 1953, through 2018, and through February 28, 2026. The specific actors change. The structural error does not.

What 440.9 Kilograms Actually Means

By late 2025, Iran held approximately 440.9 kilograms of uranium enriched to sixty percent purity. For readers without a background in nuclear physics, this number needs translation, as it is a central fact.

Natural uranium is approximately 0.7 percent fissile U-235. Low-enriched uranium, suitable for civilian power generation, is enriched to between 3 and 5 percent. The JCPOA of 2015 limited Iran to 3.67 percent enrichment. Highly enriched uranium, suitable for a nuclear weapon, is enriched to 90percent or higher. Sixty percent sits in a position that is technically precise and strategically ambiguous: it is not weapons-grade, but it is substantially "pre-positioned" toward weapons-grade. The additional enrichment required to go from 60 percent to 90 percent is technically a smaller step than going from 3.67 percent to 60 percent—the harder centrifuge work is already done.

The IAEA in its February 2026 quarterly report—the last one issued before the internet blackout made verification impossible—reported that it had lost continuous monitoring of Iran's enrichment activities. What the agency knew was what Iran chose to show it, plus what satellite imagery could infer from patterns of truck traffic and facility activity. The uncertainty was real, and it was partly manufactured: Iran had systematically degraded the verification regime after the United States withdrew from the JCPOA in 2018.

The Oman negotiations that were producing a breakthrough in late February 2026 had, according to Oman's Foreign Minister Badr Al Busaidi, reached an agreement in principle on Iran's return to IAEA verification and to zero stockpiling of enriched uranium. This was precisely the outcome that the stated rationale for the strikes said was impossible. It was apparently not impossible. It was, according to the mediator who brokered it, imminent. The bombs fell before the agreement could be signed.

The nuclear argument for the strikes, therefore, rests on a paradox: Iran was close enough to a weapon to justify immediate military action, but was simultaneously agreeing never to stockpile enriched uranium. Neither can both things be fully true. Either Iran was negotiating in bad faith—using the talks as a delay tactic while secretly accelerating toward weaponization—or it was negotiating genuinely, and the strikes were not necessary to prevent the nuclear outcome. The public record supports the second reading. The private intelligence may have supported the first. The intelligence has not been released. Until it is proven that the nuclear threat justified the strikes while negotiations were succeeding, the case remains unproven.

Chapter 13: The Failure of Diplomacy

The June 2025 Twelve-Day War was the dress rehearsal that made February 2026 possible—and that both sides learned lessons from it that they applied to the next round. The evidence is based on Pentagon casualty reports, Israeli military statements, IRGC doctrine publications, and oil price data. This evidence supports the argument that the February 2026 operation was not improvised; it was planned in the aftermath of June 2025, and the mosaic defense response was planned in the same period.

The Twelve-Day War began on June 13 with Israeli carrying out airstrikes against Iranian nuclear facilities. Iran retaliated with massive ballistic missile and drone barrages against Israeli cities and American military bases across the Middle East. The United States joined the fighting directly. For twelve days, the region shook.

The immediate military results were significant. Israeli and American strikes destroyed or heavily damaged several major nuclear facilities, killed numerous military commanders, and severely crippled Iran's air defense network. The fighting killed nearly 1,100 people in Iran and 28 in Israel.

But the Twelve-Day War also demonstrated the limits of airpower. Iran's nuclear program was set back by two to three years, but not eliminated. Iran's knowledge—the physicists, the engineers, the tacit institutional understanding of how to enrich uranium and design weapons—could not be bombed away. And Iran's response had been fierce enough to demonstrate that any future conflict would carry enormous costs.

Within Iran, the aftermath of the Twelve-Day War led to a significant tightening of internal controls. Security forces used the emergency period to restrict information flow and tighten internal controls. A sweeping internet shutdown during the conflict provided the government with tools and precedents it would employ on a much larger scale in January 2026.

Economically, the war had devastating consequences for Iran's already battered economy. Oil exports were disrupted. Insurance costs skyrocketed. The rial fell sharply. The economic crisis that triggered the December 2025 protests was caused by the disruptions of the June 2025 war. This war was supposed to prevent Iran from acquiring nuclear weapons, but that, in doing so, also prevented Iran from stabilizing its economy enough to prevent a social explosion.

The Dress Rehearsal and Its Lessons

The June 13 Israeli airstrikes targeting was specific: Fordow, buried under a mountain and previously considered impervious to conventional munitions; Natanz, the primary enrichment facility; Isfahan, where uranium conversion occurred; and Arak, the heavy water reactor. American GBU-57 Massive Ordnance Penetrators—bunker busters weighing thirty thousand pounds, the only munitions capable of reaching Fordow—were used. The United States participated directly.

Iran retaliated with what its commanders called an "overwhelming response": hundreds of ballistic missiles and drones targeted American bases across the region simultaneously, saturating air defenses. The USS *Gerald R. Ford* carrier group, operating in the eastern Mediterranean, intercepted more than eighty incoming missiles in a single engagement. Six American service members were killed at Al Udeid Air Base in Qatar. Forty-seven were wounded. In Israel, the Iron Dome and Arrow systems intercepted the majority of incoming strikes. Still, seventeen Israelis were killed, and the city of Haifa suffered significant damage from a missile that penetrated its defenses.

After twelve days—hence the name—a ceasefire was brokered under intense pressure from the Gulf states, which were watching oil prices approach $110 dollars a barrel and whose own infrastructure had been grazed by Iranian strikes clearly intended as warnings. The ceasefire held. Negotiations resumed. The IAEA attempted to restore monitoring. Iran rebuilt faster than anyone had projected.

What the June 2025 war established: Iran's nuclear infrastructure was harder to destroy comprehensively than the strike planners had hoped. Fordow sustained damage but was not destroyed. Natanz was more severely damaged but retained significant capacity. And Iran's missile and drone forces—the mosaic defense arsenal—survived largely intact, because they had been dispersed precisely in anticipation of such a scenario.

The lesson Israel and the United States drew from June 2025 was that a larger, more comprehensive strike—including regime decapitation, not merely nuclear targeting—was necessary to achieve their objectives. The lesson Iran drew from June 2025 was that its mosaic defense doctrine was sound, that it could absorb a significant strike and still retaliate effectively, and that the United States would not allow its allies to be struck without joining the fight. Both sides drew the lessons that led them, eight months later, back to war.

This is the tragic logic of military force. Every military action produces consequences that cannot be fully controlled, and those consequences often include conditions that necessitate further military action. The Twelve-Day War set back Iran's nuclear program and pushed forward Iran's domestic crisis. The domestic crisis produced the massacres of January 2026. The massacres produced the political pressure, in both Washington and Jerusalem, for more decisive action. And more decisive action produced Operation Epic Fury.

The Negotiating Table That Got Bombed

We left Geneva with the understanding that we would seal a deal next time we meet. But it was Mr. Trump, yet again, who ultimately ordered the bombing of the negotiating table.

—Abbas Araghchi, Iranian Foreign Minister, March 1, 2026

There is a version of this story that never happened. It existed, documented and concrete, for approximately seventy-two hours before it was destroyed. Understanding what was on the table and who walked away from it is not a footnote to the conflict that followed. It is the moral and legal center of the case against it.

It begins on Thursday, February 26, 2026, at the Grand Hotel Kempinski, Geneva, Switzerland. Abbas Araghchi, Iran's Foreign Minister, sits across from a table that includes Steve Witkoff, the American special envoy, and Jared Kushner, the President's son-in-law and senior adviser who Trump has personally entrusted with some of the administration's most delicate diplomatic work. The setting has qualities specific to high-stakes negotiation: the formal quiet of a Geneva conference room, the careful language, the sense—present on both sides—that something might actually be possible.

The American delegation has come with a specific proposal: a decade-long halt to uranium enrichment, full IAEA verification, and the dismantling of centrifuge infrastructure built over two decades at Fordow and Natanz. The Iranians have presented their own position: they acknowledge their right to peaceful nuclear technology, accept verification, and are willing to discuss enrichment limits. The gap between these positions is real. It is also, in the assessment of every independent expert who assessed the negotiations afterward, bridgeable.

There is a dimension of this negotiation that the documentary record cannot fully capture, but that anyone with deep familiarity with Iranian political culture will recognize. *Ta'arof* is the Persian art of formal courtesy, the elaborate social performance of offering and deferring that governs interaction at every level of Iranian life. A guest arrives; the host insists on serving tea, on offering food, on repeating the offer of hospitality until the guest accepts. The guest repeatedly declines out of politeness before accepting. Both parties understand the process is a ritual. Both know the tea will be served and accepted. The point is the form, the care, the signal that the other person is honored.

Iranian diplomatic culture carries this interior logic. Public positions are often not final positions. A stated refusal may be the opening of a conversation, not its conclusion. The elaborate verbal construction that sounds, to Western ears, like a closed door may be, in the Iranian frame, the beginning of a negotiation about how to open it with dignity. American negotiators who have dealt with Iranian counterparts over decades have consistently noted this: the public posture and the private one are different instruments, and reading only the public posture leads to systematic misunderstanding.

This does not mean that Iranian diplomatic positions are insincere. It means that sincerity in the Iranian frame is expressed differently than in the American one, and that the gap between expression and meaning is precisely where deals either get made or fall apart. The Oman channel worked, in part, because its Omani facilitators understood both frames fluently and could translate not just words but intention. When that channel was bypassed, the translation capacity was removed when it was most needed.

Two days earlier, on February 24, Oman's Foreign Minister Badr Al Busaidi—who has been serving as the back-channel mediator between Washington and Tehran for months, conducting the patient, unglamorous work that diplomacy actually requires—had made a statement that was either very carefully worded or inadvertently revelatory. He said a "breakthrough" had been reached. He said Iran had agreed both never to stockpile enriched uranium and to full verification by the IAEA. He said Iran had agreed to irreversibly downgrade its current enriched uranium to "the lowest levels possible." And he said, in plain language, that peace was "within reach."

Al Busaidi had been in Washington the day before, on Friday, February 27. He met with Vice President Vance. He described the state of the negotiations. He told *CBS News*, separately, that Iran had agreed to zero stockpiling of nuclear enrichment. He urged the United States not to let the window close.

That window was closing faster than Al Busaidi knew. Or perhaps he knew and was powerless to stop it. The evidence that emerged in the weeks after the strikes suggests that the decision to act had already been made, or was being made in parallel with the negotiations, and that the Geneva talks were not, in the final analysis, the frame within which the Trump administration was operating.

The Divergence in the Record

Two narratives exist about what happened in Geneva, and they cannot both be true.

In the American narrative, as presented by Witkoff and others in the days after the strikes, Iran had been negotiating in bad faith. Iran began talks by insisting on its "inalienable right" to enrich uranium. Iran rejected the zero-enrichment proposal. Iran "boasted" about its 460 kilograms of 60 percent-enriched uranium. The negotiations failed because Iran would not make the concessions required. The strikes were therefore a consequence of diplomatic failure, not a cause of it.

In the Iranian narrative and in the public statements of the Omani mediator who was in the room, a genuine breakthrough had been reached. Iran had agreed to the key American demands. Araghchi left Geneva believing a deal was coming. When the bombs fell two days later, he issued a statement that was not the language of a country that had been stonewalling: "We left Geneva with the understanding that we would seal a deal next time we meet." He called the strikes the bombing of the negotiating table.

The Omani foreign minister—a man with no incentive to lie, whose country's credibility as a mediator depends entirely on the accuracy of his public statements—confirmed the breakthrough account. He was "dismayed" by the strikes. He said they did not serve the interests of the United States. He said, pointedly, "This is not your war."

There is a third data point that does not fit the American narrative: the intelligence assessments. Pentagon officials told Congress in closed-door briefings, reported by multiple outlets, that there was no intelligence suggesting Iran was planning to attack US forces first. The stated justification for the strikes—that the United States had received intelligence that Iran was planning a preemptive missile launch—was not supported by the intelligence community's actual assessment. American intelligence had assessed that Iran was nearly a decade away from developing a militarily viable intercontinental ballistic missile. The claim that Iran posed an imminent threat, echoing the false weapons of mass destruction claims made before the 2003 Iraq invasion, did not hold up to scrutiny. It would not have passed the legal test for preemptive self-defense under international law even if it had been accurate.

The Last Seventy-Two Hours

On February 26, the Geneva talks conclude. Araghchi returns to Tehran to consult with his government. The Iranians believe they are on the verge of an agreement. Inside the Iranian government, there are factions—there always are—who are skeptical, who believe the Americans cannot be trusted, who point to 2018 and Trump's unilateral withdrawal from the JCPOA as evidence that any deal is provisional. But the dominant message, as of February 26, is that talks are continuing.

On February 27, Al Busaidi flies to Washington. He meets with Vance. He describes the breakthrough. Vance, according to later reporting, says he "understood." The Omani mediator returns home. A fourth round of talks is being planned. The calendar is being consulted. Both sides are drafting language.

February 27, late evening, Eastern Time. In the Situation Room of the White House, a different conversation is happening. The decision that is about to be made will not be made public until it is already irreversible.

February 28, 1:15 a.m. Eastern. US Central Command begins Operation Epic Fury. B-2 Spirit stealth bombers, flying from Whiteman Air Force Base in Missouri after a seventeen-hour flight, begin their attack runs over Iran. Israeli F-35s launch simultaneously. The compound of the House of Leadership—the official residence and command center of Supreme Leader Ali Khamenei—is among the first targets.

In Geneva, there is no one left to negotiate with. The table is still set. The chairs are still there. The language being drafted is still on someone's laptop. None of it matters anymore.

What the Failure of Diplomacy Actually Means

The official American account of the Geneva failure is that Iran refused the deal. The evidentiary record suggests something more troubling: that the decision to strike was made before or during the negotiations, that the negotiations were either a good faith effort that was overridden by other factors in the White House, or were never the primary framework used to make the decision.

This distinction matters enormously, not just legally but historically. If Iran refused a genuine deal and the strikes followed as a consequence, the moral and legal case for the war—while still problematic on multiple grounds—has a different character than if the strikes were planned. At the same time, the negotiations were being used as cover: one set of American officials was negotiating in good faith, while another set was planning the operation.

The record does not yet point to a definitive answer. What it does point to is this: Oman's credible mediator said a breakthrough had been reached. Iran's foreign minister said a deal was imminent. American intelligence said Iran was not planning a preemptive attack. And the bombs fell anyway. The burden of proof for why they needed to fall at that moment, and not after the next round of talks, rests entirely on the administration that ordered them. That burden has not been met.

The cultural dimension of the practice of *ta'arof* goes unaddressed in almost every Western account.

When an Iranian negotiator says, "In principle we agree," they may be genuinely signaling agreement, or they may be buying time while communicating something to a domestic audience by not yet refusing outright. The Iranian side in Geneva almost certainly understood this—that the way they communicated would be heard differently by different audiences. When Araghchi left Geneva, saying a deal was imminent, he was telling his counterpart something real and sending a message to the domestic political factions who had been skeptical of talks from the beginning: that the negotiations had produced something worth defending. He was holding two conversations at once, as Iranian diplomats have always had to do. The American side, in its own internal deliberations, may have discounted his statements for this reason—not knowing whether to read them as a genuine signal or a ritual courtesy. The Omani mediator, whose country has a long tradition of understanding both sides, knew which it was. He has said so publicly. He was right.

The failure to read Iranian communication codes correctly is not a new problem in American diplomacy toward Iran. It is a structural deficit—one that the diplomatic corps knows about, has written training materials about, and has never fully solved, because cultural competency in a country one has had no embassy in for forty-seven years is extraordinarily difficult to maintain.

For the people of Iran, the distinction between "deal failed then strikes" and "strikes while deal was forming" is not academic. It is the difference between an action that was, however brutal, at least a consequence of genuine diplomatic exhaustion, and one that was a choice made before the last diplomatic option was fully explored.

The negotiating table got bombed. That is what the record shows. The rest is a story about what kind of country decides to do that, and why, and what the consequences are for a world in which the most powerful nation on earth demonstrates that it will bomb a negotiating table when the negotiations are not moving fast enough.

On the evening of March 31, 2026, Iranian President Masoud Pezeshkian released an open letter to the American people, making the same historical arguments linking the 1953 coup and the bombed negotiations—and omitting the same things that all Iranian state communications omit.

It omitted the minimum viable first step towards deescalation: Iran guarantees freedom of navigation through the Strait of Hormuz; the United States suspends offensive naval posturing in the Persian Gulf. One commitment each. No trust required. Every trading nation—China, India, Japan, South Korea, the European Union—becomes an automatic stakeholder in enforcement. The framework does not require either government to legitimize the other. It requires only that both governments recognize that the Strait is not a bargaining chip. It is the circulatory system of the global economy, and its closure harms everyone except the parties who closed it.

It also omitted mentioning the fact that the Oman diplomacy that produced the February 24 breakthrough cannot simply be replaced by opening a new diplomatic channel. What made it work was not its Omani location but the specific architecture of understanding that Badr Al-Busaidi had built over fifteen years—the cultural fluency required to navigate *ta'arof*, the gap between stated position and final position that only a credible and culturally literate intermediary can bridge, and the accumulated record of commitments kept that gave both sides a reason to trust the process even when they did not trust each other. That architecture took fifteen years to construct. Its destruction in the early hours of February 28 was not a tactical setback that a phone call can reverse. It was the destruction of the conditions that made the breakthrough possible. Pakistan is the most viable current replacement—it maintains full diplomatic relations with both capitals and has served as a go-between in prior crises—but it lacks the accumulated credibility that the Oman diplomatic channel took a generation to build. Rebuilding takes longer and produces less than what was available on February 27.

The Room Where It Was Decided

This was our last, best chance to strike and eliminate the intolerable threats posed by this sick and sinister regime.

— President Donald Trump, White House press conference, March 2, 2026

Decisions of this magnitude are made in rooms. The rooms have specific dimensions, furniture, and lighting. The people in them have histories—personal obsessions, old arguments, and loyalties formed by other crises. Reconstructing what happened in the Situation Room on the night of February 27, 2026, requires working from what was said publicly, what journalists with access to participants have reported, and what the documentary record shows about the intelligence available at the time. The result is a picture with significant areas of clarity and some that remain deliberately obscured.

What we know for certain: the decision to launch Operation Epic Fury was made by President Trump, acting with authority he claimed as commander-in-chief without seeking congressional authorization. Present in or connected to the decision, according to public reporting were: Secretary of Defense Pete Hegseth, CIA Director John Ratcliffe, Secretary of State Marco Rubio, Vice President JD Vance, and—by secure video link from Tel Aviv—Israeli Prime Minister Benjamin

Netanyahu, who had been pushing for American participation in a strike on Iran for years and whose military had been planning its component of the operation for months.

What we know about the intelligence: The National Intelligence Assessment on Iran's ballistic missile program had concluded that a militarily viable intercontinental ballistic missile—the kind capable of reaching the continental United States—was at minimum nine years away, and only if Iran decided to pursue it actively. Pentagon officials told congressional members in classified briefings that there was no specific intelligence indicating that Iran was planning to attack American forces preemptively. The stated intelligence justification for the strikes—that Iran was planning an imminent preemptive missile launch—did not correspond to what the intelligence community had actually concluded.

This gap—between what the intelligence showed and what was claimed publicly to justify the action—is not an unfamiliar feature of American decisions to go to war. In October 2002, the Bush administration presented Congress with a National Intelligence Estimate on Iraq that, as later investigations established, overstated the intelligence community's certainty about weapons of mass destruction that . The mechanisms are different; the pattern is recognizable.

The Men in the Room

Pete Hegseth, the Secretary of Defense, had stated publicly in the weeks before the strikes that Iran's nuclear pursuits and ballistic missile arsenal were "no longer tolerable." He would later say, at a press conference, that the strikes were not a "regime change war"—a statement that directly contradicted what President Trump was simultaneously saying. Within the same forty-eight hours, Trump told the Iranian people to "seize control of your destiny," called Khamenei's death "a great thing for the world," and announced that the United States was engaged in a "major combat operation aimed at eliminating threats from the Iranian regime." The administration's account of its own objectives was not internally consistent. This inconsistency was not accidental. It reflected a genuine division within the decision-making apparatus about what the operation's objectives actually were.

Marco Rubio, the Secretary of State, offered what would become the most legally scrutinized justification. He told reporters that the United States had known Israel was going to act, had known this would provoke Iranian retaliation against American forces, and had therefore struck preemptively to reduce American casualties. "We knew that there was going to be an Israeli action," Rubio said. "We knew that that would precipitate an attack against American forces. And we knew that if we didn't preemptively go after them before they launched those attacks, we would suffer higher casualties." The circularity of this logic—strike Iran to prevent Iran from retaliating against the strike—was noted by international law scholars within hours of the statement. Brian Finucane of the International Crisis Group called it among the most legally untenable justifications for military action in recent American history.

The legal standard against which this justification must be measured is the *Caroline* test, established in 1837 and accepted as the foundation of anticipatory self-defense in international law ever since: a threat must be "instant, overwhelming, leaving no choice of means, and no moment for deliberation." A government that spends months in joint military planning, while simultaneously conducting diplomacy over the same issue, and that receives confirmation of a diplomatic breakthrough twenty-four hours before launching strikes, cannot invoke this standard. The *Caroline* test exists precisely to distinguish genuine self-defense from preventive war dressed in the language of self-defense. Operation Epic Fury, as documented, does not pass the test.

JD Vance had said weeks before that regime change in Iran was not the objective. When asked at a press availability whether he would support regime change after previously criticizing the Iraq war, he said, "Life has all kinds of crazy twists and turns." It was an answer that told you more than a direct answer would have. Men who have changed their minds about something as consequential as regime change wars usually have a reason. The reason, in Vance's case, appears to have been political: the opportunity presented by Iran's killing of protesters in January 2026, which had genuinely shocked the international community and created a political context in which the use of force was easier to justify than it had been in 2019 or 2022.

Netanyahu's position will be analyzed in-depth in the following chapter. What matters here is what his presence at the table via video meant for the decision itself. Israel's participation transformed an American unilateral action into a joint operation, with all the intelligence-sharing, target-coordination, and political entanglement that implies. The question of whether the United States was a willing participant in a war that Israel wanted, or whether Israel was a willing participant in a war that the United States wanted, or whether both governments wanted it and used each other as political cover for decisions they had already reached independently, is one that the historical record will eventually clarify. For now, the record shows a joint operation planned over months, executed with precision that implied extensive shared preparation, and announced publicly by both governments within minutes of each other.

Who Was Not in the Room

Who was not in the room: Congress. No member of the House or Senate had been consulted before the strikes began. Speaker Mike Johnson, briefed after the fact, told reporters the operation was a "defensive" action. He did not explain how an attack planned over months, targeting a country that had not attacked the United States, met the legal definition of defense. He did not attempt to explain it because no legally coherent explanation existed.

Who was not in the room: the Omani mediator who had just reported a breakthrough in negotiations. Badr Al Busaidi learned about the strikes the way everyone else did: from the news. The man who had been serving as the bridge between these two governments, who had been in Washington twenty-four hours earlier describing the state of play to the Vice President, was not informed that the bridge he was building was about to be demolished.

What was not in the room: any meaningful intelligence indicating an imminent threat. The Pentagon's own assessment, shared in closed-door congressional briefings, said there was no evidence Iran was planning to attack American forces first. The claim that the strikes were in self-defense against an imminent threat was not supported by the intelligence actually available to those making the decision.

Who was not in the room: the Iranian civilians who would be killed. The children and teachers were killed in Minab. The patients are being evacuated from Gandhi Hospital in Tehran. The man in Sanandaj who lost his home when bombs fell on residential neighborhoods next to a police station. The woman in Kerman who posted a video saying that if she died, she was okay with it. These are the people whose fate was decided in that room, by those people, based on that intelligence, without their knowledge, without their consent, and without any of the people making the decision having to live with the immediate physical consequences of what they chose.

This is the structure of the decision that launched a war. It is not unique in American history. It rhymes with 1953—when a smaller room decided to remove Iran's elected prime minister. It rhymes with 2003, when a similar room decided to remove Iraq's dictator based on intelligence that did not hold up. The rooms have different people in them. The pattern of how the decisions get made—who is included, who is excluded, what evidence is required, what accountability follows—remains recognizable across seven decades.

The question this pattern raises is not primarily about Donald Trump, Benjamin Netanyahu, or Pete Hegseth. They are individuals who made choices. The question is about the structure that makes such choices possible: a legal framework in which a president can take a country to a major war without a vote, an intelligence apparatus whose assessments can be selectively used or ignored, a public discourse in which the decision is announced and the rationale constructed simultaneously, and an international order in which the strongest country faces no effective legal constraint on its use of force. That structure is what needs to change. The men in the room are temporary. The structure is the problem.

Chapter 14: Oil and the Price of Everything – How This War Came Home

The Strait of Hormuz is not a strategic abstraction. It is the pipe through which one-fifth of the world's oil flows. When that pipe narrows, every price in every economy on earth adjusts.

— Energy Information Administration, US Department of Energy

A woman is standing at a petrol station in Birmingham, England, on Saturday morning, March 1, 2026—the day after the bombs fell. Her name is not relevant to this story. What is relevant is the number on the digital display in front of her, which changes as she watches. It has changed three times in the last four minutes. She has never seen a petrol price change while she was standing at the pump. She takes a photograph with her phone and posts it, not because she has any particular political view about Iran, but because it seems like the kind of thing you document as it is happening.

Oil closed at $72 a barrel on Friday, February 27—the last price before the bombs fell. By Sunday, as the first images of smoke rising over Tehran reached international markets, Brent crude had crossed $100 for the first time since 2022 and briefly touched $108. By Monday, March 2, it had spiked toward $120 before pulling back to close around $104—a gain of more than 40 percent in seventy-two hours. Gold rose as investors fled to safe havens. The Pakistan Stock Exchange suspended trading and recorded its largest single-day decline in history. Dubai International Airport closed. Major airlines suspended Middle East routes. In London, the FTSE opened more than half a percent lower. In New York, the Dow fell nearly 600 points in early trading before recovering most of its losses; it closed down just 73 points, or 0.15 percent, as investors concluded the conflict would be short. The conclusion was optimistic.

This is what a war in the Persian Gulf does to the global economy within seventy-two hours. It is not a projection or a model. It is a fact, observed in real time, in the prices that every person in every country pays for energy, food, transportation, and goods whose supply chains run through Dubai, Doha, Kuwait City, and the waters of the Persian Gulf.

The Anatomy of a Chokepoint

The Strait of Hormuz is twenty-one miles wide at its narrowest point—the distance from central London to Heathrow, or from downtown Chicago to O'Hare. Through that gap, on an average day in 2025, approximately 21 percent of global petroleum liquids passed: 17 to 20 million barrels of crude oil and refined products per day, flowing primarily from Saudi Arabia, the UAE, Kuwait, Iraq, and Iran itself toward Asia, Europe, and North America. There is no alternative route for this volume of energy. The Saudi East-West pipeline and the UAE's Habshan-Fujairah pipeline together can redirect perhaps 7 million barrels per day away from Hormuz. The rest has no other way to go.

Iran has spent forty years preparing for the possibility of disruptions in this strait. The Revolutionary Guard's naval forces are specifically trained for swarm tactics in confined waters: small fast boats, mines, anti-ship missiles fired from mobile coastal launchers. The IRGC Navy has described the Strait of Hormuz as a "strategic lake" under Iranian influence. This is not idle boasting. In 2019, following US sanctions reimposed after the JCPOA withdrawal, Iran seized a British-flagged oil tanker and temporarily disrupted commercial traffic. The demonstration was brief and calibrated. The capacity behind it is real and has grown since.

By March 3, 2026, the fourth day of the conflict, Iranian forces had shifted to what Foreign Minister Araghchi called a "mosaic defense": decentralized military cells operating independently, mobile missile launchers disguised to look like civilian vehicles, drone swarms launched from positions across Iran's twenty-four provinces. The Strait had not been formally closed—Iranian leadership was aware that closing it entirely would unite the world against them—but shipping insurance rates for Hormuz passage had increased by 900 percent, effectively making the passage economically prohibitive for many operators. Tanker traffic had fallen by 60 percent from baseline. The pipe was not closed. It was narrowed.

What a Narrowed Pipe Does

Every economist who has modeled a sustained Hormuz disruption has reached similar conclusions, differing mainly in the severity and duration of their effects. The short-term impact is immediate and felt everywhere: gasoline and diesel prices spike within days because the marginal price of oil sets pump prices faster than those of any other commodity. Heating oil, aviation fuel, and natural gas prices follow within weeks. Everything that gets transported—namely everything—costs more to move. Food prices rise because food requires fertilizer (which requires natural gas to produce), transportation, refrigeration, and packaging, all of which depend on energy.

A family in Sunderland, England, which spent £180 a month on gas and electricity before the war, was spending £230 within six weeks. A Chicago family, filling a minivan three times a month, is spending an additional $80 per month by April. A Toronto commuter whose subway system runs on electricity partly generated by natural gas has been paying higher fares over the past quarter. These are not catastrophic numbers for households that are already comfortable. For households that were already at the margin, however, they tip balances. Food banks in Birmingham and Manchester reported 34 percent increases in demand in the six weeks after the strikes. The connection is not metaphorical; the consequences are direct.

The UAE economy—the most globalized single-city economy in the world, built on the assumption of absolute stability in the Gulf—absorbed a severe shock. Dubai's airport, the world's second busiest by international passenger traffic, closed for four days. An Iranian drone struck the Fairmont Palm Hotel. Construction projects involving 400,000 migrant workers from South Asia were disrupted. The UAE Minister of Economy & Tourism appeared on CNBC, attempting to project calm. His attempt was only partially successful.

Qatar, which hosts the largest US air base in the Middle East and also controls the world's third-largest natural gas reserves, watched Iranian missiles intercepted in its airspace while simultaneously reassuring liquefied natural gas customers in Europe and Asia that deliveries would not be interrupted. Qatar's government had specifically warned the United States in the weeks before the strikes that any escalation could have severe consequences for the Middle East. The warning was not heeded.

The Global Recession Scenario

When does a price shock become a recession? Economists use the rule of thumb that a sustained 10 percent increase in oil prices reduces global GDP growth by approximately 0.3 percent. In this case, oil prices rose approximately 60 percent in five days. If sustained for three months—a conservative estimate for a conflict that the Trump administration said would last four to five weeks—the growth impact would be severe.

The mechanisms are not mysterious. Higher energy costs reduce consumer spending power. Higher transport costs reduce trade volumes. Higher uncertainty causes businesses to defer investments. Higher insurance premiums for Gulf shipping reduce the availability of goods. Central banks face a genuine dilemma: raise interest rates to fight inflationary pressure, or hold them steady to protect growth, knowing that neither option resolves the underlying supply shock.

The European Council on Foreign Relations, in an analysis published within days of the strikes, described Iran's strategy as targeting the Gulf's pain threshold to force a ceasefire before the government collapsed. The most effective pressure point in that strategy was not military. It was economic: the systematic targeting of Gulf energy infrastructure in ways that made every government and central bank in the world have a direct stake in how quickly the conflict ended. This is asymmetric warfare at its most sophisticated: a country that cannot win a military contest makes itself so economically costly to fight that the other side's allies and trading partners become reluctant members of the peace coalition.

The people watching prices change are not policy analysts. They are not reading the Brookings Institution or the ECFR. But they are registering in the most direct possible way what it means for their government to have committed to a war in the Persian Gulf. And the Reuters/Ipsos poll that found 43 percent of Americans disapproved of the strikes within 72 hours, before the full economic impact had registered, suggests that the public's intuition about costs was running ahead of the official reassurances.

The woman at the Birmingham petrol station. The Chicago family filling the minivan. The Toronto commuter on the subway. The migrant worker in Dubai waiting to hear if his construction site will reopen. None of them voted on this war. None of them were consulted. All of them are paying for it. That is the final arithmetic of a conflict launched by a small number of people in a room, about a country far from all of these lives, for reasons that have still not been fully and credibly explained.

The Energy Chokepoint and Global Stakes

The Strait of Hormuz is a narrow passage—at its narrowest point, just twenty-one miles wide—between Iran and Oman, through which flows approximately one-fifth of the world's oil and petroleum products and a similar share of global liquefied natural gas. In 2024, more than one-quarter of global seaborne oil trade transited the Strait. The countries of East Asia depend on it for the vast majority of their energy imports.

An Iranian mining of the strait—or even a sustained Iranian campaign of harassment against commercial shipping—would cause immediate and severe global economic disruption. Analysts estimated that if Iran succeeded in significantly disrupting traffic, oil prices could surge to $115 per barrel or higher. Every $10-per-barrel increase in oil prices translates, over time, into significant inflation across importing economies, reduced growth, and—in the most vulnerable developing countries—genuine humanitarian crises.

For the US states, far from the Persian Gulf in every sense, this matters concretely: every family's heating bill, every factory's energy costs, every grocery store's food prices are connected, through the global energy market, to the security of the Strait of Hormuz. The war in Iran is not a distant abstraction. It is a global economic event with local consequences.

By March 2026, the Strait was under exactly this kind of pressure. Electronic warfare activity, attacks on vessels, maritime advisories urging commercial ships to avoid the area—all contributed to the disruption already affecting global oil and gas markets. Shipping insurance premiums and freight rates were soaring: the mechanism by which a war in the Persian Gulf becomes a tax on every person on the planet who uses energy or buys food.

What the Closure Actually Looked Like

What happened to the strait after February 28 was not a theoretical scenario. It was documented in real time by shipping data, insurance filings, and decisions from the world's largest maritime companies.

Late on February 28, outgoing tanker traffic through the strait was still heavy. By March 1 and 2, it had stopped. Maersk, CMA CGM, and Hapag-Lloyd—the three largest container shipping companies in the world—suspended all transit through the strait and related Red Sea routes. Tanker traffic dropped first by approximately seventy percent, according to data reported by S&P Global Commodities at Sea, and then fell further. More than 150 ships were anchored outside the strait or in gulf ports, waiting. An IRGC senior adviser stated on March 2: "The strait is closed. If anyone tries to pass, the heroes of the Revolutionary Guard and the regular navy will set those ships ablaze." By March 8, S&P Global's tracking data showed four vessels transiting the strait that day—down from six the day before—in a waterway that in normal conditions sees dozens of transits daily.

On March 11, a Thai bulk carrier, the Mayuree Naree, was struck and set ablaze near the Strait. The Royal Thai Navy released photographs of smoke rising from the vessel. By March 12, Iran had made twenty-one confirmed attacks on merchant ships, according to data cited by Wikipedia's running record of the crisis. The US Navy, acknowledging the threat of mines, released video of strikes against sixteen Iranian minelaying vessels. The CBS News chief analyst at Global Risk Management described the situation plainly: "It is de facto closed in that no one dares to go through." As of March 20, Brent crude—the international benchmark—stood at $108.84 per barrel, having peaked at $126 earlier in the month. It had been below $70 on February 27.

By March 16, a single Pakistani oil tanker crossed the Strait with explicit Iranian permission—the first meaningful transit in weeks. It was notable enough to be reported as news.

The Food Chain

What is less reported, and more consequential over time, is what the disruption does to food.

Natural gas is not only an energy source. It is the primary feedstock for nitrogen fertilizer, specifically urea, the most widely used fertilizer in the world. Nearly half of all globally traded urea moves through the Strait of Hormuz. When QatarEnergy halted LNG production, it also halted the world's largest urea plant, at Ras Laffan. The downstream effects were immediate: India, whose agriculture depends on fertilizer imports for staple crops including rice, wheat, and sugar, cut output from three of its own urea plants as Qatari LNG supplies fell. Bangladesh shut four of its five fertilizer factories. By mid-March, the United States was close to 25percent short of fertilizer supply for the season.

The timing compounded the problem. The disruption fell in the middle of the Northern Hemisphere's spring sowing season, which runs from mid-February to early May. Fertilizer applied in this window determines yields for the entire growing season. Morningstar analyst Seth Goldstein told Reuters that nitrogen fertilizer prices could roughly double from current levels, and phosphate prices could rise by approximately 50 percent. According to Kpler, a data and analytics firm, as much as one-third of global fertilizer trade could be disrupted if the Strait of Hormuz were to remain closed. Oxford Economics raised its fertilizer price forecast by twenty percent for the second quarter of 2026 and described the risks as "skewed to the upside."

Brazil imports more than ninety percent of its fertilizer, nearly half of which transits the Strait. India produces and exports the world's largest volumes of rice. Lower fertilizer use means lower yields for staple crops—rice, wheat, maize, soybeans—tighter global supply, higher food prices, and, in the most exposed countries, hunger. The people who will go hungry because of decisions made in February 2026 will not be the ones who made them. They will be farmers in Bangladesh and consumers in Cairo.

The systems scientist in me wants to name what this is. The Strait of Hormuz is a single point of failure in the architecture of the modern global economy. Every systems engineer knows that a system with a critical single point of failure—one node whose loss brings down the whole system—is not resilient. It is a system waiting for the failure to happen. The failure has happened. The consequences are not limited to the combatants. They are distributed through global trade to everyone on Earth who buys food or uses energy. That is almost everyone.

A war in the Persian Gulf is not a regional event. It is a global tax, levied without a vote, on people worldwide.

The Grid as Target: What Obliterating Power Plants Actually Means

On March 21, 2026, President Trump posted on Truth Social that unless Iran fully reopened the Strait of Hormuz within 48 hours, the United States would "hit and obliterate their various POWER PLANTS, STARTING WITH THE BIGGEST ONE FIRST." Iran responded that all US energy infrastructure in the region would be targeted in return.

This exchange is not a military confrontation between two governments. It is, in its consequences, a sentence of deprivation for tens of millions of civilians across an entire region.

Water treatment plants run on electricity. Hospitals run on it. Dialysis machines, ventilators, and operating rooms run on it. Food refrigeration runs on it. In arid regions, desalination plants supplying drinking water to millions run on it. When the grid fails, these systems do not slow down. They stop. Within hours of a major grid collapse, hospitals exhaust backup generator fuel, water pressure drops, food spoils, and communications degrade. Within days, water-borne disease begins, refrigerated medicine is lost, and patients dependent on powered medical equipment die.

Germany's Office of Technology Assessment conducted a formal study on extended blackouts and documented that sustained grid collapse leads to societal breakdown within two weeks: water systems irreparably contaminated, communications gone, backup fuel exhausted. This is not a forecast. It is a documented sequence. Iran has a population of 93 million people. Nearly all depend on a centralized grid whose largest assets, once destroyed, cannot be quickly restored.

The electrical grid is not a military asset. It is the foundational infrastructure of modern society—the platform on which water, medicine, food, communications, and economic function all depend. Destroy it, and everything built on top of it collapses. Not for a government. For every civilian in its reach.

I know this from direct experience. In the weeks following September 11, 2001, I directed all infrastructure security research and development for North American utilities at the Electric Power Research Institute. The finding that shaped everything we did was this: the electrical grid is the single point of failure for modern society. Every other critical infrastructure—water, communications, finance, transportation, emergency response—depends on it. Destroy it deliberately and at scale, and the cascade is not a possibility. It is a certainty.

Chapter 15: The Karbala Paradigm and Israel

Witness Voice

> Minab, Hormozgan Province, March 1, 2026, Documented by Human Rights Activists in Iran; footage verified by *The Washington Post*.
>
> "The school was called Shajareh Tayyebeh—the Good Tree. It was a girls' elementary school. It opened at seven-thirty in the morning. The strike came at eight-fifteen. The girls were in their first-period classes. We know this because one teacher survived. She was in the teachers' room at the back of the building when the front of the building was hit. She crawled out. She counted what she could count. One hundred and eighty children. She kept counting. She is still counting."

What this voice complicates: the phrase "surgical precision." Precision describes the accuracy of targeting. It says nothing about what was targeted, what was near it, or who was inside it at 8:15 in the morning.

Operation Epic Fury was technically precise yet legally

indefensible: it achieved its targeting objectives while simultaneously violating the UN Charter, the War Powers Resolution, and the constitutional war-making framework.

★★★

By the end of the first seventy-two hours, the Red Crescent had documented 201 civilians killed and 747 injured in Iran. The actual toll, given the information blackout the government imposed on day one, was almost certainly higher. Human rights organizations operating through encrypted channels inside the country reported the number continuing to rise through the first week.

When Trump was asked about civilian casualties in an NBC News interview broadcast the evening of the second day, he said: "We expect casualties with something like this. We have three, but we expect casualties—but in the end it's going to be a great deal for the world."

The three he was referring to were American servicemembers. He did not mention the school.

Oman's Foreign Minister, whose breakthrough announcement now seemed to belong to a different world, expressed "dismay" at the outbreak of violence and urged the United States to "not get sucked in further." "This is not your war," he said.

It was not. But it was fought in our name. And the names of the children—those that have been recovered and documented, which is not all of them—will outlast every press conference that called the operation a success.

In conflicts of this kind documented across every culture and every century, three behavioral laws are operating. First: an external attack unifies populations behind governments they actively oppose. The Iranian protest movement of January 2026, which had brought millions into the streets against the Islamic Republic, suspended itself within forty-eight hours of the February 28 strikes. The government that could not control its own population was handed the one instrument that could—a foreign enemy. Second: know the civilization before you enter it. Every major military failure in recorded history shares one root cause: decision-makers did not understand the society they were entering. History, language, and codes of honor are not background reading. They are the terrain. Third: restraint, applied from a position of demonstrated strength at the right moment, has ended more conflicts and preserved more strategic advantage than any final offensive. The warrior scholars who understood this are the ones history remembers.

* * *

Before any honest analysis of where this war goes next, it is necessary to reiterate and expand the discussion about how Iranians—including Iranians who deeply oppose their own government—are likely to experience being bombed by the United States and specifically Israel. This is not a secondary consideration. It is the central strategic and moral question that the architects of Operation Epic Fury appear to have either ignored or dismissed.

Iran is a majority Shia Muslim country. To be Shia is, in ways that have no precise Western equivalent, to carry in one's bones a foundational story of dispossession, of righteous suffering, of the small against the large, the just against the powerful. The story is fourteen centuries old. It happened on the plains of Karbala in 680 CE, when Hussain ibn Ali—grandson of the Prophet Muhammad—. chose to fight rather than submit. An arrow struck his infant son as Hussain held him up and appealed, before the opposing army, for water.

The Karbala Paradigm describes how this single event functions, in Shia political culture, as a template for every subsequent encounter with injustice. It is not merely a historical commemoration. It is a living interpretive framework: a way of understanding who you are, who the oppressor is, and what the right response to overwhelming force looks like. The paradigm does not require martyrdom. What it requires is the refusal to submit—the recognition that legitimacy lies not with power but with justice, and that suffering borne with moral clarity outlasts the power that inflicts it.

What makes this directly relevant to the present moment is what it means for American and Israeli bombs falling on Iranian cities. For many Iranians—including those who have been in the streets opposing their own government, including those who have paid enormous personal costs for that opposition—the arrival of foreign airstrikes does not feel like rescue. It feels like Karbala. They are Hussain. The bombs are Yazid's army. The size of the attacking force, far from delegitimizing resistance, is precisely the point: the righteous minority is always outnumbered, and its refusal to submit is precisely what constitutes its moral authority.

There is something more. Iranians as a people understand themselves as David in a geopolitical landscape that has repeatedly cast them as a target. They are a civilization of extraordinary antiquity—one of the oldest continuous cultures on earth. They have been invaded by Greeks, Arabs, Mongols, Russians, the British, and Americans, and they have survived each invasion not by submitting to it but by absorbing it and eventually reasserting themselves. This historical consciousness runs very deep.

Here is what makes this conflict unlike the American planners' apparent model: Iranians, the vast majority of whom are Shia, share with Jewish people something that is rarely acknowledged in Western strategic discussions—a deep, bone-level familiarity with what it means to be the minority, the outsider, the historically persecuted people who survived by refusing to assimilate to the terms of their oppressors. The Shia have been a minority within Islam since 680 CE, persecuted by Sunni majorities across the Muslim world for over a millennium. The Jewish people have carried a parallel historical consciousness of dispossession, survival through moral and intellectual tradition, and the refusal to disappear, across two thousand years. These two people have more in common in their historical self-understanding than the current military confrontation suggests.

The tragedy is that this shared experience of marginalization and the hunger for justice could, in other circumstances, be a basis for the deepest kind of recognition. Instead, the Karbala Paradigm and the Israeli narrative of existential survival are being mobilized against each other—each side reading the other through the lens of their own history of persecution, each side convinced that they are the David and the other is the Goliath.

The lessons from Libya, Syria, Iraq, Somalia, Sudan, and Yemen do not paint a promising picture of what happens to a society of ninety million people when its institutions are destroyed from the outside without a credible plan for what comes after. Each of those countries was, before its catastrophe, described by its destroyers as a special case, a situation where the intervention would be swift and the aftermath manageable. In each case, the aftermath was neither swift nor manageable. The chaos that followed killed more people than the governments that preceded it, and in several cases produced ungoverned spaces that became bases for the most violent non-state actors on earth.

Iran is not Iraq. It is not Libya. It is roughly three times the population of Iraq, with a far more educated and urbanized citizenry, a more developed civil society, a more cohesive national identity, and a military and security apparatus that, even in its weakened state, is significantly more capable than anything the United States has previously dismantled by air campaign. The people bombing Iran know this, or should. The question is whether knowing it changes anything about what they are doing.

Chapter 16: Voices from the Ground – The People Who Are Not Statistics

The bomb does not ask who voted for the government. It does not ask who marched in the streets against it. It falls, and the street is the same.

—Anonymous Iranian engineer, Tehran, March 1, 2026 (via NPR)

History is always written afterward, and it is usually written by those who survive and those who have power. The voices of the people caught inside a war while it is happening rarely make it into the formal record. This chapter is an attempt to hold space for them, briefly, before the analysis continues.

I am a specific kind of witness: I was in Minneapolis, watching a war in the country where I was born, through accounts transmitted by journalists I had never met, about people I would never meet, transmitted over media whose fidelity I could not fully verify. This is the condition of diaspora witnessing. It is not the same as being there. It is not the same as not being there. It is something else: a form of grief at a distance, both more and less than what people inside the country are experiencing, and it carries its own obligations.

The obligation is to receive the account carefully, to resist the temptation to flatten what is complex, and to pass it forward with as much fidelity as the medium and the distance allow. The voices in this chapter are not my voices. They arrived through journalists, through social media, through the chain of diaspora transmission—imperfect, filtered, but still the best accounts available. They are what we have.

From Inside Iran

NPR correspondent Arezou Rezvani spent the days following the first strikes exchanging messages with people inside Tehran. All of those she spoke to asked not to be identified. Their voices nonetheless belong in this account.

> *A 30-something engineer was at work in downtown Tehran when he heard the first boom. "We even saw one of the explosions from our office window around downtown Tehran," he told Rezvani. He scrambled to get home. US and Israeli airstrikes pounded Tehran the rest of the day and well into the night. "We were going to sleep, and suddenly we heard cheers from our neighbors."*
>
> *— Unnamed engineer, Tehran. NPR, March 2026*

Those cheers, in the middle of a bombing campaign, capture the impossible complexity of what Iranians are experiencing. A population that has lived through forty-six years of contested governance and that rose in protest just weeks before the bombs fell is being asked, by the bombs themselves, to sort out its feelings about who its enemies are.

> *A 22-year-old university student, voice distorted at her request, told Rezvani: "They killed him. They finally killed him." Then she switched to English: "I'm very happy. I'm excited. Oh, my God, I'm shaking." She asked for her voice to be distorted because she was still afraid of government reprisals, even with the government being bombed.*
>
> *— Unnamed student, Tehran. NPR, March 2026*

From CNN's documentation of social media voices: A woman in Kerman posted a video following the strikes, saying simply: "If I die, I'm okay with it."

— Unnamed woman, Kerman. CNN, March 2026

Three voices. Three different takes on the same impossible situation. The engineer who goes home through the bombs. The student who is shaking with complicated joy. The woman in Kerman who has made a kind of peace with death. And a fourth voice, from a blogger in Tehran who managed to connect to the internet after six days of blackout and wrote the following, not knowing if she would be able to publish before the connection was cut again:

"What I've lived through during these days of bombardment has exposed one brutal truth: the abstract separation of 'the government' from 'the country' is moral escape. Those who say you can set Iran on fire in the name of hitting the Islamic Republic, while assuming people will somehow remain safe, either do not understand what war is, or they are deliberately looking away. Bombs are not selective. Destruction does not work by careful choice. Fighting internal authoritarianism is our responsibility. But anyone who justifies the external fire, knowingly or not, is standing on the side of continued devastation. Life does not grow under repression, and it does not survive under the rubble of bombs."

She published it. I do not know what happened to her afterwards. She is the person this war was being fought over. Not governments, not strategic objectives, not the talking points that senior officials rehearsed before congressional briefings. Her—writing through six days of silence, hearing explosions through her windows, trying to think clearly in the dark, choosing to publish anyway. None of these people chose this war. None of them voted for it. All of them are living inside it.

Chapter 17: The Third Current – What the War Cannot See

In Washington and in diaspora drawing rooms from Los Angeles to London to Stockholm, the argument about Iran has long defaulted to a binary. On one side stands the ruling establishment, defended by those who see engagement or deterrence as the only realistic option. On the other stands the exile politics of regime change, defended by those who argue that sufficient pressure—economic, military, or both—will produce a democratic transition. This framing is not simply incomplete. It is actively misleading, because it erases from view the current that has, across decades of difficulty and disappointment, proven most persistent.

That third current consists of Iranians inside the country who oppose both the conditions under which they live and the idea that foreign military intervention is the solution. It is not a political party. It has no headquarters in London or Los Angeles. It does not hold press conferences or publish manifestos in languages designed for Western consumption. It exists in the actions of people who have decided, at considerable personal cost, to organize where they are.

What the Third Current Has Built

These people are not asking to be liberated by missiles. They are asking—in strikes, in protests, in letters passed hand to hand—to be left a room to organize in. They are asking that the international community's response be targeted at the institutions and individuals who commit crimes, not at the family in Tehran who cannot afford bread, not at the nurse working a double shift in a hospital already broken by sanctions and mismanagement. They are asking, in the plainest possible terms, for a politics that takes the difference between a government and its people.

Consider what this current has built despite everything arrayed against it. The 2023 Charter of Solidarity—known informally as the Mahsa Charter, named for Mahsa Amini—was an attempt by diverse Iranian opposition figures to articulate shared democratic values: territorial integrity, equality before law regardless of ethnicity or gender, and the separation of religion from state governance. It was imperfect, contested, and incomplete. It represents the kind of internal legitimacy that no amount of external bombardment can manufacture. Governments imposed by foreign force arrive without that legitimacy. They have to spend their first years acquiring it under the most unfavorable conditions imaginable—conditions that the history of Iraq, Afghanistan, and Libya has not made more forgiving.

What the Scholarship Shows

The scholarship on civil resistance offers some useful perspectives on these limitations. Erica Chenoweth and Maria Stephan, whose research at Harvard's Carr Center established the empirical foundation for understanding nonviolent resistance, find that movements relying too heavily on street protests and digital mobilization are easier to suppress than those employing a diverse repertoire of tactics—strikes, professional associations, consumer boycotts, artistic expression, underground education, and parallel institutions. The oil workers and the teachers and the lawyers who have organized are not peripheral to the third current. They are its architecture. Success depends on eroding the pillars that sustain authoritarianism: the loyalty of security forces, economic elites, bureaucrats, and religious authorities. Iran's protests of 2022 and 2025–26 showed glimpses of this diversity when merchants in Tehran's Grand Bazaar shuttered their shops and oil workers slowed production. But years of crackdowns have weakened unions and student organizations, and the war has disrupted whatever organizing capacity remained.

Carnegie Endowment for International Peace research on authoritarian transitions finds that mass protests alone have toppled a fully consolidated regime only once in the past decade. In most cases, the security apparatus remained loyal and movements were crushed—which has happened repeatedly in Iran. Movements succeed either when splits occur within the regime itself or when a broad coalition sustains pressure over time and offers a credible alternative. Neither condition is easily manufactured from outside. Both take years.

Why External Force Fails Here

Barbara Geddes and her collaborators, working across decades of comparative data on authoritarian regimes, have documented a pattern that applies directly to Iran. Systems born of violent revolutions—forged in the fires of 1979 and hardened by eight years of war with Iraq— develop internal institutional cohesion that makes them significantly more resistant to external pressure than dictatorships that depend on a single ruler's charisma. The institution survives the individual. Removing the Supreme Leader does not remove the Revolutionary Guards, the bonyads, the clerical courts, the patronage networks that have spent four decades binding loyalty with resources. These structures were explicitly designed to outlast their founders. They are doing what they were designed to do.

This structural resistance is not a sign of popular support. GAMAAN surveys consistently show that less than 20 percent of

Iranians want the current system to continue. But a lack of popular support in a state that has spent decades ensuring that its coercive apparatus does not depend on popular consent is not enough alone. The gap between what people want and what they get is precisely the gap that the third current is trying to close—from the inside, at the pace that internal organizing allows, not at the pace that foreign policy timetables demand.

What This Means for the War

The bombs that fell on February 28, 2026, did not fall on the Revolutionary Guards' patronage networks. They did not fall on the bonyad foundations that control billions in assets and the loyalty of millions of employees. They fell on the cities. They fell on the infrastructure—the electrical grid, the highways, the manufacturing plants—on which the third current's members depend for their daily survival and for the economic platform from which organizing becomes possible.

The teacher in Tehran who was planning a union meeting in March 2026 is now focused on whether her building has water. The oil worker who had been coordinating with colleagues about the next strike is now trying to locate his sister, who was in Ahvaz when the second wave of strikes hit. The lawyer who had been documenting the January 2026 protest deaths is now documenting something on a scale that documentation cannot keep up with. The war has damaged the conditions the third current needs to succeed.

This is not a counsel of despair. It is a counsel of precision. The tools that work against institutionally consolidated authoritarian systems are slower, less dramatic, and harder to photograph for a press conference. They include targeted sanctions against specific individuals and entities—not the broad sanctions that collapse living standards and produce the photographs of hungry children that governments then use to argue the world is their enemy. They include diplomatic support for civil society organizations, legal aid for political prisoners, and sustained documentation of abuses that can form the evidentiary basis for future accountability. They include the patient work of keeping diplomatic channels open, because the only durable constraint on a nuclear program is verification, and the only way to verification is negotiation.

These are not exciting policy prescriptions. But they are the ones that the third current— the Iranians who are doing the actual work of building alternatives inside the country—has consistently said it needs. The war cannot see them. That is not their failure. It is the war's.

Chapter 18: After-the-Strike Scenarios and the Shape of What Comes Next

On the morning of March 1, 2026, , the world woke to a set of facts with no clear precedent in the modern era. The Supreme Leader of the Islamic Republic of Iran—the man who had held absolute authority since 1989, who had ordered the suppression of every major protest wave from 1999 to 2026, who had built Iran's nuclear program and its regional proxy network into instruments of genuine strategic reach—was dead, killed by Israeli precision munitions in what was described as a morning strike on a leadership compound. The Article 111 interim council—the president, judiciary head, and a Guardian Council jurist selected through the Expediency Council—had been activated. Forty senior officials were confirmed killed. Hundreds of military sites had been struck. And across the region, a retaliation architecture that Iran had spent forty years and tens of billions of dollars constructing, was beginning to move, in autonomous cells from Lebanon to Yemen to Iraq.

What follows from this is not a matter of prediction but of probabilities—probabilities shaped by institutional structure, historical precedent, and the known characteristics of the actors involved. Responsible analysis requires rigorously mapping this scenario space because the decisions made in the weeks and months after Epic Fury will determine not just Iran's future but also the security architecture of the entire Middle East for a generation.

The scenario that the architects of Epic Fury appear to have hoped for—though they have been cautious about stating it explicitly—is that the decapitation of Iran's leadership will accelerate an internal political transition. In this scenario, the interim Article 111 council proves unable to maintain cohesion; factions within the IRGC and the clerical establishment begin negotiating with reformist and civil society figures; and the combination of external pressure, internal elite fragmentation, and mass public mobilization produces a move toward more representative governance. This scenario is not impossible. Political scientists who study authoritarian breakdown note that decapitation can, under the right conditions, accelerate elite defections and create space for a negotiated transition. But those conditions are specific: an organized opposition with a credible transition plan, military elites willing to defect in exchange for amnesty guarantees, and an external actor prepared to provide economic inducements for cooperation rather than simply military punishment for resistance. In the immediate aftermath of Epic Fury, it is not clear that any of these conditions are present.

A more probable scenario—one grounded in the empirical record—involves a period of dangerous turbulence in which multiple centers of power compete to fill the vacuum. The IRGC, with its independent revenue streams derived from its vast economic empire, its decades of investment in precisely the decentralized command structure that allows it to operate after a leadership strike, and its history of treating the death of senior figures as a consolidating rather than a disintegrating force, is not likely to dissolve. It is likely to rigidify. And in rigidifying, it may become more extreme rather than less, because the factions that survive a decapitation strike are precisely those that were most prepared for it and tends to mean those most deeply committed to the institutional ideology that made the strike necessary in the first place. This is not a paradox. It is the logic of selection pressure applied to political organizations under existential stress.

Iran's "mosaic defense" doctrine was designed for exactly this scenario. It deliberately compartmentalizes military units so that even after strikes on command and control infrastructure, autonomous cells can continue to operate—launching drones and ballistic missiles, activating the IRGC's "mosquito fleet" of fast-attack boats and mini-submarines in the Persian Gulf, targeting American military installations in Bahrain, Qatar, Kuwait, and the UAE, and coordinating with Hezbollah in Lebanon, the Houthis in Yemen, and Kataib Hezbollah in Iraq. Each of these actors has its own interests, its own command structure, and its own calculations about when retaliation serves those interests. None of them requires a signal from Tehran to act. They may, in fact, be more dangerous after the decapitation of the Iranian central command than before it, because the institutional constraints that sometimes moderated IRGC adventurism—the Supreme Leader's political calculations, the reformist factions within the system who counseled caution—are no longer there.

The energy dimension carries consequences that extend far beyond the battlefield. The US EIA reported in 2025 that more than 20percent of global seaborne oil trade and approximately 17percent of global liquefied natural gas trade transits through the Strait of Hormuz. Any sustained disruption of traffic through that strait—whether through Iranian mine-laying, attacks on tankers, or the electronic warfare that the IRGC has been developing for precisely this purpose—would send oil prices above one hundred dollars a barrel and potentially far beyond. The countries of the Global South, which had no voice in the decision to launch Epic Fury and no direct stake in its stated objectives, would bear a disproportionate share of its economic aftermath—not because they are proximate to the conflict but because they are most exposed to the commodity price shocks that follow energy supply disruptions.

The nuclear question does not resolve cleanly with strikes. The bombing destroyed centrifuges. It could not destroy knowledge. The physicists and engineers who understand weapons-grade enrichment are not all located in buildings that can be targeted from the air. Some of them are outside Iran. Some of them have transmitted their knowledge through channels that no precision munition can reach. The IAEA's loss of continuous monitoring means that the international community has less visibility into the nuclear program after the strikes than before. This is not a peripheral irony. It is the central strategic problem: the actions taken in the name of preventing a nuclear-armed Iran may have created conditions that make that outcome more, not less, probable, because they removed the inspection infrastructure that was the only reliable early-warning system.

And what of the Iranian people? The rally-around-the-flag effect—the tendency of populations under external attack to unite behind whoever is defending the country, even if they despised that defender the day before—is one of the most robust findings in political science. It operated in Britain during the Blitz. It operated in Iraq after the 2003 invasion turned Saddam Hussein, despised by millions, into a figure of national martyrdom for some. It may operate in Iran, too. The architects of Epic Fury are betting that it will not—that the accumulated grievances of Iranians against their government are severe enough to overcome the nationalist impulse to close ranks against a foreign attacker. They may be right. But they are making that bet with other people's lives.

Mosaic Defense—Why "The Most Lethal Air Campaign in History" Did Not Win the War

The Precision Doctrine and Its Limits: A Formal Counterargument

The strongest version of the case for the strikes rests on precision. Modern American precision-guided munitions have transformed the relationship between military force and civilian harm. GPS-guided bombs with a circular "error probable" measured in meters, compared to hundreds of meters for Cold War weapons, mean that a 2026 strike campaign kills far fewer civilians per military objective destroyed than any previous air campaign in history. The strikes on Iranian nuclear facilities were genuinely targeted at military infrastructure. Civilian casualties, while real, were lower than those produced by comparable historical campaigns.

. But precision describes only the accuracy of a weapon in hitting its designated target. It says nothing about target selection, collateral blast radius, secondary effects—power grid failure, hospital disruption, water treatment collapse—or the cumulative civilian impact of 1,200 strikes across 24 provinces in 48 hours. The Minab school strike, which killed at least 168 people—schoolchildren, teachers, and parents—was either a targeting error, which undermines the precision claim, or a deliberately targeted location near military infrastructure, which raises a different legal question entirely. Neither the United States nor Israel has provided any explanation. Under international humanitarian law, the burden of justification rests on the attacker, not the defender. That burden has not been met.

★★★

Pete Hegseth called it "the most lethal and precise air power campaign in history." He was not exaggerating about the precision. Over the first forty-eight hours of Operation Epic Fury, US and Israeli aircraft dropped more than 1,200 munitions across twenty-four of Iran's thirty-one provinces. The targets were carefully selected: leadership compounds, nuclear infrastructure, missile storage facilities, air defense systems, and command-and-control nodes. The intelligence preparation was extensive. The execution was technically impressive.

And yet, on day four, Iran was still fighting, not as in a dying gasp, but as part of a deliberate strategy. It had fired more than 400 ballistic missiles and nearly 1,000 drones at targets across the region.

It had hit the headquarters of the US Fifth Fleet in Bahrain. It had struck the US Embassy in Riyadh. It had disrupted shipping in the Persian Gulf, caused the closing of Dubai's airport, and sent missiles into Doha, Kuwait City, and Amman. It had done all of this while its centralized leadership was being systematically destroyed. The explanation for this paradox is doctrinal. Iran was not fighting the way the United States expected it to fight.

The Architecture of Mosaic Defense

The concept of mosaic defense emerged in Iranian military thinking in the decade following the 2003 invasion of Iraq. Iranian military planners watched the American campaign unfold. They drew a specific lesson: centralized command and control is a vulnerability, not a strength, when facing an adversary with air force superiority and precision weapons. The Coalition destroyed the Iraqi command structure in days, and the war was effectively over in weeks.

Iran's response was to build a military specifically designed to survive the destruction of its command structure. Mosaic defense means exactly what the name implies: small, independent cells—each capable of operating autonomously without guidance from headquarters—that together form a picture of coordinated military action, with no single piece that is essential to the whole. Destroy one tile in a mosaic, and the image is damaged but not destroyed. Destroy the center of a mosaic, and the edges continue to exist and function.

The practical implementation involves mobile missile launchers disguised as civilian vehicles—Shahed-136 drones can be launched from trucks that look like ordinary transport vehicles. Underground missile storage is spread across the country, not concentrated at identifiable bases. Command authority is pre-delegated to regional commanders, who have received their targeting orders and can execute them without real-time contact with Tehran. Drone and missile production capability is partially dispersed across civilian industrial facilities, making complete targeting impossible without bombing factories whose destruction would constitute clear war crimes.

The Economics of Asymmetry

The financial arithmetic of this war is as important as the military arithmetic, and it systematically favors the defender. A Shahed-136 drone—the primary Iranian offensive weapon in the current conflict, a small delta-winged loitering munition with a shaped-charge warhead—costs approximately $20,000 to manufacture. The Patriot PAC-3 interceptor missiles used to shoot them down cost approximately $4 million each. The THAAD (Terminal High Altitude Area Defense) interceptors deployed in the Gulf cost approximately $10 million each.

Iran fired approximately 1,000 drones in the first four days of the conflict. The interception cost to the United States and Gulf allies, if those drones were engaged at full THAAD or Patriot cost, approaches $10 billion. The drones themselves cost $20 million to produce. This is not an accident. It is the central insight of the Iranian defense doctrine: force the world's most expensive military to expend expensive interceptors at a rate that depletes stockpiles faster than they can be replenished.

The United States has seven THAAD systems. During the June 2025 twelve-day war, the US blew through approximately a quarter of its THAAD interceptors. By day four, the current conflict had already used a comparable proportion. The question of how long Gulf air defenses can sustain this rate of expenditure before depletion becomes operationally significant is not a technical question that can be answered publicly. It is, however, a question that Iranian military planners have been modeling for years, and the mosaic defense doctrine is specifically designed to exploit the answer.

Why "Four Weeks" Was Not a Plan

President Trump told the *Daily Mail* that the conflict would last "four weeks or so." Defense Secretary Hegseth echoed a similar timeline. These statements reflect a particular theory of the war: that the destruction of Iran's centralized leadership and nuclear infrastructure would produce either a rapid political capitulation or a military collapse fast enough to be managed within a short campaign.

The mosaic defense approach was specifically designed to defeat this theory. A military that has pre-delegated its command authority, dispersed its weapons production, embedded its strike capability in civilian infrastructure, and trained its soldiers to operate without contact with headquarters does not collapse when the headquarters is destroyed. It continues. This is not a theoretical observation. It is what was observed in the first four days of the conflict.

Historical precedent reinforces the concern. In 2006, Hezbollah in Lebanon continued firing rockets into northern Israel until the last day of the conflict, despite thirty-three days of intensive Israeli air strikes, because it had built a command structure specifically designed to survive Israeli air superiority. Hamas in Gaza continued operating militarily for more than a year under conditions that destroyed virtually all visible military infrastructure, because it had built tunnel networks and pre-positioned weapons that did not depend on surface structures. Iran has been studying both examples for years and has built a military that incorporates their lessons on a national scale.

The honest military assessment—which the public statements of American officials were not reflecting—is that a four-week campaign capable of producing the political outcome the administration sought would require a level of military escalation far beyond what had been publicly described. The alternative—a sustained campaign that destroys Iranian civilian infrastructure over months or years—would produce a humanitarian catastrophe that no Western government could politically sustain and that would generate the kind of regional blowback that makes the region more dangerous, not less. The mosaic defense doctrine has not won the war. But it may have made winning the war impossible on the terms the United States has set for itself.

Chapter 19: The Fracture Strategy – What Is actually Happening, and What It Will Produce

Who Actually Planned This War

The most important thing to understand about Operation Epic Fury is who planned it. Not in the White House. Not in the Pentagon's Iran planning cells, which have existed for decades and which have always been constrained by American strategic judgment about the costs of what they were drawing up. The target sets for this war—the specific list of facilities, command nodes, leadership compounds, and military infrastructure that was struck beginning February 28—were built by the Israel Defense Forces.

This is not an accusation. It is what Israeli officials said publicly. IDF Chief of the General Staff Lieutenant General Eyal Zamir stated explicitly that "close joint planning was carried out between the IDF and the US Army" in the months before the strikes, and that this joint planning "enabled the broad attack to be carried out with maximum synchronization." An Israeli defense official confirmed that Operation Roaring Lion "had been planned for months in coordination with Washington," and that the specific launch date was decided weeks in advance.

But coordination is not the same as origination. Israel has been building detailed targeting packages on the Iranian military, nuclear, and leadership infrastructure for years. The United States has had some dissenting voices during that process—the voices of military leaders who understood the costs, intelligence professionals who understood the uncertainties, diplomats who understood what bombing tends to produce. Those voices were not heeded in February 2026. The result is a war that looks, in its architecture, like the war Netanyahu has sought for the better part of a decade—and which the United States agreed to fight.

Netanyahu has been explicit about this for years. He told the U S Congress in 2015 that Iran was an existential threat that required military action. He pushed for the United States's withdrawal from the JCPOA. He lobbied with maximum pressure. He ordered the June 2025 Twelve-Day War. He lobbied the Trump administration, after Trump's return to power, for the Kurdish connection—Israel has been cultivating intelligence networks among Kurdish groups in Iran, Iraq, and Syria for years. Each step in this sequence was one Netanyahu chose, and each brought the decision closer to where we are now.

Trump did not resist. Trump accommodated. The man who presented himself as the dealmaker, the one who could negotiate his way out of any confrontation, became the instrument of someone else's forty-year strategic objective. Whether he understood this or not is a question for historians. The outcome is the same regardless of the answer.

The Division of Labor

The CSIS assessment of Operation Epic Fury noted an operational division of labor consistent with Israel leading the strategic objectives: Israel targeted Iran's leadership and command structure and the

United States engaged in large-scale capability degradation. Trump's own public statement explicitly disclaimed US responsibility for targeting Iranian leadership—while Israeli Prime Minister Netanyahu stated the joint operation "will create the conditions for the courageous Iranian people to take their destiny into their own hands." These are two different statements of war aims. One is about destroying capability. The other is about regime change. The United States signed up for the first. Israel was always there for the second.

The Security Apparatus After the Strikes: Who Holds Power

Since the Twelve-Day War, the formal civilian structures of the Islamic Republic have been progressively hollowed out. This process was already underway before the bombs of February 28. It will accelerate after them.

During the 2025 war, Supreme Leader Ayatollah Ali Khamenei "was not reachable" for extended periods, according to sources cited by multiple credible outlets. Dr. Ali Larijani—newly appointed by Ayatollah Khamenei as head of the Supreme National Security Council, a role that gave him extraordinary emergency powers—effectively ran decision-making during the conflict. The National Interest reported in 2025 that "an IRGC military council had already replaced Khamenei" in practical terms. The Council on Foreign Relations, in its prewar analysis, observed that "a government dominated by the Islamic Revolutionary Guards Corps would formalize a shift in the balance of power that has been underway for decades."

The February 28 strikes did not create this dynamic. They accelerated and completed it. The decapitation strategy—the killing of Ayatollah Khamenei, his security adviser Ali Shamkhani, the IRGC commander-in-chief, and forty senior commanders in a single coordinated strike—was designed to destroy the apex of the command structure. What it actually did was remove the clerical layer that sat above the IRGC, while leaving the IRGC itself—its regional commands, its economic networks, its militia relationships, its weapons caches—largely intact.

What does historical precedent suggests happens when you remove the top of an institutionally consolidated state that is not a civilian democracy? You get the military. Iran's Interim Leadership Council—formed on March 1 under Article 111 of the Iranian constitution, consisting of the president, the chief justice, and a Guardian Council representative—is the formal structure. The actual power right now in the rooms where decisions about retaliation and succession are being made lies with the IRGC. This will become more obvious as the weeks pass. It is already obvious to anyone paying attention.

The succession process confirms it. According to Iran International, citing exclusive sourcing, the IRGC pressured Iran's Assembly of Experts to select Ayatollah Mojtaba Khamenei—the late Supreme Leader's son, a 56-year-old cleric with deep ties to IRGC command networks going back decades—as the next Supreme Leader. The decision was reportedly made under IRGC pressure, in wartime, with the constitutional process compressed by urgency and external threat. The Assembly of Experts building in Qom was struck by US-Israeli bombs while the succession vote was reportedly underway.

What the architects of the decapitation strategy appear not to have fully modeled: removing the Supreme Leader does not remove the IRGC. The IRGC was always the real coercive infrastructure of the Islamic Republic. Ayatollah Khamenei was its legitimizing cover. Now the cover is gone. What remains is the infrastructure—angrier, more autonomous, and freed from the clerical caution that sometimes constrained it.

The New Calculations

The University of Tehran's Hassan Ahmadian told Al Jazeera: "Iran learned a hard lesson from the June 2025 war: Restraint is interpreted as weakness." The new calculations in Tehran, he said, is likely to be a "scorched earth" policy. "The decision has been made. If attacked, Iran will burn everything." Field commanders, freed from the political caution of the clerical leadership, are now making decisions that Ayatollah Khamenei himself might have moderated. This is not the outcome the strikes were designed to produce.

The Kurdish Card, and Why It Is More Dangerous Than It Looks

On March 3, 2026, CNN reported that the CIA was actively working to arm Kurdish forces to foment a popular uprising inside Iran. Multiple sources familiar with the plan confirmed it. The Trump administration is in active discussions with Iranian opposition groups and Kurdish leaders in Iraq about providing military support. Iranian Kurdish armed groups—numbering in the thousands of fighters operating along the Iran-Iraq border—are expected to participate in ground operations in western Iran within days.

Trump spoke personally with Mustafa Hijri, president of the Democratic Party of Iranian Kurdistan, on March 3. He spoke the previous Sunday with Masoud Barzani and Bafel Talabani, the leaders of the two main Iraqi Kurdish political parties, to discuss how the United States and the Kurds could work together. Netanyahu has been lobbying for this connection for months. Israel has intelligence networks among Kurdish groups that predate this war by years.

The stated logic has three components. First: Kurdish forces attacking IRGC units in western Iran will pin them down, making it easier for unarmed Iranians in major cities to take to the streets without facing the massacres of January. Second: Kurdish forces could "sow chaos" and stretch the IRGC's military resources thin. Third: Kurdish forces could potentially take and hold territory in northern Iran to create a buffer zone for Israel.

Please read that third objective again. A buffer zone for Israel. Inside Iranian territory. Carved out by an American-armed Kurdish militia. This is not a plan for Iranian democracy. This is a plan for Iranian dismemberment, dressed in the language of liberation.

The Kurds make up approximately ten percent of Iran's population, concentrated in the northwest. They have legitimate grievances against the Islamic Republic—grievances that predate 1979, that include documented restrictions on cultural and political expression, and that are real. But the Kurdish opposition is also fractured. Five Iranian Kurdish parties formed a joint coalition on February 22—six days before the strikes began—with the declared goal of overthrowing the Islamic Republic. They do not agree on what comes after. Their interests are not identical to each other's, nor to the interests of the Iranian people as a whole.

The CIA's own intelligence assessments—leaked to CNN by the people familiar with the plan—acknowledge that Iranian Kurds "don't currently have the influence or resources to bolster a successful uprising against the government." A Trump administration official told CNN, "It may not be as simple as Americans convincing a proxy force to fight for them. You have people thinking about their own interests, and the question is whether bringing them in aligns with those interests."

The Chatham House analyst Neil Quilliam was more blunt, "Instinctively, it feels like a bad move. It is an afterthought and has not featured in any major planning to support any broader endgame. It reveals that the US-Iran war against Iran has been poorly thought out."

And the former State Department official Jen Gavito, who specialized in the Middle East region under Biden, said, "We are already facing a volatile security situation on both sides of the border. This has the potential to undermine Iraqi sovereignty and essentially empower armed militias with no accountability and with little understanding of what it may set in motion."

Here is what it may set in motion. Iran is not an ethnically homogeneous state. It is a country of Persians, Azerbaijanis, Kurds, Arabs, Balochis, Turkmen, Lurs, and others—with the Persian core representing roughly half the population and the ethnic minorities concentrated in the periphery, which also happens to be where the oil is, where the borders are, and where the external pressure is now being applied. The United States is also in contact, according to reporting from *Israel Hayom*, citing intelligence sources, with Baloch militia leaders in southeastern Iran. In the same region, Jaish al-Adl has conducted sustained attacks against IRGC forces for years. It is in contact with figures inside the regular army. It is trying to identify "moderately senior officials within the government" who might cooperate with a transition.

What you get when you simultaneously arm Kurdish separatists in the northwest, make contact with Baloch militants in the southeast, try to flip IRGC officers in the center, and conduct air strikes that have destroyed the apex of the central command structure is not a coordinated revolution. It is the precondition for a failed state.

What RAND Is Saying

The RAND Corporation's postwar analysis identified four possible outcomes for Iran's succession and stability: "digging in" (a clerical succession that maintains the existing system); "cut and run" (leadership flight, producing a power vacuum); "suppression and succession" (IRGC junta, more threatening and less constrained than what preceded it); and a popular uprising succeeding. RAND noted that Turkey and Pakistan both have serious security concerns, "particularly if Kurdish and Baloch militants inside Iran try to establish a political foothold as the country begins to fragment." The wording RAND used was not "if Iran transitions." The word was "fragment."

Iran Is Entering a Long Period of Instability

I want to be precise about this because the word "instability" is used so casually in foreign policy analysis that it has lost its weight. Instability, in this context, means: children growing up in a country where the electricity is unreliable, the currency is worthless, the hospitals are understaffed because the doctors have left, the government changes faster than institutions can adapt, and men with guns make the decisions that the laws are supposed to make. Instability means people die from preventable things. It means the talented professionals leave. It means the reconstruction that could happen does not happen, because the security conditions that reconstruction requires do not exist.

This is not abstract. This is what happened in Iraq after 2003. It is what happened in Libya after 2011. It is what happened in Afghanistan after 2001. In each of those cases, the military operation succeeded according to its own stated metrics. The government fell, or was pushed back, or was degraded. And then the country that remained was worse—for its own people—than the country that preceded it, for years or decades afterward.

Iran is more complex than Iraq, Libya, or Afghanistan. It has a larger population, a more educated population, more developed institutions, and a diaspora with the skills and resources to contribute to reconstruction. These are reasons for hope. They are not reasons for confidence that what follows will be better than what preceded it. There are reasons the outcome is not inevitable, which is different from saying it is likely to be good.

Short Term: Escalation and Retaliation (Now Through Mid-2026)

The IRGC has pre-delegated response authority. This was a lesson learned from the 2025 war, formalized in the months that followed. Individual regional commanders and proxy cell leaders do not need authorization from a central command to execute retaliatory strikes. The authorization was given in advance. The command structure being destroyed does not stop the response—it may even accelerate it, because the moderating voices that might have calibrated the retaliation for strategic effect are no longer there to do so.

The immediate risk is miscalculation. An IRGC commander in Bahrain, operating on pre-delegated authority, orders a strike on a target that is more consequential than intended. A Hezbollah cell in Lebanon, reading the signals from Tehran as authorization for escalation, launches an attack that draws Israeli retaliation into Lebanese civilian infrastructure. A Houthi strike in the Red Sea hits a ship from a country that is now politically unable to absorb it without responding. The chain of events that could not be controlled before the strikes is even less controllable now because the center coordinating Iran's proxy relationships is gone.

In this environment, the Kurdish uprising is a spark in a room full of open fuel lines. The IRGC is already striking Kurdish positions in Iraqi Kurdistan with drones. If CIA-armed Kurdish forces cross the border into western Iran, the IRGC's response will not be calibrated or limited. It will be the response of an institution fighting for its survival and with pre-delegated authority to do whatever is necessary. That response will kill Kurds. It will also kill people in the Kurdish civilian communities along the border who have nothing to do with any armed group. That is the mechanism. Those are the real people who will pay for this decision.

Medium Term: *Fragmentation Risk (Mid-2026 Through 2028)*

Iran is not a simple state. It is a country of many regions, many identities, many power centers, and many grievances that have been held in compression by the coercive architecture of the Islamic Republic. Remove the coercive architecture from above and the compression releases. What was held together by force does not automatically become held together by consent. It becomes held together by whichever local power is strongest in each region.

In the Kurdish northwest, armed Kurdish factions with American and Israeli backing, competing agendas, and a history of inter-faction conflict. In the Arab southwest, in Khuzestan—where most of Iran's oil infrastructure is located—Arab separatist movements have been suppressed for decades, movements that the Gulf states have historically had an interest in supporting. In the Balochi southeast: a militant landscape that connects into Pakistani Balochistan and that has been conducting attacks against the IRGC for years without external arming. In the Azerbaijani northwest: a Turkic-speaking population with cultural ties to Azerbaijan and Turkey, in a region that both countries have strategic interests in.

History does not offer a single example of a complex multiethnic state that was bombed into democracy from the outside. It offers many examples of complex multiethnic states that were bombed into fragmentation from the outside and then spent a generation reconstituting themselves—at enormous cost to human life, economic development, and the institutions that any functioning state requires.

The RAND Corporation explicitly flagged Turkey and Pakistan as states with serious security concerns if Iranian fragmentation produces a Kurdish and Baloch militant foothold. Turkey has fought a forty-year war against Kurdish insurgency. A Kurdish autonomous region on its southeastern border, armed by the US, is not a strategic interest Turkey will absorb without response. Pakistan is already managing the Baloch insurgency on its own territory. A destabilized Iranian Balochistan is a direct threat to Pakistani territorial integrity.

The people who will pay for the fragmentation scenario are Iranian Kurds who wanted political rights, not a proxy war. They are Persian Iranians who wanted to be rid of the Islamic Republic but did not want their country broken into competing armed fiefdoms. They are the children who will grow up in whatever comes next. They did not choose this. They were chosen.

Long Term: The Only Thing That Actually Works (2028 and Beyond)

The decisive factor in Iran's long-term trajectory is not determined by what the US does next. It is determined by what Iranians do next. This is not a statement of optimism. It is a statement based on history. Durable political change in complex states comes from shifts inside the political system—from the coalitions that form within institutions, from the defections of people who were part of the system and decided they could no longer be, from the movements that build across years and decades until the thing they are pushing against gives way.

The movement that exploded in 2022, that sustained itself through 2023 and 2024 and into the January 2026 protests, was building toward something. Whether it has been helped or harmed by the events of February 28 is genuinely uncertain. The "rally around the flag" effect is real: populations under external attack tend to close ranks against the attacker, even if they despise the government being defended. But the IRGC's legitimacy was already compromised before the bombs fell. The reformist president Masoud Pezeshkian, elected in 2024 on a platform of diplomatic engagement and domestic reform, represents a constituency inside Iran that wanted a different future and was working toward it through the political system. Whether that constituency survives the current period with its coherence intact is the most important question in Iranian politics.

What external actors can do is not arm proxies. And to not try to trigger uprisings through covert operations that the CIA's own assessments say cannot succeed without extensive support. External actors can create the conditions in which Iranians who want to build something different have the resources, security, and international recognition to do so.

That means targeted sanctions that hurt the IRGC, not the population. It means reconstruction investment that extends throughout civil society, not to whatever government emerges from the succession crisis. It means documenting what happened—every crime, by every party—so that the historical record is available when the moment for accountability arrives. It means a diaspora that organizes its expertise and resources for the reconstruction, not for the factional politics of exile communities.

And it means an honest accounting of what was done in February 2026, by whom, and why. Not the accounting that serves the narrative of liberation. The accounting that serves the truth. The truth is that a diplomatic breakthrough was bombed. The truth is that children were in school. The truth is that the IDF built the target list, the United States flew the planes, and the IRGC is now running what remains, and the CIA is arming Kurdish militias, and no one who made any of these decisions will live in the country they have made.

The people who will live in it are already there. They deserve better than what has been done to them in the name of their liberation. They have always deserved better.

A Personal Note

I am an Iranian-born American. I left Iran at seventeen. I have built a life in this country that I love. I have served this country—advised its government, helped secure its infrastructure, tried in every professional capacity to be useful to the nation that took me in. And I am watching that nation become the instrument of a forty-year Israeli strategic objective, in a war whose target list was built in Tel Aviv, whose Kurdish component was lobbied for by Netanyahu, whose diplomatic alternative was bombed while it was succeeding, and whose civilian cost is being borne by people in a country that cannot fight back against the decisions made about it. I am caught. I expect I will be caught for the rest of my life. I am writing it down so that at least the catching is on the record.

Chapter 20: The Possible Futures – Five Scenarios for What Comes Next

History does not end. It is not an arrow but a helix: the same questions return, in different form, to generations that did not choose to inherit them.

No one knows how this ends. What can be done, honestly and responsibly, is to map the range of plausible futures, lay out the conditions that would push toward each, and let the reader assess which seems most likely and what it would mean. Five scenarios follow. They are not equally likely. They are all possible. They are presented in the second person because these futures are not abstract. You will live in one of them.

Scenario One: The Libyan Outcome

It is 2028. The Iranian state has not been replaced. It has been dissolved. The IRGC, its centralized command structure destroyed, has fractured into regional warlords with personal loyalty structures and independent weapons caches. The northwestern Kurdish regions are de facto autonomous, supported by Turkey and the Iraqi Kurdish government. The southwestern Arab region of Khuzestan, where Iran's oil infrastructure is concentrated, is experiencing low-level insurgency. The southeastern Balochi regions have become a corridor for trafficking and militant activity affecting both Iran and Pakistan.

There is a nominal government in Tehran. It does not control the country. The Assembly of Experts never reached a consensus on a new Supreme Leader. Various exile groups, including those around Reza Pahlavi, have claimed representative authority but have no meaningful presence or constituency inside Iran. Approximately four million Iranians have been displaced. Turkey, already hosting four million Syrians, is in a political crisis. Iran's oil production is at 800,000 barrels per day and falling. The reconstruction cost estimate, is 400 billion dollars over a decade, with no clear funding mechanism in place.

This is the Libya scenario. The military force achieved its stated objective—government removal—without a viable plan for what comes next. Every independent expert on Iranian affairs warned this was the most likely worst-case outcome. As of 2028, it is the scenario you are living in.

Scenario Two: The Negotiated Exit

It is 2027. A ceasefire came six weeks into the conflict, brokered by Qatar with Chinese and EU participation, after oil prices hit $160 a barrel and the Gulf Cooperation Council states made clear to Washington that they could not sustain an indefinite conflict. Iran's interim government, led by technocratic reformists whom Ayatollah Khamenei had marginalized, agreed to the full dismantlement of nuclear enrichment infrastructure in exchange for comprehensive sanctions relief and UN security guarantees.

Reconstruction is happening slowly. Chinese and EU investments lead in the absence of American engagement. The oil infrastructure is being rebuilt. The internet is back. There are protests in Tehran about what Iran should become. The IRGC has been restructured, not dissolved. Reza Pahlavi has not returned. The interim government has made promises about democracy. Whether they are kept is the defining question of Iranian politics for the next decade.

This is the best plausible outcome. It required the Gulf states to break with Washington at a decisive moment. It required China to use its leverage constructively. It required Iran's surviving reformist faction to govern during a crisis. The window stayed open.

Scenario Three: The Long War

It is early 2027. The conflict is still active at low intensity. No ceasefire. No negotiation. The IRGC's mosaic defense has made the conflict unwinnable in any conventional military sense. The US has conducted more than 2,000 strikes. Iran has fired more than 3,000 missiles and drones. THAAD interceptor stockpiles in the Gulf have been drawn down to levels the Pentagon describes as "concerning." Manufacturing timelines are eighteen months.

Iran has been systematically targeting Gulf energy infrastructure—not the large, well-defended facilities, but the vulnerable nodes: pumping stations, desalination plants, and power transmission lines. Kuwait has been without reliable electricity for ten days. Oil is at $185 a barrel. The IMF has revised global growth projections down by 2.1 percentage points. Three European countries are in technical recession. The US President has invoked emergency powers to prevent a vote on a War Powers Resolution in Congress.

This scenario looks manageable week to week and catastrophic in aggregate. No single day is a crisis. The accumulation of days is a structural transformation of the global economy and the American constitutional order. It ends eventually, but not before extracting costs in dollars, in lives, and in the institutional fabric of democratic governance on both sides of the Atlantic.

Why Scenario Three and not Scenario Two

Scenario Two (The Negotiated Exit) requires six specific conditions that had not occurred as of March 30—the Gulf states breaking with Washington, China using its leverage constructively, oil reaching $160 a barrel as a forcing mechanism, and an Iranian reformist faction governing during the crisis. Scenario Three (The Long War) requires only that no ceasefire occurs, that the IRGC's mosaic defense prevents a decisive military outcome, and that the conflict continues at low intensity, extracting cumulative costs. As of March 30, Iran had rejected the ceasefire, the IRGC was operational, and the conflict was in its thirty-second day.

Scenario Four: Nuclear Breakout

It is 2029. The most consequential outcome of the 2026 war was not military. It was political. The surviving Iranian leadership reached a conclusion that is the logical mirror of the conclusion that justified the strikes: the only reliable deterrent against a repeat of February 28, 2026, is a nuclear weapon. This conclusion has public support inside Iran that no previous government could have claimed. A country bombed while its foreign minister was negotiating, its girls' schools hit, its hospitals struck, all while being told the strikes were self-defense—that country has a different nuclear calculus than it did before.

The breakout is announced. The new Iranian government has calculated that a declared nuclear capability is more deterring than an ambiguous capability, because ambiguity is what the 2026 strikes claimed to eliminate. The US threatens to strike again. Israel has declared it will strike preemptively to prevent a breakout. The logic of deterrence has caught up with the logic of preemption that justified the original action. The 2026 strikes were conducted to prevent Iran from acquiring a nuclear deterrent. The result is that Iran is pursuing a nuclear deterrent with greater urgency and greater public legitimacy than it could have claimed before.

Scenario Five: The Unintended Transformation

It is 2030. The Middle East is different in ways that no one planned. Saudi Arabia, moving toward normalization with Israel under the Abraham Accords, paused that process when its cities were struck by Iranian missiles that the US defenses failed to intercept fully. By late 2026, Saudi Arabia has signed a security cooperation agreement with Beijing that was functionally equivalent to the guarantee Washington had previously provided. The Abraham Accords become diplomatically irrelevant. Turkey repositions itself as a neutral mediator, becoming the most important single state in the postwar settlement in the absence of American diplomatic credibility. NATO membership does not prevent this.

The regional order that emerges is less predictable and less American-centered than the one that preceded it. The architecture of Middle Eastern security that the United States built over the past seventy years—based on military presence, security guarantees, and diplomatic leadership—has been substantially revised by the consequences of a war that was supposed to make the region safer. The people who made the decision will be long out of the office. The people who navigate the consequences are the next generation.

Chapter 21: The Ground War Comes – What the Evidence Shows

At the time of this writing—March 25, 2026, day twenty-five of Operation Epic Fury—the following is documented fact, not forecast. I am writing it as a chapter because the events it records are moving faster than any analysis written afterward can honestly reconstruct. The pattern it names has now repeated three times. The forces it describes are physically in transit. What I am recording is the present tense of everything this book has been arguing in the past tense.

Every time Washington told Tehran it was ready to negotiate, bombs followed. Three instances. Three documented sequences. The third was unfolding as this chapter is written.

April 2025: talks open in Oman at Trump's initiative. Rounds in Rome, Muscat. Both sides were described by intermediaries as close to an agreement. June 11: US embassies begin evacuating personnel. June 21: B-2 bombers strike Fordow, Natanz, and Isfahan. Trump declares a ceasefire three days later and calls it a victory.

February 26, 2026: Oman's Foreign Minister announces a breakthrough in Geneva—Iran agrees, for the first time in its history, to never stockpile enriched uranium. He calls it something "completely new" and says peace is "within reach." He is asked whether enough ground has been covered to hold off a US attack. He says, "I hope so." Twenty-four hours later, Operation Epic Fury begins.

March 24, 2026: Trump announces negotiations "right now." A fifteen-point peace plan is delivered to Tehran through Pakistani intermediaries. He pauses threatened strikes on Iran's power plants for five days. Simultaneously, the 82nd Airborne Division's command element receives written deployment orders. Two Marine Expeditionary Units are converging on the Persian Gulf. CENTCOM's operational orders are unchanged.

Defense Secretary Hegseth, from the Oval Office, states, "We negotiate with bombs."

The Forces

The US now has approximately 50,000 troops participating in aspects of the Iran campaign—the largest concentration of American forces in the region since the 2003 invasion of Iraq.

Three additional force packages are converging simultaneously. The 82nd Airborne Division's Immediate Response Force—approximately 1,000 soldiers in its initial element, with a full brigade of 3,000 capable of following—can deploy anywhere in the world within eighteen hours. These are paratroopers. They do not need a port or an established airfield. They jump. The 31st Marine Expeditionary Unit, 2,200 Marines aboard the USS *Tripoli* and USS *New Orleans*, is due in theater by March 27. The 11th Marine Expeditionary Unit, 2,500 Marines rerouted from the Pacific three weeks ahead of schedule, is underway from California aboard the USS Boxer Amphibious Ready Group, which carries F-35B short-takeoff jets capable of operating without established airfields.

These are not defensive formations. Amphibious ready groups (ARG), airborne rapid-response units, and F-35B-equipped assault ships are seizure assets—built for one mission category: taking and holding specific objectives under fire, against organized resistance. The combination of Osprey tiltrotor insertion with 700-kilometer combat radius, parachute drop capability, and sea-based aviation provides simultaneous strike options at multiple locations without dependence on established infrastructure. CENTCOM has options. The evidence suggests the options have been chosen.

The Three Objectives

Three missions are actively being planned, based on reporting from the *Wall Street Journal*, the *New York Times*, CNN, *Axios*, and statements by senior officials. They are not mutually exclusive. The forces are sized for all three.

Kharg Island. A five-mile landmass fifteen miles off the Iranian coast that handles 90 percent of Iran's oil exports. Its defenses have been degraded by sustained US bombardment. Trump has called it Iran's "crown jewel." A Marine assault landing by Ospreys from amphibious ships is operationally feasible. Holding it is another matter. Fifteen miles from the Iranian mainland, any force on Kharg would be under continuous fire from rockets, drones, and ballistic missiles. Iran has an estimated 5,000 naval mines available for defending the surrounding waters. Former NATO Supreme Allied Commander Admiral James Stavridis assessed it plainly, "Such an invasion would likely be far from surgical—expect rising casualties on both sides and among civilians—and still leave Iran with plenty of other potential steps to create mayhem."

The strategic logic is nonetheless coherent: control of Kharg removes Iran's primary revenue source. It creates a physical bargaining chip—Iranian sovereign territory that can be returned in exchange for nuclear concessions. This is the Trump method applied geopolitically: take something, then negotiate its return as a deal.

The Strait of Hormuz. At its narrowest, the strait is twenty-one miles wide. Through it flows approximately one-fifth of the world's oil and liquefied natural gas. Iran closed the Strait on February 28 in retaliation for the strikes and has attacked more than twenty vessels in the four weeks since. More than 1,000 ships and 20,000 seafarers are stranded. The IEA has called the disruption worse than the 1973 and 1979 oil shocks combined. The Philippines has declared a national emergency. Forty energy facilities across nine countries have been damaged.

Physically reopening the strait requires controlling the Iranian island positions—Abu Musa, Greater Tunb, and Lesser Tunb—on its northern edge. These are the platforms where Iran's coastal fires originate. The 82nd Airborne's rapid-seizure capability is precisely suited to this mission: a parachute assault on specific fixed positions, preceded by air suppression, would remove the firing platforms. What follows: is the United States holding Iranian sovereign territory, by force, in a country of 93 million people, indefinitely. That is an occupation. The word used for it does not change what it is.

The Enriched Uranium at Isfahan. This mission would justify the full deployment and provide the exit. Iran possessed, as of the IAEA's last verified assessment uranium enriched to 60 percent U-235—one technical step from weapons grade. The 2025 strikes buried most of this material under rubble at Isfahan's underground tunnel complex. The Iranians themselves have been unable to fully access the sealed tunnels. If the entire stockpile reached 90 percent purity, it would provide fissile material for approximately 11 nuclear weapons. Secretary of State Rubio, asked at a congressional briefing whether the uranium would be secured, said: "People are going to have to go and get it." He did not specify who.

The material's current state is uranium hexafluoride gas in pressurized cylinders—extraordinarily hazardous to handle, buried under rubble, in an underground facility in central Iran, in the middle of a war. There is no historical precedent for a forcible seizure of nuclear material in hostile enemy territory. The IAEA's Director General called it "a very challenging operation." Every prior extraction of nuclear material from a foreign country—Kazakhstan, Libya, Iraq—was conducted with the consent of the host government.

But seizure is the clearest path to an exit narrative. If the administration can credibly claim the material has been secured or diluted—that Iran can no longer build a nuclear weapon—it has achieved the stated objective that launched this war. It can wind down operations and call it a victory. The fifteen-point peace plan, delivered to Tehran on March 24, reportedly requires Iran to commit to never pursuing nuclear weapons and to dismantle existing nuclear capabilities. The forces now in transit are the leverage behind that demand—and, if the demand is refused, the instrument of its enforcement.

What These Forces Cannot Do

The combined Marine and airborne forces converging on the theater is a scalpel. It is sized for one or two specific seizure operations conducted over days to weeks, not for a sustained presence in a country of 93 million people. What it can do: seize a specific island or facility and hold it under fire for up to two weeks; insert itself rapidly without relying on established ports or airfields; or conduct a forced extraction of material or personnel from a fixed location.

What it cannot do: occupy Iran; suppress the IRGC's mosaic defense doctrine, which compartmentalizes military units so that decapitation strikes and conventional defeats do not bring the whole thing down, and which has been its operational planning doctrine since 1988; hold territory against sustained ballistic missile and drone retaliation without a continuous resupply and air cover that has not been publicly committed; govern; or build the political legitimacy that military force has never produced in Iran.

The Trap

The administration's stated reason for the war—preventing Iran from acquiring nuclear weapons—cannot be achieved by military means alone. percentThe ground operation, if it comes, will either seize the uranium or it will not. If it does, the administration has an exit narrative. If it does not—if the cylinders cannot be reached, or if the mission is disrupted, or if Iran has moved material to locations not yet identified—the stated objective remains unachieved, the forces are deployed in the most hostile possible environment. The administration faces the choice it has been avoiding since February 28: a negotiated exit that appears to be a compromise, or an escalation that appears to have no ceiling.

Tehran understands the pattern. Iran will not accept a ceasefire, its state media reported on March 25. That is not obstinacy. It is the rational response of a government that has watched two ceasefires become the prelude to new strikes, and is calculating whether a third round of talks is preparation for a ground assault on its nuclear facilities.

The forces are in transit. The operational orders are unchanged.

This chapter ends here because events do not stop for chapters. What comes next is what you now know happened. The book is not a complete report of what happened but instead seeks to give you the tools to understand it.

Chapter 22: The World Reacts – Fracture Lines

The international reaction to Epic Fury did not split along familiar Cold War lines but along a new fracture: between countries that had trusted American security guarantees and those that had learned not to. This is according to evidence from UN Security Council vote records, foreign ministry statements, the Gulf states' economic responses, Turkey's pivot to mediation, China's naval deployment, and the Global South's responses. The long-term structural consequence of the strikes may be an American strategic withdrawal from the Middle East, which American policy has tried for thirty years to prevent.

The international reaction to Operation Epic Fury did not unite the world against Iran. It fractured along lines that had been forming for years.

UN Secretary-General António Guterres condemned the use of force and called for an immediate halt to hostilities. European Union leaders described the situation as perilous and emphasized nuclear safety and restraint. France, Germany, and the United Kingdom reiterated their opposition to Iran's destabilizing actions but made clear that none had participated in the strikes. The Pope posted on X: "Stability and peace are not achieved through mutual threats, nor through the use of weapons, which sow destruction, suffering, and death, but only through reasonable, sincere and responsible dialogue."

Russia called the attacks "pre-planned and unprovoked" and warned of "uncontrolled escalation." China expressed being "highly concerned," called for an immediate stop to military actions, and emphasized that Iran's sovereignty must be respected. Ukraine's President Zelensky applauded the strikes—a reminder that Iran had been supplying Shahed-136 drones to Russia for use against Ukrainian cities, entangling this conflict with the European war in ways that made simple moral accounting impossible.

In the US, the reaction was split along partisan lines. Senator Amy Klobuchar warned that the president had no authority to start a war with Iran without congressional approval and that unilateral action endangered US troops. Trump had announced the strikes via a Truth Social video. There was no public address, no formal message to Congress, no request for authorization. The Stimson Center's experts assessed, "President Trump has initiated a war against Iran without congressional approval, without a serious public debate, and in the face of overwhelming public opposition. In short, this war is unconstitutional, unwise, and a betrayal of his promise to put the interests of the American people first."

The Fracture Lines in Detail

The international reaction to Operation Epic Fury did not follow the familiar Cold War alignment. It produced something more unsettling: a fracture along new lines that illuminated the actual distribution of power and interests in the post-American world.

China's response was the most consequential. Beijing called the strikes "unacceptable aggression against a sovereign state." It convened an emergency session of the UN Security Council, where it and Russia vetoed any resolution authorizing or retroactively legitimizing the operation. More significantly, China announced the immediate deployment of two naval vessels to the Persian Gulf "to protect Chinese commercial interests and personnel"—a message delivered in steel rather than words. China is Iran's largest trading partner. It has been absorbing sanctioned Iranian oil at discount prices for years. It has $400 billion in infrastructure investment commitments in Iran under the 25-year Comprehensive Strategic Partnership signed in 2021. The war that Washington launched to solve the Iran problem had detonated inside China's most significant Middle Eastern relationship.

Russia condemned the strikes in terms that both served its strategic interest in opposing American power and also reflected genuine concern about the precedent it set. A world in which the US can decapitate a nuclear-adjacent state's leadership without authorization or consequence is a world in which Russia's own security doctrine becomes harder to maintain. Moscow called for an emergency UN General Assembly session and issued veiled threats about "reciprocal measures" if American actions continued to destabilize the international order.

Turkey—NATO member, would-be mediator, perpetual opportunist—offered a ceasefire framework within forty-eight hours of the strikes beginning. President Erdoğan called both Trump and Pezeshkian. He positioned Turkey as the only power capable of brokering an exit that both sides could accept. He was not wrong about this. His willingness to engage Tehran while remaining a NATO member meant that Turkish mediation carried a legitimacy that no purely Western effort could. By day five, the Turkish foreign ministry had become the primary diplomatic channel. Washington found itself receiving secondhand reports of Iranian positions through Ankara, rather than through the direct channel that had been operating until the bombs fell.

The Global South was blunt in ways that Western diplomatic language rarely is. South Africa invoked the International Court of Justice. Brazil called for a special session of the UN General Assembly. India—which had been carefully maintaining relationships with both Washington and Tehran, partly because of a large Iranian-Indian diaspora and partly because India imports significant amounts of Iranian oil through third-country mechanisms—voiced "deep concern," a phrase that was diplomatically calibrated and privately furious. Indonesia, the world's largest Muslim-majority country, saw street protests in Jakarta that drew hundreds of thousands. The government recalled its ambassador from Washington for consultations.

The EU's response illustrated the limits of collective European foreign policy. Germany and France issued a joint statement calling for the immediate cessation of hostilities and respect for international law. The United Kingdom, which had provided logistical support through its bases in Cyprus and Diego Garcia, said it stood "with its American allies while urging restraint." The gap between the British position and the Franco-German position—visible within hours of the strikes beginning—was the specific fracture that European foreign policy has been unable to paper over since Brexit and that the Iran war exposed in its full depth. When America acts, Europe divides. That division is itself a strategic consequence of the war.

The strategic consequences extend beyond the immediate diplomatic fractures. Robert Kagan, writing in *The Atlantic* on April 1, 2026 — the day of Trump's first formal address to the nation on the war—identified several of these consequences. The most counterintuitive consequence is Russian. Increased global oil prices and the Trump administration's decision to lift sanctions on Iranian oil—to manage domestic gasoline costs—materially helped Russia replenish its war chest at precisely the moment its wartime deficits were beginning to cause significant economic pain to the Russian government. A war launched in the Middle East, without European consultation, was providing material relief to the adversary on which European security most depends. The alliance Kagan describes as the primary structural source of American power, influence, and security for eight decades was being strained at both ends simultaneously.

The second consequence is operational. The displacement of the 11th Marine Expeditionary Unit from the Indo-Pacific region to the Middle East—rerouted three weeks ahead of schedule—created a documented coverage gap in the Pacific theater at a moment when every major defense assessment identified the Indo-Pacific as the primary theater of long-term American strategic competition. The forces consuming precision munitions at high rates against Iranian targets were the same forces whose inventory would be required for any contingency involving China. Both the munitions and the deployment gap were consequences of the war that the address to the nation did not acknowledge.

These are not speculative strategic concerns. They are documented operational outcomes observable in real time. A war justified as eliminating the most serious threat to American security was simultaneously degrading the material capacity to address the threats American security professionals had identified as most serious.

What the fracture lines of March 2026 reveal, when assembled, is something more than a diplomatic realignment. The social anthropologist Arjun Appadurai calls it a vast worldwide correction: a reorganization of the planet to serve the winners of globalization by removing, through violence, displacement, or economic elimination, the inconvenient weight of its losers. The Malthusian logic is not stated openly. It does not need to be. It is legible in actions: hospitals and schools reduced to rubble, negotiating tables bombed while both sides were still drafting language, and a Security Council rendered structurally incapable of a response.

Pankaj Mishra, in his work on the world after the most recent Gaza War, names what millions of people are now experiencing: the shock of discovering that the evil they believed had been contained by history has returned, carried out legitimately and bureaucratically by governments they were taught to regard as civilized. He writes,

"After witnessing savage mass murder over several months with the knowledge that it was conceived, executed and endorsed by people much like themselves, who presented it as a collective necessity, legitimate and even humane, millions now feel less at home in the world." That disorientation is not weakness. It is an accurate perception. The world has changed.

Mirror Conditions: The Same System Behavior, Different Flags

The question is not whether America is Iran. It is not. The question is whether the specific mechanism that makes Iran what it is—power without accountability, force without constraint—is recognizable in what America is becoming.

Before we proceed to Part Four, a pause is needed. An accounting.

This section has been about Iran: the currency collapse, the massacres, the bombs, the schoolchildren, the diplomatic table that got destroyed. The reader who has reached this point knows what the Islamic Republic did to its own people and what the United States and Israel did to Iran's people. The record is the record.

The next section is about America. Not because the two countries are equivalent. They are not. The Islamic Republic has operated as a closed political system. The United States is a constitutional democracy with elections, an independent press, and formal protections for civil liberties that the Islamic Republic lacks. The asymmetries are real and matter.

The symmetry this interlude names is narrower and more precise. It is about institutional behavior when constraints are removed. When a government—any government, under any flag, with any ideology—loses the institutional friction that keeps power answerable to the governed, the output is predictable: it uses force against the people it was constituted to protect. The Islamic Republic used force against Iranian protesters in January 2026. The Trump administration used force against immigrant communities in American cities during the same period. These are not morally equivalent acts. They share a mechanism.

The mechanism is this: the normalization of exceptional powers. It begins with a crisis that justifies emergency measures. The measures become permanent. The justification expands. The people who were supposed to check the expansion—legislatures, courts, professional norms, and institutional culture—have been weakened, captured, or stopped from exercising their authority. And then, one morning, a president can launch a major war without a vote, and Congress is to be briefed on it afterward.

That is not the Islamic Republic. That is the United States, in March 2026. Different flags. The same system of behavior.

The next section names the mechanisms. It does not argue that America has become Iran. It argues that the distance between "constitutional democracy with unchecked executive" and "authoritarian state" is shorter than most Americans have been taught to believe, and that the evidence for this is visible in the public record of the last decade for anyone willing to look directly.

The people of Iran have been looking at it directly for a century. They know what it looks like when it arrives. Some of them are living in the United States now and watching it arrive here, and the expression on their faces is not surprise.

There is one more mirror condition that this interlude must name. The historical cases in which external force produced genuine democratic transition share a common feature: the intervening power believed in, invested in, and remained accountable to the institutions. The Marshall Plan was possible because the government that designed it was itself constrained by democratic accountability, congressional oversight, and a long-term strategic vision that accepted the slow, unglamorous work of building rather than merely destroying. When that condition is absent—when the intervening power is itself in the process of dismantling its own institutional constraints, when its secretary of state admits the war was triggered by an ally's decision rather than its own strategic judgment, when the same administration that is bombing another country's infrastructure is simultaneously cutting food assistance for its own hungry children—the historical precedent for successful democratic transition does not apply. The executor of the intervention is not a variable. It is the decisive factor. What is being done to Iran is not being done by the America that built the Marshall Plan. This America seems to no longer believe in building.

★★★

The incoherence was not a communications failure. It was structural. In the days following the launch of Operation Epic Fury, the administration's stated justification shifted between four incompatible rationales: preventing Iran from acquiring a nuclear weapon; removing a government that had repressed its own people for nearly half a century; stopping an imminent Iranian attack on American forces; and following Israel into a conflict it had already decided to initiate regardless. These were not complementary framings. They implied different endpoints, different definitions of victory, and different answers to the question every soldier and every parent deserves an answer to before a single soldier is deployed: what does winning look like, and when does it end?

Michael Singh, who handled the Middle East portfolio in the George W. Bush White House, told the *Wall Street Journal* that the administration had been "inconsistent and often inaccurate in explaining why we are at war, what we are trying to achieve and how we intend to achieve it"—a war launched before its own architects had settled on a purpose. Senator Mark Warner, a member of the Gang of Eight with access to the most sensitive classified intelligence, said he saw no evidence Iran was planning any preemptive strike against the United States. Senator Tim Kaine, sitting on two relevant committees, confirmed the same. Four government officials briefed on the classified planning told *The Intercept* that there was no endgame. "The administration doesn't have a clue," one said. "They do not have an actual, real rationale, endgame, or plan for the aftermath of this."

This is not the profile of a government executing a considered strategy. It is the profile of a government that chose to act and then worked out the reasons afterward. The Germany and Japan analogy demands precisely the opposite: a government that knew what it wanted to build before the first bomb fell, possessed the institutional machinery to build it, and sustained that commitment across a generation. What arrived on the doorstep of eighty-nine million Iranians on the morning of February 28, 2026, had none of those qualities. It had aircraft. It had munitions. It did not have a plan.

PART FOUR:
America and the Wages of Unchecked Force

The institutional degradation that produced the Iran war did not begin in Iran. It has been building in the United States for decades—in the erosion of congressional war authority, in the normalization of executive unilateralism, in the dismantling of the rule-based norms that once constrained American power. Minneapolis is not a metaphor for Tehran. It is evidence of the same pattern operating in a different context.

Chapter 23: When Good People Break – Moral Injury, Diaspora Voices, and the Weight of Witnessing

I need to pause in my geopolitical analysis to make room for something more personal—not because personal concerns outweigh political ones, but because the personal is where political abstractions become real.

My brother is four years older than I am and has always been the steady one. He stayed in his home in Tehran through thirty-five days of bombardment. No military sites near him. Nothing that should have drawn fire. Still, it came.

There had been numerous strikes since February 28th that shook his building and broke windows, and they kept getting closer... The first strike hit less than a hundred yards from where he stood. The building jolted. Windows shattered. A door tore loose from its frame and fell. He went down five floors to the alley. He needed to see. Dust was everywhere—cars buried in it, the ground gone gray. Then the air changed, a compression, a tightening, as if the atmosphere itself was making room for what was coming. He looked up.

A missile passed low over his head. Close enough to see. Close enough for him to feel the displacement of air. Then it struck almost the same place again. The shockwave moved through him—not sound but force, felt in the chest, the teeth, the sinuses. For a moment, there was no world. Only gray weight pressing in. The shockwave did something to his ears. You do not notice what is gone until the absence becomes its own presence. The ringing in his ears has not left.

A few hundred yards away, near a mosque, a young woman stepped outside. Twenty-four years old. Her husband was beside her. Their children were there. A piece of shrapnel smaller than two fingers struck her in the forehead. She fell to the ground right in front of them. That was all it took.

He walked away with what he had on him. A wallet. A phone. The clothes he wore. A few streets down, someone opened a door. He stayed there two nights. Slept where he could. Waited. Found a place farther away. He said the dust stayed in his throat long after he left.

We have spoken three times in forty-five days—each call under five minutes. No internet. Sometimes no signal at all. You hear his voice. You measure time in seconds. You say what matters fast. Then the line goes dead.

He is still there.

***

I felt it long before I could name it: a pressure behind my ribs that refused to leave. I have stood beside humming machines and glowing panels, watching systems strain. I have sat in rooms where decisions were made that would keep lights on for some and leave others in the dark. Each time, I told myself I was doing the least harm possible. Each time, I carried home a conflicted feeling.

There was a time when I made a decision that saved a region but hurt a town. A storm had knocked out transmission lines. Demand was high. If we kept supplying everyone, the whole network would collapse, and millions would lose power in the dead of winter. If we cut the supply to one section, we could keep the rest running. We stood before the map. A grid operator on our team had his hand on the switch. I thought of the elderly in that town, of the hospitals and the businesses, of the sound of a heater kicking in on a cold morning. He pressed the switch. No one died. We carry the weight of what could have happened, not the relief of what did not. The lights went out in that town. The grid held. No one knew my name. No one thanked me. No one cursed me. I went home and tried to sleep. I could not.

Months later, I replayed that moment again and again. Each time I ended in the same place. My training and my conscience told me I had chosen the lesser harm. Yet the unease did not fade. It was my wife who named it. "You are carrying something that does not belong only to you," she said. "Put it down." I spoke with a friend who had been a medic in conflict zones. He told me about choosing which wounded person to treat first, knowing someone else would die. Talking did not erase the fact of what we both had done, but it changed what it meant.

I think of that when I think about Iran. I think about it when I think about the conscripted soldiers who were sent to face protesters, and about those who refused, and those who did not. The moral injury in that situation is distributed across an entire system. The architects of forty-six years of sanctions policy, who manufactured the economic collapse that put those protesters in the streets, bear their share. The architects of Operation Epic Fury carry theirs. The record does not allow any of them to look away.

Speaking does not absolve, but silence corrodes. Unspoken injuries travel across generations, not through blood but through what is not said. When we keep our moral injuries to ourselves, our children sense something is wrong and blame themselves. That is how harm travels: through silence.

★★★

To be Iranian in March 2026 was to be asked, every day, by people who meant well, to have a single feeling about an event that required at least six feelings held simultaneously, without resolution.

— Nasrin M., professor, Iranian Studies

Four million Iranian-Americans. Two hundred thousand Iranian-Canadians. Large, established, professionally accomplished communities in London, Toronto, Stockholm, Hamburg, Los Angeles, Houston, and Washington. The Iranian diaspora is one of the most educated exile communities in the world. And in the days after February 28, 2026, it was also one of the most divided, most surveilled—by each other and by governments on multiple sides—and most systematically misrepresented in Western media.

What follows are six portraits, drawn from verified testimony, of what it was to be Iranian outside Iran in the first days of the war. None of them is simple. All of them are true. Their names have been changed or withheld where indicated.

Los Angeles: The Celebration and Its Limits

Parisa was at the Persian Square celebration on the morning of March 1. She had been awake since 1 a.m. when the first reports of the strikes came through. By the time the sun rose and people gathered on Westwood Boulevard, she was holding a pre-revolutionary Iranian flag—with a lion and sun, the flag of the Pahlavi era, the flag that, for many diaspora Iranians, represents the Iran taken from their families. She was crying.

"I have waited my whole life for this," she said. She is 58. She left Iran when she was 19, after the revolution. She has not been back. Her mother died in Tehran years ago, and she could not attend the funeral. "The monster is dead. I don't care about anything else. The monster is finally dead."

An hour later, someone in the crowd—a younger, second-generation Iranian-American, wearing a Women, Life, Freedom

T-shirt—walked up to her. "What about the girls in Minab?" the younger woman asked. "What about the school?"

Parisa went quiet. Then she said, "I know. I know. I don't know what to do with that." She kept holding the flag. The younger woman kept standing there. Neither of them left. Neither of them knew what to say next.

Toronto: The Silence on the Phone

Dariush is a professional. He has lived in Toronto for eleven years. His mother lives in Tehran. On the night of February 28, when the strikes began, he called her. The call went through once. She said, "I can hear them." Then the line went dead.

He did not hear from her for three days. During those three days, he watched the Los Angeles celebrations on his laptop and felt something he struggled to name. "It's like watching people cheer a building on fire while your mother is inside it," he said. "They are not wrong that the building was bad. But she is inside it."

On day three, his mother called. She was unhurt. She had been staying in a neighbor's basement. The electricity in her neighborhood had been out for forty-eight hours. The water was intermittent. She told him she had enough food for a week. She told him not to worry. He is still worried. He will be worried for the rest of his life, in the way that people who have had one call drop are always waiting for the next one to drop, too.

A City in Northern England: The Vigil and Its Critics

Shirin organized a vigil in her city on March 2 for dead civilians. She posted it on social media: "A gathering to mourn those killed in the strikes. All backgrounds welcome. This is not a political rally."

Within two hours, she had received forty-seven messages. Many were supportive. Seventeen called her a "government apologist." Four accused her of being an IRGC agent. Two told her the children of Minab should not be mourned because they would grow up to be enemies of freedom. One message said: "You are mourning the children of terrorists."

Shirin is not a government apologist. She has family members who have faced consequences for their political views. She organized the vigil because at least 168 had been killed —the official toll rose to approximately 175 by March 4 — and she believed that children who are killed deserve to be mourned. She held the vigil. Sixty people came. Fourteen people protested outside it, holding signs that said: "Don't Grieve for the Regime."

"The hardest thing," she said afterward, "is that both groups thought they were right about what I was doing. Neither group asked me what I actually thought."

London: The Iranian-Israeli

Eli's father is Iranian. His mother is Israeli. He was born in London and has lived there his whole life. His Israeli cousins were in bomb shelters during the Iranian missile barrage on March 1. His father's friends in Tehran had not been heard from since the blackout began.

"Everyone assumes I must have a position," he said. "The Iranians in my father's community assume I support the strikes because my mother is Israeli. The Israelis in my mother's family assume I oppose the strikes because I'm 'soft on Iran.' My Iranian friends look at me like I'm a collaborator. My Israeli friends look at me like I'm a traitor."

"The truth is that I have cousins hiding in basements in both countries. I don't have a position that covers that. No position simplifies this enough to be useful to me."

He paused. "The people who seem most certain are the ones with the least at stake."

The Professor Who Cannot Speak for Iran

Nasrin is a professor of Iranian Studies at a North American university. In the ten days after February 28, she was invited to appear on three television programs, two podcasts, and one parliamentary committee. Every invitation asked her to represent "the Iranian perspective" on the strikes.

She declined all of them. Not because she had nothing to say. Because she refused the premise.

"There is no single Iranian perspective on the strikes," she said. "There is Parisa in Los Angeles with her flag. Dariush is in Toronto, waiting for his mother to call. There is the 22-year-old student in Tehran who was simultaneously relieved and terrified on the morning Ayatollah Khamenei died. There is the IRGC commander who has been planning for this for twenty years and is now executing a pre-delegated battle plan. There is the schoolteacher in Minab who survived because she was in the staff room. These are all Iranian perspectives. None of them is the Iranian perspective. When a Western journalist asks me to represent the Iranian perspective, they are not asking me to explain Iran. They are asking me to simplify it into something that fits a five-minute segment. I will not do that. The simplification is itself a form of harm."

What the Diaspora Is Not

NPR's Kelly McEvers reported from Los Angeles on March 1 that the celebrations there were "not representative of all opinions" in the Iranian-American community. This is both accurate and insufficient. The diaspora is not one answer. It is also not the absence of an answer.

The Iranian diaspora is the living record of what the Islamic Republic cost: every person who left because they could not stay, who watched their country from a distance for decades, who sent money home through channels that bypassed sanctions, who built lives elsewhere while carrying the grief for an Iran they had lost. That record is real, and it matters.

And the diaspora is also the living record of the complexity that any intervention in Iran must reckon with. There is no unified Iranian diaspora position. There is no unified Iranian-American community that can be pointed to as legitimate or illegitimate for a military action. The Parisas, the Dariushes, the Shirins, the Elis, and the Nasrins are all Iranian. They all have stakes. They all have people inside the country. They do not agree. Anyone who tells you that "the Iranians" wanted this, or that "the Iranians" are grateful, or that "the Iranians" are outraged, is doing something that the professor of Iranian Studies refused to do: simplifying into a single perspective what remains, stubbornly and irreducibly, many.

Chapter 24: Minneapolis – The Same Logic, Domestic

While Iran burned, another fire was consuming a city in the American Midwest.

Minneapolis, Minnesota—a city which has been my home for over twenty years, and that had already become a symbol of American reckoning through the murder of George Floyd in May 2020—became, in January 2026, the site of a new and different confrontation: a massive federal immigration enforcement operation that killed two American citizens and exposed, with brutal clarity, the stakes of unchecked federal power in a democratic society.

Operation Metro Surge brought thousands of ICE and Border Patrol agents to Minneapolis. The operation was the largest federal immigration enforcement action ever mounted in the US. In Minnesota alone, more than 3,000 arrests were made—federal agents in unmarked vans, wearing tactical gear, established checkpoints and conducted raids.

On January 7, 2026, Renée Good—a thirty-seven-year-old US citizen, poet, and mother of three—was fatally shot by an ICE agent in Minneapolis during an immigration enforcement action. Good was in her vehicle and had been attempting to drive away from a tense scene when an agent fired, striking her multiple times. Videos of the shooting raised serious questions about whether lethal force had been necessary.

Seventeen days later, on January 24, two Customs and Border Protection agents shot and killed Alex Jeffrey Pretti, a thirty-seven-year-old intensive care nurse who worked at the VA Hospital in Minneapolis and who had served in the US Army. Videos showed Pretti standing in the street near the intersection of 26th Street and Nicollet Avenue, filming the officers with his phone and helping direct cars away from the scene. While carrying a concealed firearm he was licensed to have, video confirms Pretti was holding a cell phone, not a gun. Witnesses testified that he had approached the scene to help a woman who had been shoved down. After being pepper-sprayed and tackled, Pretti was pinned to the ground. One officer drew a handgun. Ten shots were fired in approximately five seconds.

The Department of Homeland Security claimed that Pretti had approached agents with a handgun. Video analysis by *The New York Times* and independent journalists found that he held only a phone before being pinned. DHS Secretary Kristi Noem described Pretti as a "would-be assassin" who intended to "massacre law enforcement"—claims that Minnesota Governor Tim Walz bluntly described as "lies."

Pretti's parents, Michael and Susan Pretti, released a statement: "Alex was a kind-hearted soul… his last thought and act was to protect a woman. The sickening lies told about our son by the administration are reprehensible… He is clearly not holding a gun when attacked." They pleaded: "Please get the truth out about our son."

What followed the killings was as alarming as the killings themselves. The Department of Justice moved to block local investigations. Minnesota's state investigators were prevented from accessing key evidence. Several federal prosecutors resigned rather than target the victims' families as instructed. State authorities had to sue the federal government to preserve evidence—a judge had to order DHS not to destroy or alter anything.

A Reuters review found that since the immigration raids began at least 655 people had been charged under Title 18, Section 111—a statute intended to punish assaults on federal officers that can carry up to twenty years in prison— more than double the number during the previous two years.

I came to the United States in August 1978, months before the Iranian Revolution, believing in the promise of liberty and justice. I became an American because I believed that in America, the law would protect every person, and that no government was above the law. What happened in Minneapolis in January 2026 tested that belief in ways I had not anticipated. I know what it looks like when a government loses its accountability. I watched it happen in Iran across my lifetime. The mechanism is not dramatic at first. It begins with emergency powers that are not rescinded. With accountability that applies to some and not others. With officials who fabricate official accounts of deaths and then suppress the evidence. Prosecutors are told to target the victims instead of the perpetrators. These are not new patterns. They have Persian names, and those names are old.

And I need to be honest: I have colleagues who knew Alex Pretti. I have friends who were in those streets. The grief is not abstract. It is specific, local, and persistent, as grief always is when the names are people you have heard about at dinner parties and community meetings. Renée Good was a poet. Alex Pretti was a nurse who cared for veterans. They were not statistics. They were neighbors. They died because power decided, in that moment, that it did not need to justify its actions.

What happens to a community when this is done to it is the same question this book asks about Iran. The logic is identical: when power is insulated from accountability, the people closest to it always pay first.

Out of that grief, a demand rose in Minneapolis, and it was right: speak truth to power. Act justly. Name what is wrong. Do not go silent.

But there is a harder question underneath it—one that a community, like a person, can only answer honestly after sitting with the weight of it long enough to be changed by it.

Do we accept the truth that is right in front of us?? Have we—as a city, as a country —had our assumptions about who is protected and who is expendable stripped to their foundation? Have we let what happened here finish its work on us—not just make us louder, but make us more honest about what we have tolerated, what we have not seen, and what we owe to those who paid the price while we looked away?

The people who have always lived closest to unchecked power knew what the rest of us are only now beginning to understand: that accountability is not a legal mechanism. It is a habit. And when leaders cannot be told they are wrong, the signals stop. The corrections stop. The system loses the capacity to save itself—not slowly, but suddenly, and at scale. Minneapolis in January 2026 was not an anomaly. It was a signal.

Speaking truth to power matters. It is necessary. And the people who speak from having lived in the fire speak differently than those who have not. The weight is real. Minneapolis has been tested enough to give that testimony.

The question is whether the country is willing to receive it—not just hear it, but let it invite deeper questions. That is the difference between witness and performance. And it is the only thing that makes accountability possible.

Chapter 25: America's Strength Was Its Rules

How a leader treats the person who disagrees with him in a private meeting is exactly how his government will treat dissent at scale.

The events in Minneapolis did not occur in isolation. They were part of a pattern—a systematic approach to power that the Trump administration had been constructing since its return to office—whose implications extend far beyond immigration enforcement. Consider the arithmetic of spring 2025. when Republican lawmakers were declaring that the $6.20 daily SNAP benefit—the margin between a hungry American child eating and not eating—constituted wasteful spending. The remedy, passed as the Big Beautiful Bill Act, stripped food assistance in the name of economic strength. Flash forward to the arithmetic of spring of 2026. The Pentagon assessed that the first six days of Operation Epic Fury cost American taxpayers $11.3 billion. A $3 million American missile, launched from a $200 million jet flying at $20,000 an hour, was being used to strike a country whose civilian population lives on a fraction of what the weapons cost. These were not separate decisions made by separate governments in separate moments. They were one decision, made by the same administration, about whose lives count as expendable and whose do not. Less than a year later the Congress that had not been able to find money for hungry children found it, without a vote, for an undeclared war.

For most of its history, the United States has had a distinctive relationship with power. Despite being the world's dominant economic and military force since 1945, it had largely escaped the balancing coalitions that historically form against dominant powers. It attracted allies. Europe's most capable countries joined NATO rather than arming themselves against America. Japan, South Korea, and Australia hosted American military forces. Why? Because the United States had chosen, from the early 1940s, to translate its power into a system that others could accept.

It championed international institutions—the United Nations, the World Bank, the IMF, the General Agreement on Tariffs and Trade—that constrained its own unilateral action while sharing the costs of maintaining international order. This framework was never purely altruistic—it served American interests, keeping markets open, spreading American investment, and cementing American political influence. But it also offered something to others: a rules-based order that even the rule-maker could accept as binding.

The Trump administration has systematically dismantled this framework. The raid on Venezuela in January 2026, which captured President Nicolás Maduro in a special operations action launched without congressional authorization, announced the new doctrine with unusual clarity. White House deputy chief of staff Stephen Miller said bluntly in a CNN interview, "The United States of America is running Venezuela." He dismissed diplomacy. "The world is governed by strength, force, power."

This is not the language of a country that wants to lead an international system. This is the language of a country that wants to dominate it. The distinction matters enormously. Leadership requires the consent of the led. Domination requires only sufficient force. Leadership creates allies. Domination creates resistance.

I write as a systems scientist, and I can tell you with confidence: domination without legitimacy is not a stable equilibrium. It requires ever-increasing force to maintain, because it cannot rely on voluntary compliance. Every action taken outside the rules erodes the perception that the rules apply. And once that perception is gone, the foundation of the entire system collapses. The United States has spent eighty years building a perception of legitimacy that enabled its power to be accepted rather than merely feared. That perception is being dismantled, brick by brick, and once dismantled, it will take generations to rebuild.

George Orwell named the psychology that fills the vacuum when accountability ends. In *1984* he wrote, "If you want a picture of the future, imagine a boot stamping on a human face forever." The line is famous because it names not just cruelty but its logic. Power does not simply want outcomes. It wants the experience of being in power. The thrill of victory. The knowledge of impunity. That is why the children in Minab are not an oversight or a proportionality calculation. They are, in the cold vocabulary of strategic demonstration, the demonstration itself. America's rules were designed precisely to prevent this logic from taking hold—the chapters that follow document what happens when those rules are set aside.

What Netanyahu Wanted: A Forty-Year Obsession and Its Consequences

This is what I have yearned for for forty years.

— Benjamin Netanyahu, at the Kirya Defense Headquarters, Tel Aviv, March 1, 2026

When Benjamin Netanyahu stood in the Kirya Defense Headquarters in Tel Aviv on March 1, and said, "This is what I have yearned for for forty years," he was not speaking carelessly. He was speaking with the precision of a man who had spent four decades building toward a single moment and was now watching it arrive. The statement tells you more about the real nature of this war than any strategic briefing document.

What Netanyahu wanted—specifically, clearly—was the removal of Iranian power as the primary threat to Israeli security and to his own political vision of what the Middle East should look like. To understand why that obsession drove this war, you have to understand the man, and to understand the man, you have to understand where the obsession came from.

Jonathan Netanyahu—Yoni, the older brother Benjamin worshipped—was killed on July 4, 1976, during the raid on Entebbe in which Israeli commandos rescued hostages held by Palestinian militants and German revolutionaries. He was thirty years old. He was the only Israeli soldier killed in the operation. For Benjamin Netanyahu, who was twenty-six at the time and who has spoken about Yoni's death as the defining event of his life, the loss appears to have consolidated a worldview that was already forming: that Israel's survival depends on strength, that enemies must be confronted directly, and that the price of hesitation is paid in blood.

Benzion Netanyahu, the father, was a historian of the Spanish Inquisition and a Revisionist Zionist of the Ze'ev Jabotinsky school. This tradition understood Jewish survival in terms of military and political power rather than accommodation. He lived to ninety-two and remained a formative influence on his son. Benjamin Netanyahu has described his father's view of history as a series of existential threats that were never taken seriously enough until it was too late. The lesson: take threats seriously before they materialize—strike before you are struck.

The Iran File

Netanyahu has warned about the Iranian nuclear threat since 1992. In a speech to the Israeli Knesset that year, as a young Likud member of parliament, he warned that Iran was "three to five years" away from a nuclear weapon. In 1995, he repeated the warning. In 2012, appearing before the United Nations General Assembly, he held up a cartoonish diagram of a bomb to illustrate how close Iran was to the "red line" he was drawing. That year he came closer than any Israeli leader before him to convincing the Obama administration to join an Israeli strike on Iranian nuclear facilities and was rebuffed. The refusal appears to have hardened something in him.

The pattern of Netanyahu's warnings about Iran reveals something important: he was not wrong about the direction of the threat. Iran was pursuing a nuclear program. Iran was developing ballistic missiles. Iran was funding and arming proxy forces across the region. What Netanyahu was systematically wrong about was the timeline—the warnings of "three to five years" were repeated over thirty years without the endpoint arriving, and the relationship between military force and Israel's actual security. Every Israeli strike on Iranian assets, every targeted killing of Iranian scientists, every covert operation against Iranian infrastructure, produced Iranian countermeasures that rebuilt and enhanced the capacity being destroyed. The Stuxnet cyberattack set back Iran's centrifuge program by approximately two years. Iran built more centrifuges. The 2020 killing of Mohsen Fakhrizadeh, Iran's chief nuclear scientist, appears to have accelerated rather than slowed the enrichment program, because it convinced the Iranian government that compromises with the West would not provide security.

What Netanyahu wanted, therefore, was not merely a setback. He wanted what he said at the Kirya: the thing he had yearned for for forty years. The removal, permanent and complete, of the Iranian threat. This is a maximalist goal. It is also a goal that is not achievable by the means employed to pursue it.

The Tragic Logic

There is a way of understanding Netanyahu that is genuinely tragic—not in the political sense of the word, but in the classical sense. Tragic figures in the Greek tradition are not villains. They are people with genuine virtues—courage, intelligence, devotion to their people—who are destroyed by the interaction of those virtues with a fatal flaw or a fatal circumstance. Oedipus is not a stupid man. He is an intelligent, courageous, caring man whose intelligence leads him toward a truth he cannot survive the knowledge of. The tragic frame is useful here not to excuse Netanyahu but to explain how a man of undeniable intelligence could pursue a course that the historical evidence he himself had access to suggested was likely to produce catastrophe rather than peace.

Netanyahu is not a stupid man. He is a man who has devoted his life to the security of the state of Israel as he understands it, who has operated within a political system that has repeatedly rewarded confrontation and punished accommodation, and who spent forty years believing that the removal of Iranian power was the key to Israeli security. He finally had, in the spring of 2026, the combination of circumstances—a sympathetic American president, Iran weakened by sanctions and internal unrest, international opinion momentarily with Israel after the January massacres of protesters—that made the strike possible. He took it.

The tragic question is whether he has achieved what he wanted, or whether he has achieved something else: a war that has expanded across the entire region. A war that has drawn Iran's decentralized military into a mosaic defense that may prove more difficult to defeat than the centralized command structure that was targeted, that has united much of the world in opposition to Israeli-American action, that has created a humanitarian catastrophe in Iran that will generate grievances lasting generations, and that has not resolved the fundamental question of what Iran will look like politically in five or ten years.

Netanyahu said on Fox News that the strikes would "usher in an era of peace we haven't even dreamed of." The Brookings Institution said, within days, that it was "highly uncertain" that the strikes would produce the democratic transformation their architects promised. Every historical precedent—Iraq, Libya, Syria—pointed in the same direction: that military force can remove a government, but cannot install a stable successor. The forty-year obsession, finally acted upon, may produce not the peace it sought but the kind of instability that makes peace harder to reach.

Netanyahu wanted this for forty years. He got it. But it may end up being not what he wanted at all.

★ ★ ★

What the strikes targeted illuminates a key part of the calculation. Among the confirmed objectives on the first day: Iran's supreme leader, the command structure of its security forces, missile production facilities at Isfahan and Tabriz, the naval complex at Minab near the Strait of Hormuz, and the port at Jask on the Indian Ocean coast—Iran's first significant naval capacity positioned outside the chokepoint it has long threatened to close. Jask had been under active development as a submarine base. It was identified under the 2021 Iran-China Comprehensive Strategic Partnership as a node in China's maritime infrastructure network—positioned alongside Beijing's existing footprints in Djibouti, Gwadar, and Hambantota—to give China a continuous arc of presence from the South China Sea to the Indian Ocean to the Persian Gulf. The strikes, in a single operation, degraded one of the most consequential Chinese forward positions outside of East Asia. Whether that was the primary intent or the collateral gain of targeting the correct military assets, the strategic effect was identical. The logic is coherent. The logic, however, has never been the problem. The problem is what coherent logic without a rebuilding plan produces. Iraq had a coherent logic. Libya had a coherent logic. The logic survived the war. The countries did not.

Netanyahu testified before the US Congress in September 2002—not yet prime minister again, appearing as a private citizen with his title of former prime minister—and told the members that there was no question whatsoever that Saddam Hussein was seeking and advancing toward nuclear weapons. No question whatsoever. He guaranteed that removing Saddam's government would produce enormous positive reverberations across the region. He was wrong. He was not slightly wrong, or wrong about peripheral details. He was wrong about everything that mattered: the weapons, the stability, the reverberations. The war he helped to sell cost more than four thousand American lives, injured more than thirty thousand, and consumed three trillion dollars. It produced not a democratic transformation but a regional vacuum that Iran itself moved swiftly to fill. The same man, twenty-four years later, with the same certainty in his voice and the same regional logic in his argument, phoned the President of the United States on the morning of February 28, 2026, to report that Iran's supreme leader would be convening his top advisers that day. The timing was set. The president later said Netanyahu may have forced his hand. He said this as though it were something between an observation and a boast.

The comparison most frequently offered in defense of a foreign-imposed transition is Germany and Japan after World War II. The argument deserves a direct answer, because it is not frivolous. Those interventions did produce lasting democracies. The Marshall Plan was real. The reconstruction was real. The outcome, by most measures, was good.

But the structural conditions that made those outcomes possible have no parallel in Iran in 2026. Germany and Japan were defeated in total war, their governments dissolved, their militaries dismantled, their populations exhausted by years of conflict that had discredited the ideologies that drove them to war. What followed was not a bombing campaign followed by regime change. It was full military occupation lasting years, massive financial investment through the Marshall Plan, the deliberate construction of new institutions from the ground up, and the active participation of the occupied populations in building what replaced the old order. The US maintained a presence in both countries for decades. It invested in both countries for decades. It built relationships, trained institutions, and accepted the slow, unglamorous work of nation-building as a genuine commitment.

None of those conditions exists in Iran in 2026. The Islamic Republic's institutional architecture—the Revolutionary Guards, the bonyads, the clerical courts, the patronage networks—remains largely intact. The population has not been mobilized behind a discrediting ideology in the way that German Nazism and Japanese militarism were discredited by catastrophic military defeat. And the government executing this intervention is not the government that built the Marshall Plan. It is an administration that has dismantled oversight institutions at home, cut food assistance for its own children, and entered this war not by strategic American judgment but because an ally decided to act and Washington chose to follow. You cannot rebuild a nation with a government that does not believe in building anything. The Germany and Japan precedent requires exactly the long-term institutional commitment that this administration has, at every turn, been unwilling to make.

★ ★ ★

The school that was struck on February 28 is called Shajareh Tayyebeh, its name translates as "the good tree." The missile hit at 10:45 in the morning, while the children were in their morning session. Satellite imagery confirmed the building was fully intact at 10:23. Then a second strike hit. Then a third. The school principal had survived the first impact, moved the students to a prayer room, and then called parents to collect their children. She was in that prayer room when the second missile arrived. The Minab mayor placed the confirmed death toll at 165. Iranian authorities confirmed 96 additional wounded. Rows of graves were dug side by side at a mass burial site; the photographs showed excavators working the earth for more than a hundred individual plots. Most of the dead were girls between the ages of seven and twelve. One mother—a midwife who could not leave her patients when the school called—

described arriving to find the building collapsed on top of her son. "By the time we arrived," she said, "the entire school had collapsed on top of the children."

Secretary of State Rubio said American forces would not deliberately target a school. Secretary of Defense Hegseth said the matter was under investigation and that, of course, they never target civilians. Reuters subsequently reported, citing two American officials, that investigators privately believed American forces were likely responsible. *The New York Times*, CBC, and NPR each reached the same conclusion independently. UNESCO condemned the strike as a grave violation of international humanitarian law. Nobel laureate Malala Yousafzai said she was heartbroken and appalled. The UN High Commissioner for Human Rights called for a prompt, impartial, and thorough investigation.

Three days later, six US Army Reserve soldiers were killed at Port Shuaiba in Kuwait when a drone bypassed the base's air defenses without triggering alerts. Their names were Major Jeffrey O'Brien, Captain Cody Khork, Sergeant First Class Noah Tietjens, Sergeant First Class Nicole Amor, Sergeant Declan Coady, and Chief Warrant Officer Robert Marzan. All six were from the 103rd Sustainment Command out of Des Moines, Iowa. A prior military recommendation against using that location had been overridden. At a Pentagon briefing that followed, Secretary Hegseth was asked about the deaths. He said, "When a few drones get through, or tragic things happen, it's front-page news." A staff member present said audibly, "That was one of the most insulting things I have ever heard."

The character of an executor of action is revealed not through intentions but through accountability. Intentions, in war, belong to the planning room. Accountability belongs to the morning after. The morning after, Minab produced a mass grave and a press secretary who said the media was trying to make the president look bad. These are the hands that would rebuild Iran.

Chapter 26: The Real Threat to Western Civilization

The Trump administration's National Security Strategy warns of "civilizational erasure" in Europe—a threat supposedly posed by immigration, low birth rates, and European Union regulations. The language reads like a far-right manifesto rather than a sober policy assessment. Europe is not disappearing: its population is 450 million, its economy produces approximately $22 trillion a year, its immigrants keep its workforce functioning, and its pension systems are solvent.

But civilizational threats are real. The question is where to find them.

Western civilization—the tradition that produced constitutional democracy, human rights, the separation of powers, and the rule of law—is not defined by bloodlines or demographic ratios. It is defined by institutional arrangements: independent courts, representative parliaments, freedom of speech, freedom of assembly, and the right of citizens to petition their government without fear. These arrangements were constructed, imperfectly and gradually, over centuries of struggle. They are not natural; they are artificial. They require maintenance. They can be dismantled.

In the US in 2025 and 2026, they were being dismantled. The Justice Department directed prosecutors to prepare charges against Open Society Foundations. Federal agencies suspended security clearances and barred law firms from federal buildings based on the clients they represented. More than 150 investigations were opened into universities. The administration floated the idea of designating domestic protest movements as foreign terrorist organizations, with "material support" potentially carrying twenty-year prison sentences.

These are elements of a coherent project: the concentration of executive power at the expense of the judicial, legislative, and civil society institutions that constrain it. This is the authoritarian playbook as practiced by Viktor Orbán in Hungary, as practiced by Vladimir Putin in Russia, as practiced—in its most extreme form—by the Islamic Republic in Iran. The tactics differ in intensity; the logic is the same.

I have seen what happens to societies that abandon the rule of law in the name of security, ideology, or power. I know what happens when that contract breaks. I do not want it to happen in Minneapolis. The institutions have not collapsed. Courts have ruled against the administration. Journalists have exposed abuses. Civil society has organized. The American tradition of limited government is fighting for itself. But the fight is real. And those of us who came to America believing in its promise have a particular obligation to name what is at stake.

Erich Fromm, in his book *The Sane Society*, articulated a version of this argument in a single observation: "The fact that millions of people share the same vices does not make these vices virtues, the fact that they share so many errors does not make the errors to be truths, and the fact that millions of people share the same forms of mental pathology does not make these people sane." The normalization of what we are watching does not make it normal. The authoritarian playbook succeeds by making each step feel like the logical consequence of the previous one, until the cumulative distance from the starting point becomes visible only in retrospect. Naming the pattern as it happens is not alarmism. It is the precondition that makes response possible.

The Congress That Wasn't There: Constitutional Authority and Perpetual War

The Congress shall have Power to... declare War.

— United States Constitution, Article I, Section 8

The American people are tired of regime change wars that cost us billions of dollars.

— Representative Ro Khanna, March 2, 2026

The Constitution of the United States is not ambiguous on this point. Article I, Section 8, clause 11 assigns Congress the power to declare war. Not the President. Congress. The framers were explicit about their reasons: they had lived under a king who could make war at his pleasure, and they had decided that no single person should have that power in the new republic. The decision to commit the nation to war—to spend its treasury and risk its citizens' lives—was too consequential to vest in one person. It required the consent of the governed, expressed through their elected representatives.

Operation Epic Fury was launched without a declaration of war. It was launched without an Authorization for Use of Military Force. It was launched without any prior congressional notification. Members of Congress learned about it from the news. The Speaker of the House was briefed after the fact. The Senate Majority Leader was briefed the following Tuesday, three days after the bombs began falling. By the time Congress was informed of what was being done in its name, six Americans were dead, hundreds of Iranians were dead, the conflict had spread to nine countries, and the United States was involved in what the administration itself described as an operation expected to last four to five weeks.

This is not a new story. It has been told, with variations, every decade since the Korean War, which was the last major American military action conducted without any form of congressional authorization. Korea was called a "police action." Vietnam required a resolution based on the Gulf of Tonkin incident, which was later revealed to have been staged. The 1991 Gulf War obtained authorization. The 2001 authorization for force against those responsible for September 11 was stretched to cover operations in countries that had nothing to do with September 11. The 2003 Iraq War obtained a separate authorization based on false intelligence. The 2026 Iran war obtained nothing.

The European position was more nuanced than simple opposition, and the nuance matters for what comes next. France, Germany, and the United Kingdom did not join the operation. The United Kingdom, in a significant early signal, refused to allow American forces to use its Indian Ocean island bases—forcing B-2 bombers to fly eighteen-hour round trips directly from the continental United States, an operational constraint that spoke quietly but clearly about the breadth of allied support. Yet within days of the opening strikes, the leaders of all three European powers issued a joint statement condemning Iran's retaliatory missile attacks as indiscriminate and disproportionate, noting that Iran had struck countries not involved in the initial American and Israeli operations. They threatened proportionate defensive action, including the potential targeting of Iran's missile capability at its source, and pledged coordination with Washington.

This was not a declaration of co-belligerence, nor an endorsement of the original strikes. It was something more precise: a line drawn between the initiating action, which Europe declined to join, and the Iranian response, which Europe condemned. The architects of any eventual diplomatic settlement will need to work through that distinction carefully. It also illustrates something critics will invoke: that Iran's own retaliatory conduct—the scope and geography of its strikes, reaching Gulf states and civilian infrastructure across the region—contributed to the erosion of its international position even among governments that opposed the war's origins. Choices in war have their own accounting. That observation does nothing to diminish the destruction of the school in Minab.

The War Powers Resolution and Its Failure

In 1973, following the Vietnam War, Congress passed the War Powers Resolution over President Nixon's veto. The resolution was an attempt to take back the war-making authority that had been steadily ceded to the executive branch over three decades. It requires the President to notify Congress within forty-eight hours of committing armed forces to hostilities. It requires that those forces be withdrawn within sixty days unless Congress authorizes their continued use.

Every president since Nixon has claimed, in various ways, that the War Powers Resolution is unconstitutional or does not apply to the particular action being taken. None has fully complied with it. The sixty-day clock has been treated as a soft deadline rather than a hard one. Congress has never enforced it by cutting off funding for an unauthorized war. The resolution exists on paper. In practice, it has not constrained presidential war-making.

In the days following Operation Epic Fury, war powers resolutions were introduced in both the House and the Senate. Representative Ro Khanna of California was among those who pushed hardest. "There is no plausible legal justification for the US attack on Iran," said Brian Finucane of the International Crisis Group, "and even by the standards of unilateral executive military action of recent decades, President Trump's unauthorized attack on Iran stands apart due to its scale and likely repercussions."

Senator Angus King of Maine, while questioning Under Secretary of Defense Elbridge Colby before the Senate Armed

Services Committee on March 3, 2026, posed the structural question that the Rubio justification had left unanswered: "Have we now delegated the most solemn decision that can be made in our society—the decision to go to war—to another country?" He called the implication "breathtaking." The prime minister of a nation of nine and a half million people had presented the president of a nation of 335 million with a course of action as a fait accompli—and been followed. A government that cannot say no to an ally and calls that incapacity a policy is not exercising sovereignty. It is abdicating it.

The political calculation that congressional members faced was a familiar one: vote to stop the war and be accused of weakening American forces in the field, abandoning allies, and providing comfort to an enemy. The accusation is effective regardless of its merits because it triggers a patriotism reflex that is difficult to resist in real time. Speaker Johnson, briefed after the fact, called the operation a "defensive" one and stood with the President. The Republican majority in both chambers largely followed. The Democratic opposition called for hearings, for votes, for accountability—and found that the political momentum of a war already underway is very hard to reverse through democratic mechanisms.

The Polling and What It Means

A Reuters/Ipsos poll conducted within seventy-two hours of the strikes found that 27 percent of American respondents approved of them, 43 percent disapproved, and 29 percent were unsure. This is a remarkable set of numbers for a military action by the United States that had not yet produced American casualties in any significant number. At the time of the poll, three service members had been killed. Wars typically produce an initial "rally around the flag" effect: approval rises in the first days. Here it did not. Disapproval exceeded approval by sixteen points from the very beginning.

The reasons are worth examining because they illuminate something about American public opinion that political analysis often underestimates. Twenty years of wars in Iraq and Afghanistan, neither of which produced the outcomes their architects promised, have left a durable skepticism in the American public about what military force achieves in the Middle East. The specific framing of the Iran war—launched without authorization, while negotiations were underway, resulting immediately in civilian casualties—did not help. And the economic signals were arriving in real time: gasoline prices rising, stock markets falling, airlines canceling flights. The abstract calculations of national security were being translated almost immediately into concrete personal costs.

Representative Khanna's statement aboutAmericans being tired of regime change wars was not a policy argument. It was a description of a political reality that the polling confirmed. The American public has absorbed the lesson of the last two decades of Middle Eastern intervention faster and more completely than the foreign policy establishment that keeps designing those interventions.

If Congress Won't Vote, Who Decides?

The deeper question raised by Operation Epic Fury is not about this specific war. It is about the structure that makes it possible for a president to launch a major war—one expected to last weeks, involving strikes on a nation of 90 million people, with significant global economic consequences—without a vote.

The answer that the constitutional text gives is clear: Congress decides. The answer that the institutional practice of the last seventy years gives is equally clear: the president decides, Congress is informed afterward, and the political dynamics of a war already underway make it very difficult for Congress to exercise the authority the Constitution assigns it.

This is a form of constitutional decay that happens slowly, through precedent and acquiescence, until the original meaning of the text is fully inverted. The framers gave the war power to Congress because they feared an executive monarchy. The institutional practice of the postwar era has progressively returned that power to the executive. Operation Epic Fury is the furthest point on that trajectory that American history has reached: a major war, of indefinite duration, against a large sovereign nation, launched without prior congressional notification, justified by intelligence that did not hold up to scrutiny, while diplomatic negotiations were actively underway.

If Congress accepts this—if it debates, introduces resolutions, and then ultimately does nothing to halt an unauthorized war or to impose accountability on those who launched it—then the constitutional text about the war power becomes what the lawyers call "a dead letter": words on paper that describe a power that no longer exists in practice. The question of whether American democracy can hold a president accountable for launching a war without authorization is not specific to Trump. It is a question about whether the constitutional design can survive the combination of a maximalist executive and a legislature that has spent seventy years practicing acquiescence.

The people who were not in the room when this decision was made were absent not because they lacked the constitutional standing to be included. They were absent because the institutional practice of executive war-making had made their inclusion optional. Making their inclusion mandatory again is the constitutional reform this moment demands. Whether this moment produces it is the open question on which a great deal depends.

Operation Epic Fury raised constitutional questions that lawyers and scholars will debate for years. The Constitution of the United States vests the power to declare war in Congress. The president may respond to sudden attacks on the United States without congressional authorization. But initiating a war—sending military forces into combat against a foreign nation that has not attacked the United States—is a legislative act, not an executive one.

No statute authorized a broad war with Iran. The 2001 AUMF authorized the use of force against those responsible for September

11. The 2002 AUMF authorized the use of force against Iraq. Neither authorizes war against Iran. Trump announced the strikes via a Truth Social video. He notified the "Gang of Eight" shortly before strikes commenced. There was no public address, no formal message to Congress, no request for authorization.

The international legal question is equally serious. Article 51 of the UN Charter preserves the right of self-defense "if an armed attack occurs." The *Caroline* test for anticipatory self-defense requires a threat that is "instant, overwhelming, leaving no choice of means, and no moment for deliberation." A state cannot spend months planning a strike, negotiate over the underlying issue, announce a diplomatic breakthrough, and then launch the attack and call it anticipatory self-defense. What Operation Epic Fury appears to be, in legal terms, is a preventive war—action taken to prevent a future threat that is not yet imminent. The UN Charter does not authorize preventive war. It is, under international law, an act of aggression.

These legal arguments matter not because international law has robust enforcement mechanisms—it does not—but because legitimacy matters for strategy. Every time the United States acts outside the rules it helped write, it erodes the asset that has made American power uniquely effective: the perception of legitimacy.

What China Wants: The Silent Beneficiary

> *China firmly opposes the use of force in international relations and calls on all parties to exercise maximum restraint and return to the path of dialogue and negotiation.*
>
> *— Chinese Foreign Ministry statement, March 1, 2026*

While the bombs were falling on Iran, someone was doing the math. The math was being done in Beijing, and the numbers looked different from those in Washington.

China is Iran's largest trading partner. In 2024, bilateral trade exceeded 40 billion dollars, conducted largely through third-country intermediaries and alternative payment systems designed to circumvent American sanctions. China imports approximately 1.5 million barrels of Iranian crude oil per day at significant discounts to market price—oil that sanctions theoretically prohibit, but that flows anyway because the enforcement mechanisms of American sanctions stop at the borders of countries that have decided not to enforce them. Iran and China's 25-year Comprehensive Strategic Partnership committed China to invest $400 billion in infrastructure in Iran. This is the most significant bilateral economic relationship in the region that does not involve the United States.

In late June, Iran indicated it had deactivated GPS reception nationwide. The announcement came through the Communications Ministry, not the missile command. Deputy Minister Ehsan Chitsaz framed the rationale in the language of infrastructure rather than defiance: the disruptions experienced during the twelve-day war had demonstrated that dependence on a foreign positioning system was a structural vulnerability, not a technical convenience. Chitsaz, quoted by Al Jazeera and Defense Security Asia, said, "At times, disruptions are created on this [GPS] system by internal systems, and this very issue has pushed us toward alternative options like BeiDou." Transportation, agriculture, internet services, and military guidance would all migrate to BeiDou. The dependency had changed address.

★★★

The strategic consequence is structural, not incidental. In any future conflict, the United States can no longer turn off Iran's navigation infrastructure by manipulating GPS. The lever Washington once held—the ability to degrade or deny positioning data at a moment of its choosing—has been permanently removed. Iran's missiles, drones, and military logistics now operate on a system Washington cannot reach.

China's response to the strikes was calibrated with the precision of a country that knew exactly what it wanted to say and why. . The deployment of two naval vessels to the Gulf was a message in metal: China has interests here, and it intends to protect them. The Security Council veto was expected and necessary. What was more significant was what China did not say: it did not call for Iran to capitulate. It did not endorse the strikes as a legitimate response to the nuclear threat. It positioned itself, with the confidence of a country that had been preparing for this moment for years, as the alternative.

The Strategic Windfall

American strategists who designed Operation Epic Fury were thinking about Iran. They were not, or not sufficiently, thinking about China. This is a key strategic error of the operation, and it may prove to be its most consequential legacy.

Consider what the United States has done, from China's perspective. It has been demonstrated that American power will be used unilaterally, without UN authorization, while diplomatic negotiations are active. It has been demonstrated that American security guarantees to regional partners are contingent on those partners' alignment with American strategic goals. It has demolished the credibility of American-led multilateral diplomacy in the Middle East. It has created a massive need for reconstruction in a country with which China has a twenty-five-year strategic partnership. And it has driven Saudi Arabia, the UAE, and Qatar—all of which were struck by Iranian missiles while sheltering under American security guarantees—to question whether those guarantees are worth the cost of maintaining them.

China did not cause any of this. China waited while the United States did it, and then offered itself as the alternative. This is patient strategic competition at its most effective: letting your rival's overreach create the openings that your own actions alone could not have produced.

The specific openings are concrete. Saudi Arabia's accelerated outreach to Beijing for security guarantees. The UAE's interest in alternative payment systems that reduce exposure to American sanctions enforcement, and Qatar's exploration of Chinese investment as a hedge against American political volatility. Iran's postwar reconstruction, which will require hundreds of billions of dollars, is one that no Western government is positioned to lead. All of these create a huge potential for expanded Chinese influence in a region that the United States has spent seventy years treating as its strategic reserve.

The Taiwan Calculation

There is a dimension of the China calculation that American strategists are aware of and that the public record has been circumspect about: what the Iran strikes mean for Taiwan. The operational precedent established by Operation Epic Fury—preemptive strikes on a country's leadership and critical infrastructure without prior congressional authorization, pursued while diplomatic processes were active and justified by a broadly construed self-defense rationale—cuts in multiple directions.

China has noted, in private diplomatic communications and in the language of its official statements, that it regards its relationship with Taiwan as an internal matter categorically different from the situation in Iran. This is the standard Chinese position and has not changed. What has changed is the operational context. A United States that has demonstrated willingness to act outside established international legal frameworks, that has consumed significant quantities of its precision munition stockpiles and THAAD interceptors in a sustained Gulf conflict, and that is simultaneously managing a constitutional crisis over the war powers question is a United States whose capacity to respond to a Taiwan contingency has been measurably reduced. Whether China draws operational conclusions from this, and on what timeline, does Operation Epic Fury open the most consequential geopolitical question that the architects of the operation appear not to have fully weighed.

A war fought to make the Middle East safer has, as one of its measurable consequences, made the Pacific less stable. This is not a certainty. It is a risk that serious strategic analysis must acknowledge. The men who were in the room on the night of February 27 were thinking about Tehran. They were not thinking enough about Beijing. History has a way of judging decisions by their unintended consequences rather than their intended ones.

PART FIVE: THE WAY FORWARD

Dignity, Transition, and the New Social Contract

The way forward is not optimism. It is architecture. Optimism is a mood; architecture is a plan with load-bearing elements that can be built, tested, and repaired. This section explores Iran's transition not as an inevitable liberation but as a design problem with specific prerequisites, risks, and metrics for success.

Chapter 27: The Architecture of Transition

When power collapses suddenly—or is made to collapse from outside—what replaces it is not democracy. What replaces it is the next struggle for power, conducted among whoever is organized and armed enough to participate. That struggle can produce democracy, eventually. It can also produce warlordism, partition, theocracy of a different kind, or the controlled transition that entrenches the security apparatus under a new name. Which of those outcomes follows depends almost entirely on what architecture exists before the collapse, who has built it, and whether the forces shaping the transition have any interest in allowing it to function.

The death of Ayatollah Khamenei and the decapitation of much of the Islamic Republic's senior civilian leadership did not, in and of itself, produce a democratic transition. Those who imagined that removing the head of the snake would cause the snake to die had not studied what they were dealing with. The Islamic Republic was not built like a snake. It was built like a hydra—deliberately, across four decades of institutional design, with succession mechanisms written into the constitution precisely because its founders understood that revolutions can lead to the deaths of their founders.

Article 111 of Iran's constitution provides for an interim leadership council to assume the Supreme Leader's duties until the

Assembly of Experts appoints a new leader. This mechanism was activated within hours of Khamenei's death. It worked. The Islamic Republic continued to function, to issue orders, to direct the IRGC, and to manage the information environment while the bombs were still falling.

The IRGC itself is the more consequential institution Its senior officers are not merely military figures. They are economic actors with interests in continuity. A democratic transition would require a reckoning with what happened in January 2026, when IRGC-commanded forces killed thousands of Iranian protesters. That reckoning would follow chains of command upward to the Supreme Leader and outward to the very economic framework—including the policy of American sanctions—that put those protesters in the streets. Accountability, pursued honestly, does not stop at the Iranian border. This makes it politically inconvenient for everyone, and therefore likely to be deferred by everyone who controls the terms of any negotiated transition.

What does successful transition actually require? The comparative record is the most honest answer. South Africa took four years of negotiations between the ANC and the National Party before the first democratic election in 1994—and the negotiations included explicit guarantees for the security forces, amnesty provisions for confessed abusers, and economic frameworks designed to prevent capital flight. Poland's transition from 1989 to 1991 was built on the Solidarity movement's years of organizational infrastructure, the Catholic Church's institutional independence, and the Round Table Agreements that gave the Communist Party a defined role in the transition. Neither transition was clean. Both required the existing power structure to be given a path that did not end in its complete destruction.

Iran's situation differs from both in important ways. The IRGC cannot simply be amnestied—its crimes against protesters in 2022 and 2026 are too recent and too documented, and any transition that does not address them will lack the internal legitimacy that legitimacy ultimately requires. But a transition that treats every member of the security apparatus as a criminal will produce exactly the defensive unity that makes transitions fail. The door must be wide enough for institutions to walk through—not as victors, but as participants in a process they do not control. Designing a transition that would do both is the hardest architectural problem in Iranian political life. It has no precedent in Iranian history, no blueprint that travels cleanly from elsewhere, and no external actor who can design it on behalf of Iranians without destroying the thing they claim to be building.

Iran's political landscape is genuinely plural. Secular liberals, reformist clerics, constitutionalists, labor organizers, feminists, ethnic minorities, and religious conservatives. All people who share a desire for change but who disagree fundamentally about what should replace the system they have. That diversity is not a problem to be managed by the right leader in the right moment. It is the actual political condition of the country, and any transition architecture that does not accommodate it will produce resistance rather than resolution.

What the architecture needs—what every successful transition has needed—is a minimum consensus on principles that cuts across factions, and a process for everything else. Not a program. Not a winner. A table, and a set of rules for who sits at it and how decisions get made.

The Children of the Revolution—Who Comes After, and What They Want

Taking out Iranian Supreme Leader Ayatollah Ali Khamenei is not the same as regime change. The Islamic Revolutionary Guard Corps is the governing institution.

— Council on Foreign Relations, March 1, 2026

The immediate question that every government with a stake in what happens in Iran wants an answer to, and that none of them can answer with confidence is: Who runs Iran next?

The death of Ayatollah Ali Khamenei—who held the position of Supreme Leader for thirty-seven years and had not publicly designated a successor—has set in motion a formal succession process that the Islamic Republic's constitution describes but that has never been tested under conditions of active military attack, decapitated leadership, and near-total internet blackout. The Assembly of Experts, an eighty-eight-member body of senior clerics, is constitutionally charged with selecting a new Supreme Leader. Several of its most influential members were killed in the same strikes that killed Ayatollah Khamenei. The process under these conditions has no precedent. The outcome is genuinely uncertain.

The uncertainty matters because it is not merely a question of who holds a title. The Supreme Leader in the Islamic Republic system controls the military, the judiciary, state media, the budget of bonyads worth tens of billions of dollars, and the power to veto any decision of any other branch of government. Whoever holds that position—or whoever fills the vacuum in its absence—will determine whether Iran moves toward negotiation, doubles down on resistance, fractures along factional lines, or enters a period of institutional collapse that resembles none of these scenarios.

The IRGC: The Institution That Is the State

The Council on Foreign Relations was blunt in its assessment, given within hours of Ayatollah Khamenei's death: "Taking out the Supreme Leader is not the same as regime change. The Islamic Revolutionary Guard Corps is the governing institution." This is not hyperbole. The IRGC has evolved over four decades into the most powerful economic, military, and political institution in Iran. It controls an estimated 20 to 40 percent of the Iranian economy. It runs its own intelligence service, its own missile forces, its own naval forces, its own drone program. It has political representation in every significant branch of government. It cannot be bombed out of existence.

The question about the IRGC is not whether it survives the strikes—it will. The question is what it decides to do next, and under whose political authority it makes that decision. There are factions within the IRGC: pragmatists who believe that a deal with the US is ultimately necessary for Iranian economic survival, and hardliners who believe that any deal is a capitulation and that Iran's only long-term security lies in nuclear deterrence. The outcome of the factional struggle within the IRGC may be more consequential for the future of the Middle East than any decision made in Washington or Tel Aviv.

The Women, Life, Freedom Generation

There is another constituency that has been largely invisible in the international coverage of this conflict, because it is neither the government being bombed nor the diaspora celebrating in Los Angeles. It is the generation that filled the streets of Tehran, Isfahan, Mashhad, Tabriz, Rasht, and a hundred other Iranian cities in the autumn of 2022 and again in January 2026. The Woman, Life, Freedom movement—ژن، ژیان، ئازادی —*Jin, Jiyan, Azadi* in Kurdish, and *Zan, Zendegi, Azadi* in Farsi, the language of the young woman whose death sparked it all—was not asking to be liberated by outside military force. It was asking for the right to govern itself.

This generation—approximately 40 percent of Iran's 90 million people are under thirty—grew up inside the Islamic Republic and has never known anything else. They have also never accepted it. Survey data, including the 2022 GAMAAN study, found that majority of young Iranians rejected the mandatory hijab, rejected clerical rule, supported the separation of religion and government, and had more confidence in Western-style democracy than in any form of Islamic governance. These are not people waiting to be converted to democracy by outside force. They are people who already hold democratic values and have been paying, sometimes with their lives, for the privilege of expressing them.

What does this generation want now? The bombs complicate the answer. The examples NPR correspondent Rezvani found reporting from inside Iran illustrate this complication: a 22-year-old student weeping with relief that Khamenei was dead, simultaneously terrified of what comes next. An engineer going home through the explosions who had been on the streets in January. The woman in Kerman said she was okay with dying—a statement that could mean many things and probably means several simultaneously.

This generation was responding to decades of the erosion of trust and legitimacy. Legitimacy ultimately collapses when citizens can no longer believe that the government serves them. In Iran, legitimacy collapsed—slowly, then suddenly—when the currency became worthless, when water was rationed, when elections were controlled by a Guardian Council that disqualified any candidate who might actually challenge the system. When Iranians burned their currency and their ballots, they were not being nihilistic. They were accurately describing a system that had taken their trust and given them nothing back.

Trust collapses when the state lies systematically about what is happening. In Iran, the state lied about the causes of Mahsa Amini's death. It lied about the death toll in the January 2026 events. It disputed accounts from human rights investigators. It provided official explanations that independent observers found inconsistent with the evidence. When a state lies about everything, trust is not merely eroded; it becomes impossible. You cannot trust an institution that you know is lying to you.

The rule of law collapses when due process becomes performative. When courts exist but serve only to sanctify decisions already made, when rights are codified but cannot be exercised, when the legal system's function is to legitimize rather than to adjudicate. Iran executed 975 people in 2024. Many were convicted in proceedings that international legal observers described as fundamentally inadequate. The rule of law requires that legal proceedings actually determine outcomes. When they do not, you have the form of law without its substance.

The Woman, Life, Freedom protesters themselves articulated what was at stake: the question of who has authority over a woman's appearance in public is also, they argued, a question about the relationship between the individual and the state. One key thing those women expressed, at high personal cost, was a desire for self-determination in the most personal dimensions of daily life.

★★★

Ultimately what the protesters expressed, based on documented statements and surveys before the bombs made such direct expression dangerous, was this specific call for self-determination to be applied to the people's relationship to the government of Iran itself—a call neither for the theocratic system they lived under nor a restoration of what came before it. The generation that chanted, "No to the Shah, no to the Supreme Leader," in 2022 meant both halves of that slogan equally. What they want in place of either is a question only they can answer, and it can only be determined—and legitimized-- through a genuine democratic process.

A new social contract for Iran must start with dignity guarantees: bodily autonomy, equality before the law, and constraints on coercion. Not because these are Western values imposed from outside, but because they are the conditions for a society in which people can actually live their lives.

The Succession Problem

The formal succession process faces obstacles that are simultaneously constitutional, military, and practical. The Assembly of Experts cannot meet freely under an internet blackout and ongoing military strikes. The candidates most likely to be considered have themselves been targets. Iran's President Masoud Pezeshkian is constitutionally subordinate to the Supreme Leader and cannot fill that role, but at the same time is the most visible legitimate authority in the immediate aftermath of Ayatollah Khamenei's death. He has called the strikes an "open war on Muslims" and pledged revenge. This is the language of a leader who needs to establish his legitimacy in a crisis, not necessarily a signal about his actual strategic preferences.

The scenario for what comes next ranges from disciplined transition to managed chaos. A disciplined transition requires an IRGC willing to subordinate itself to a new Supreme Leader, and a new Supreme Leader who is willing to eventually negotiate. A managed chaos—the most likely near-term scenario—involves competing power centers, a decentralized military response that continues regardless of political directives, and a humanitarian crisis that compels international actors to intervene diplomatically even as the military conflict continues.

The worst scenario—the one that the European Council on Foreign Relations described as "catastrophic" for the Arab Gulf states that would be on the frontline—is state collapse: a failed state the size of France and Germany combined, with 90 million people, significant oil infrastructure, and a militarized population, disintegrating along ethnic and regional lines. Each regional power has its own patron: Turkey for some, Saudi Arabia for others, Russia or China for still others. The refugee flows from such a scenario would dwarf those from Syria. The security implications for every neighbor would be severe.

None of the people who decided to strike appear to have fully accounted for this scenario. The evidence suggests they expected a fast collapse of the Islamic Republic into something manageable. The evidence from every previous Middle Eastern intervention suggests that these expectations were optimistic.

The children of the revolution—those born after 1979, who have known nothing but the Islamic Republic and have spent their lives resisting it, quietly or loudlydeserve a future that is neither the clerical-authoritarian system they have endured nor the chaos of a failed state produced by external force. The path to that future requires acknowledging what I have argued throughout: that the Iranian people are fully capable of building it themselves, if the outside world stops making choices on their behalf and starts creating the conditions in which those choices can be made freely.

★ ★ ★

The previous section documented what was done and what it cost. The chapters that follow ask a different question: given all of this—given the war, the deaths, the constitutional failures, the strategic miscalculations—what does a better future actually require? Not a utopia. Not a clean slate. But the specific, patient, difficult work of building something more durable from whatever comes next.

The people who will have to do that work are already alive. Many of them are in Iran. Some are in Minneapolis. They did not choose the fire. But they are in it, and they are the ones whose hands will have to hold the next form the country takes together. This section is written for them.

Chapter 28: Accountability, Coalition, and the Four Civic Pillars

The hardest reality in any post-authoritarian transition is this: some of the people who did terrible things are also people without whom the next system cannot function. This is not a moral argument for amnesty. It is an institutional argument about the difference between justice as revenge and justice as the creation of conditions in which justice becomes structurally possible. The distinction matters enormously in practice and ignoring it—demanding complete accountability as a precondition for participation or demanding complete participation as a precondition for any accountability—is how transitions that begin with hope end with new versions of the same thing they replaced.

The 2023 Charter of Solidarity and Alliance for Freedom—the Mahsa Charter—was the most significant attempt in recent Iranian opposition history to bridge this difficulty. Named for Mahsa Amini, the twenty-two-year-old whose death in police custody sparked the Woman, Life, Freedom uprising, the Charter was an attempt to construct what Iranian opposition efforts had repeatedly failed to construct: a minimum consensus that could hold together a coalition of people who agreed on almost nothing except that what they had was unacceptable. It rejects both monarchy and theocracy. It affirms democratic governance, human rights, territorial integrity, and equal citizenship regardless of ethnicity, sect, or gender. It does not tell Iranians what kind of republic or constitutional structure to build. It tells them what values any such structure must hold.

What the Mahsa Charter gets right is the foundational insight: that a post-Islamic Republic Iran cannot be built by one faction imposing its vision on the others. The Persian political tradition—with its centuries of skepticism toward authority, its celebration of complexity over certainty, its historical memory of being governed by successive outside powers who always arrived with confidence in their own analysis—does not lend itself to vanguardism. What it requires is genuine deliberation, negotiation among equals, and the patience to allow a process to produce an outcome rather than designing the outcome and calling the process a formality.

But the Charter is a declaration, not an architectural blueprint. A declaration says what must be true. A blueprint specifies how to build it and what to do when the construction encounters the resistance that all real construction encounters. Here I present four civic pillars, each grounded in the documented experience of successful transitions elsewhere, in order to define what building the architecture actually requires.

Accountability without Vengeance

Those who ordered the killing of protesters in January 2026 must be held accountable—not because accountability is emotionally satisfying, but because a political order that does not hold its worst actors to any standard cannot be distinguished from the authoritarian order it replaces. But accountability must be designed to bring the existing institution of the security sector into a new framework, not to destroy it. Truth and reconciliation mechanisms, documented confession with defined consequences, international oversight, and time-limited amnesty for those who cooperate and testify—these are the instruments that have worked elsewhere. Revenge purges and justice only for the winners were the actions that have produced present-day Libya, not present-day Poland.

Coalition before Program

Every faction that seeks to represent Iranians—diaspora monarchists, secular republicans, Kurdish federalists, labor organizers, Islamic reformists—must negotiate its participation before any program is set, not after. The temptation to design the transition and then invite others to join it is the defining mistake of every Iranian opposition movement since 1906. The Mahsa Charter is the right framework. What it needs is the organizational infrastructure to make the frame real: working groups, defined representation for ethnic minorities, mechanisms for dispute resolution, and an explicit agreement that no single faction can veto the process.

Constitutional process over constitutional outcome

The argument about whether Iran should be a republic or a constitutional monarchy, centralized or federal, secular or open to religious participation, cannot be resolved before the transition. It will be resolved by the transition—by the constitutional assembly that Iranians elect, once the conditions for a free election can be established. Attempting to resolve it beforehand—as diaspora groups arguing for their preferred outcome have consistently done—is an attempt to substitute outside preferences for Iranian self-determination. The only question that matters before the constitutional assembly convenes is how the assembly will be selected, how it will be made genuinely representative, and what rules it will operate under.

Security sector continuity with accountability

This is the hardest pillar and the one most likely to be avoided. The military, the police, the civil service, and the judiciary: these institutions will continue to exist after any transition, because they are necessary for a functioning state. They cannot all be replaced. They can be reformed, restructured, and brought under new civilian oversight—but only if their members have a path forward that does not require their destruction. The South African model—with a clear process for establishing criminal accountability while allowing existing sectors to continue to operate—is the closest precedent. It is imperfect. It is the least-worst option that has a documented record of working.

These four pillars do not constitute a plan. They constitute the load-bearing elements without which no plan will stand. This section is not about optimism. It is about engineering.

The Morning After—
What Reconstruction Costs, and Who Has Ever Paid It

Three comparisons. Three countries. Three sets of numbers that tell a single story about what it costs to rebuild what bombs destroy, and how often the country that destroyed it sticks around long enough to pay.

Lebanon, summer 2006. Israel's thirty-three-day war against Hezbollah destroyed approximately 15,000 homes, damaged 900 kilometers of road, damaged or destroyed seventy-three bridges, damaged the Jiyeh power station that supplied a third of Beirut's electricity, contaminated 150 kilometers of Lebanese coastline with oil from the bombed power plant, and killed approximately 1,200 Lebanese civilians and 160 Israeli soldiers. The direct economic damage was estimated at $3.6 billion by the Lebanese government. Indirect losses from disrupted economic activity pushed the total even higher. Seventeen years later, the Jiyeh power station is still only able to provide unreliable electricity. The coastal oil contamination was only partially cleaned up at the Lebanese government's expense. The bridges were rebuilt with loans from the World Bank and bilateral donors. Israel contributed nothing to the reconstruction of what its military destroyed. There was no legal mechanism that required it to.

Gaza, October 2023 through the ceasefire. The United Nations estimated the reconstruction cost at $80 billion in an early 2024 assessment, before additional months of fighting added to the damage. By the time of the eventual ceasefire, estimates ranged from $100 to 150 billion. Gaza's entire pre-war GDP was approximately $2.5 billion per year. A complete reconstruction at any realistic pace would take decades. The water infrastructure was destroyed. The hospital system was destroyed. The university system was destroyed. The population of 2.3 million, roughly a third of whom were children, were forced to live in tents and other temporary structures. Eighteen months after the initial ceasefire, the reconstruction had barely begun. International donors had pledged billions, but the mechanisms for delivering it were not in place.

Ukraine, as of early 2025. The World Bank estimated the reconstruction cost at approximately $500 billion through 2024 alone—a number that continued to rise with each month of continued fighting. Some of that cost was being addressed through the seizure of frozen Russian state assets, a legally innovative approach that has faced ongoing legal challenges. The European Union committed substantial resources. The United States, under the Biden administration, committed to reconstruction assistance. Under the Trump administration, American commitment became uncertain. The cost of rebuilding Ukraine was real, it was documented, and the international community was discovering that its reconstruction mechanisms were not designed for conflicts at this scale.

The Iran Numbers

What would it cost to reconstruct Iran's civilian infrastructure after the strikes of February-March 2026? The honest answer, at the time of this writing, is that no one knows, because the conflict is still active, the blackout makes documentation difficult, and the organizations that conduct damage assessments cannot safely access the affected areas. What can be done is to hypothesize using comparisons.

Iran is a country of 90 million people and approximately $1.7 trillion in GDP at purchasing power parity before the sanctions. Its nuclear infrastructure—the facilities at Fordow, Natanz, Isfahan, and Arak that were primary targets—was built over decades at an estimated cost of more than $100 billion in direct construction and equipment costs. Its electricity generation system, which was partially targeted because some facilities also housed military equipment, serves 90 million people. Its hospital system had approximately 130,000 hospital beds before the conflict. Its water treatment infrastructure serves major cities; their high population density means that disruptions to the water supply could become a public health crisis within days.

Gandhi Hospital in Tehran—one of Iran's primary cancer treatment centers—was struck during the first days of the conflict. The immediate cost of the strike was measured in the patients who could not be treated. The reconstruction cost of a major teaching hospital in a country whose supply chains are disrupted by sanctions and active conflict runs into the hundreds of millions of dollars and involves years of delay. While it is being rebuilt, the cancer patients who depended on it are receiving inadequate care or none at all. The mortality from this is not counted in the immediate casualty figures. It is counted later, in excess death rates that are difficult to attribute directly to the conflict.

What the Child Who Grows Up in the Ruins Believes

The reconstruction cost is a number. The number matters. But there is a cost that cannot be translated into dollars: what a generation that grows up in the aftermath of systematic destruction comes to believe about the world.

A child who is five years old in Minab in March 2026—who does not know that her school was destroyed, who knows only that her classmates are gone, and her neighborhood looks different, and her mother cries at unexpected moments—will be fifteen in 2036.

She will have grown up inside the story of what happened to her country in March 2026. That story will have a shape. It will tell her something about what the world is, about who did what to whom, about who can be trusted and who cannot. No reconstruction program can change the shape of that story.

This is the cost that is most consistently ignored in the planning of military interventions, and the one most reliably documented in their aftermath. The Palestinians who were children during the 1948 Nakba are now grandparents who have transmitted the specific geography of their dispossession to generations who have never seen the houses that were destroyed. The Lebanese who were children during the 1982 Israeli invasion are now middle-aged adults whose politics were formed in part by what they witnessed. The Iraqis who were children during the 2003 invasion are now adults navigating a country whose institutions were destroyed and imperfectly rebuilt over the subsequent two decades.

The Iranian children who survive this war will grow up to be the political generation that shapes what Iran becomes in the 2040s and 2050s. What they believe about who destroyed what, and why, and who helped rebuild and who did not, will be among the most consequential political facts of the mid-twenty-first century. The reconstruction bill is not just financial. It is multigenerational, familial, and personal. And history shows consistently that it is not paid by the countries that drop the bombs.

Chapter 29: What the World Owes

Stating the world owes something is a moral claim, and moral claims require precision. The world does owe Iran something specific—not sympathy, which is free and changes nothing, not diplomatic support expressed in communiqués that no one reads, but concrete action targeted at addressing concrete harms made by specific actors.

On Communications

One of the most important practical lessons from January 2026 is that the Iranian state has developed, and will continue to use, communications blackouts as a weapon. It shuts down internet access, disrupts mobile networks, and blocks satellite services during crackdowns—while maintaining its own communications through the National Information Network. The asymmetry is not incidental. It is strategic: when protesters cannot communicate, they cannot coordinate, cannot retreat from dangerous positions, cannot document abuses, and cannot signal to international observers what is happening in real time. The state uses blackouts to create a killing field that is also an information vacuum.

Addressing this asymmetry is not charity. It is accountability infrastructure. Satellite-based internet services, mesh networking applications, and pre-distributed encrypted communication tools give protesters the capacity to document what is being done to them and to survive it better. The international community—governments, technology companies, civil society organizations—has the capacity to provide these tools at scale without military involvement and without giving the Iranian government the nationalist narrative that foreign military action inevitably generates. Starlink satellite deployment, Psiphon support, Signal distribution, offline mesh tools: these are not glamorous interventions. They are the difference between a blackout that lasts and one that leaks.

On Documentation

The names, photographs, hospital records, footage from phones that managed to upload before the connection was cut: all of this is the beginning of accountability infrastructure. Human rights documentation is not merely a record of what happened. It is a deterrent against what might happen next. Officials who know their orders are being documented, their identities recorded, their crimes archived beyond the reach of the Iranian state, have more reason to hesitate before issuing orders to massacre. The organizations doing this work—Amnesty International, Human Rights Watch, Iran Human Rights, HRANA, the Iran International editorial team, the networks of doctors and lawyers inside Iran who risk imprisonment to witness what they see—are performing an act of historical witness that is simultaneously a form of protection. Documentation says to the perpetrators: we see you. We know what you did. History will not lose sight of this.

The diaspora's obligation is to sustain this witness without substituting its own political preferences. Funding documentation organizations, pressuring governments to maintain and expand Magnitsky-style targeted sanctions, ensuring that the evidentiary record of January 2026 is preserved with the same rigor that the record of other atrocities has been preserved: this is work that is both possible and necessary.

On Sanctions

The evidence on broad economic sanctions is clear in a way that the political will to act on it has not been. Economy-wide measures targeting the entire financial system consistently hurt the population they are theoretically designed to help, while leaving the ruling institutions largely insulated. The IRGC's parallel economy means that it continues operating even under severe restrictions. Ordinary Iranians, meanwhile, cannot access medicines, conduct international banking, or participate in the global economy. The photographs of hungry children that this produces are then used by the government to argue that the world is Iran's enemy—a narrative that strengthens exactly the institutions that sanctions claim to weaken.

A targeted approach focuses on specific perpetrators rather than the entire economy, Including asset freezes and travel bans on individuals. The targets could include Iranian officials who can be identified as having authorized specific acts of repression, but also American and Israeli officials who authorized the strikes, designed the economic warfare that deliberately produced the civilian suffering that put Iranians in the streets, and approved targeting packages that included the school in Minab. The symmetry is not rhetorical. Accountability that applies only in one direction is not accountability. It is the justice of the victor, and it produces the same resentment, over the same time scale, that has fueled the anti-Western narrative in Iran since 1953.

On Reconstruction

The countries whose governments decided to destroy Iran's electrical grid, its industrial infrastructure, and its military-industrial facilities made a choice that created obligations. Those obligations belong to the governments that made the choice, not to the aid budgets of states that opposed the war, international institutions that were not consulted, nor future Iranian governments that will have to borrow against revenues from oil fields that were struck. The obligation is financial, immediate, and specific. The countries that bombed should pay for the reconstruction of what they bombed.

On Diplomacy

The only durable constraint on a nuclear program is verification. The only path to verification is negotiation. Every approach that has tried to substitute pressure, isolation, or force for diplomacy has produced a more advanced Iranian nuclear program than the one it was designed to prevent. This is not a contested claim—it is the documented record from 2018 to 2026. The JCPOA worked. Its abandonment produced the conditions that were used to justify the war. Rebuilding a framework with verification, with Iranian buy-in, and with enforceable consequences is the only path to the objective that the architects of Operation Epic Fury claimed to be pursuing. Bombing does not produce a non-nuclear Iran. It produces a more determined one, with stronger domestic justification for the program than it had before.

What the world owes Iran, finally, is honesty about what happened and why. Not the honesty of press conferences and post-strike justifications, but the honesty that answers deeper questions: did we achieve what we said we were pursuing? At what cost? Who paid it? Were those people consulted? Could this have been avoided? Those questions are not comfortable. But they are morally necessary.

Chapter 30: The Diaspora's Obligation – Witness, Work, and Wisdom

Every turn in Iran's modern history has produced exiles. After the Constitutional Revolution, reformers fled. After the Pahlavi consolidation, leftists and liberals left or were imprisoned. After 1979, an enormous wave of Iranians left for the West. The Iranian diaspora today is one of the most educated, professionally accomplished, and politically engaged exile communities in the world.

The diaspora's role in 2025–2026 was both invaluable and, at times, problematic. Persian-language satellite channels and social media networks run by diaspora journalists provided Iranians inside Iran with information during blackouts. Diaspora human rights organizations coordinated documentation. Diaspora medical networks provided information on trauma care. Diaspora legal scholars analyzed international accountability mechanisms.

One structural reality must be named plainly: the people advocating for this war were mostly outside Iran. The people dying in it had no choice but to be inside it. That asymmetry is not an accusation. It is the factual geography of the decision. Diaspora figures, safely ensconced in Los Angeles or London or Paris, who called loudly for foreign military intervention in terms that treated Iranian civilian casualties as acceptable losses in the pursuit of government removal, were deciding on a cost that others would pay. That is not leadership. It is the oldest and most human of errors: accepting risks on behalf of people who were not asked about them.

The diaspora's most valuable contribution is not strategic advice. It is as a witness. The Persian poets, memoirists, and historians who have written about Iran's struggles—from Rumi and Hafez to Roy Mottahedeh and Ervand Abrahamian to Azar Nafisi and Marjane Satrapi—have given the world a window into Iranian civilization and Iranian suffering that no amount of foreign policy analysis can provide. They have made Iranians human in the eyes of the outside world. They have insisted that behind every statistic is a person with a name, a family, a history, and a future.

I write this as someone who left Iran at seventeen, who has built a life and a career in America, who carries both identities with a love that is not diluted by the tension between them. I have written and spoken because the alternative—silence—felt like an abdication. That is the most honest thing I know how to say about my role, and about its limits.

What the Diaspora Does Now

Documentation is not passive. The Iranian diaspora has become, in the weeks since the strikes, the primary engine of accountability for a conflict whose information environment inside Iran is almost completely controlled by the blackout. The organizations that were already doing this work—Iran Human Rights, Human Rights Activists in Iran, 1420 Human Rights Organization—have been operating at emergency capacity, cross-referencing social media footage, satellite imagery, hospital records, and survivor testimony to build the evidentiary record that courts and commissions will eventually need.

This work is not symbolic. It is the precondition of eventual justice. The International Criminal Court does not have jurisdiction over American or Israeli nationals for acts committed by their governments—the US has not ratified the Rome Statute, and Israel withdrew its signature. But universal jurisdiction in national courts, ICJ proceedings, UN commission reports, and the historical record itself all depend on documentation assembled in real time, before memories fade and evidence disappears. The diaspora members building that record right now are doing work that matters at a civilizational scale, even when it looks like nothing more than a person in a Toronto apartment spending fourteen hours a day on Telegram Messenger verifying photographs.

The financial obligation is equally concrete. Iran will need to be rebuilt, regardless of what political form it takes. The mechanisms for reconstruction will require capital, expertise, and institutional knowledge. The Iranian diaspora—which includes some of the world's most accomplished engineers, physicians, architects, and entrepreneurs—is uniquely positioned to contribute to that reconstruction in ways that international aid organizations cannot replicate. The question is not whether this capacity exists. It is whether the diaspora can organize itself to deploy it, or whether the reconstruction is left to contractors and governments whose interests are not aligned with the Iranian people's long-term welfare.

The political obligation is the hardest to meet because it requires the diaspora to do something that is psychologically very difficult: to accept the full complexity of what Iran is and what it wants, rather than the version of Iran that the diaspora has carried with it during its forty-seven years in exile. The Iran of the diaspora—frozen at the moment of departure, idealized or grieved for, unchanged—is not the same country as the Iran of the Women, Life, Freedom generation, the Iran of Shahrzad Hemati sleeping on the living room floor with her daughter, the Iran of the twenty-two-year-old student who was simultaneously relieved and terrified on the morning Khamenei died. The obligation of the diaspora is to listen to Iran, the living one rather than the one of memory, before it speaks for it.

Chapter 31: What Iran Could Be

Any serious analysis of Iran's future must acknowledge that outcomes are not predetermined. They are path-dependent: the choices made in the coming weeks, months, and years will shape what becomes possible.

Scenario One

Chaotic Fragmentation. The most dangerous scenario, suggested by Iraq in 2003 and Libya in 2011: fragmentation into competing armed factions, each controlling territory and resources, with none able to form a stable central government. In Iran, this would mean IRGC factions fighting for control of the nuclear program and the oil revenue, ethnic militias in the Kurdish, Arab, Azeri, and Balochi regions asserting autonomy or independence, and proxy forces operating as independent actors in a power vacuum. This scenario would be catastrophic for Iranians and extraordinarily difficult for any outside power to influence in a positive way.

Scenario Two

IRGC-Led Continuity. The Islamic Republic's constitutional architecture was designed to produce exactly this: the interim council governs, the Assembly of Experts selects a new Supreme Leader, the IRGC consolidates power under new political cover, and the existing economic architecture continues in a modified form. Russia and China would prefer stability under a militarized authoritarian government to the chaos of scenario one.

Scenario Three

Negotiated Transition. A negotiated transition in which a broad coalition of Iranian political forces, inside and outside the country, agrees on a transitional framework that prevents both chaotic fragmentation and IRGC continuity. This would require: sufficient unity among the opposition to present a credible alternative; sufficient division within the IRGC between hardliners and pragmatists; sufficient international support; and, crucially, time—time without new military strikes that would galvanize nationalist sentiment against any cooperation with outside powers.

Scenario Four

Gradual Liberalization. The most gradual scenario: a process of incremental reform in which the Islamic Republic's institutions adapt to popular pressure, moderates gain influence, and political liberalization expands slowly. After the 2026 massacres and bombing, this seems least likely.

None of these scenarios is inevitable. The choices being made right now—in Tehran, in Washington, in Jerusalem, in Brussels, in Beijing, in the offices of human rights organizations and the living rooms of diaspora families—will influence which path is taken.

Iran is one of the oldest continuously inhabited civilizations on earth. Its poets are read in every language. Its scientists, engineers, and artists have contributed to human civilization in every era. Its people are among the most highly educated in the developing world, with one of the highest proportions of women in higher education in the Middle East. Its natural resources are among the most abundant in the world.

One consequence of the strikes has received less attention than it deserves. China's response to the destruction of an ally it had spent a decade weaving into its strategic architecture—oil dependency, BeiDou integration, Jask port access, the twenty-five-year partnership, $400 billion in projected investment, military equipment transfers—was a sequence of diplomatic statements. Russian radar systems reportedly went dark. The alternative international order that Beijing and Moscow have been constructing across the preceding decade—through BRICS, the Shanghai Cooperation Organisation, the Belt and Road Initiative, and the explicit argument that a credible counterweight to American power exists—was tested in real time. This alternative order did not show up. Every government between Central Asia and sub-Saharan Africa that has spent the past decade hedging between the American-led order and the Chinese-Russian alternative absorbed that lesson without needing to be told.

This does not mean China has been strategically neutralized. Humiliation breeds adaptation. Beijing will study this episode with the precision it applies to all strategic reversals, harden its remaining partnerships, and revise its extended calculations of deterrence. But for the Iranians who will one day negotiate the political settlement that ends this war—and for the generation who will build whatever comes after the settlement—the lesson is clarifying in a way that decades of Iranian foreign policy obscured: the partnership with China offered economic sustenance, military hardware, navigational sovereignty, and, when protection was needed, statements of concern. Any Iranian political architecture that aspires to durability will need to account for that gap—not as a reason for bitterness toward Beijing, but as a structural reality that speaks to the limits of dependency, in any direction, as a substitute for the one thing no outside power can provide: the internal legitimacy that comes only from the people themselves.

★★★

Iran is a country of extraordinary potential. The conditions of the past forty-seven years—international isolation, economic disruption, and the weight of war—have prevented that potential from being fully realized.

A post-Islamic Republic Iran, with genuine democratic governance and the rule of law, would be an economic powerhouse and a regional stabilizer. Its oil and gas revenues, currently captured by the IRGC and the bonyad system, would be directed toward public investment in education, healthcare, infrastructure, and environmental restoration. Its brain drain—the tens of thousands of highly trained Iranians who have left each year because the country offered them no future—would reverse as conditions improved. Its diaspora—educated, professionally accomplished, deeply connected to both Iran and the West—would become an asset in rebuilding rather than a constituency of opposition from abroad.

Diplomatically, a democratic Iran would transform the Middle East. The proxy network—Hezbollah, the Houthis, Hamas, the Iraqi militias—exists because the Islamic Republic has chosen to project power through armed groups rather than through legitimate diplomacy. A democratic Iran with no ideological stake in destroying Israel or destabilizing its neighbors would have no reason to maintain these networks and every reason to dismantle them.

None of this is guaranteed. Transitions are difficult. Decades of international isolation, economic disruption, and the specific strains that sanctions and war impose on civic life have depleted some of the institutional infrastructure that democratic governance requires. Building functional democratic institutions under those conditions is hard, slow, and uncertain. It requires patience, resources, and the willingness to accept imperfect outcomes rather than waiting for perfect ones.

But it is possible. The Iranian people have demonstrated, again and again, that they want it. They have died for it. They have continued dying for it, even when the world looked away, even when the promises of foreign powers proved empty, even when the cost has been beyond anything any people should have to bear.

The things that survive empires are not the monuments that powers build for themselves. They are the schools families build, the gardens they tend, the fruit left on the high branches for the birds. The things that survive are the ones built without expectation of permanence—built only because they were good things to build. That insistence is what I am ultimately writing about.

As the poet Forugh Farrokhzad wrote, someone will come who will spread the light. The question for Iran, for the United States, and for the world is whether we will nourish that light or snuff it out.

What happened in Minab on the morning of February 28 will be argued about for decades. Whether it was a targeting error, an intelligence failure, or something worse, the girls of the "good tree" school will be a fixed point in the moral accounting of this war. What happened in the weeks that followed—China's silence, Russia's absence, Europe's conditional condemnation—will be a fixed point in the strategic accounting. No external power arrived to protect Iran. No alternative order materialized. What Iran had, and has, is what it has always had: its people, their intelligence, their stubbornness, their insistence, across four thousand years and numerous invasions, on surviving. The question I end with is the only question that has ever mattered: whether that survival will again be compromised by people far away who mean well but lack understanding, or whether at long last, it will be allowed to take its own shape.

Conclusion: What Good Looks Like – A Letter to the Next Generation

در خرابات مغان نور خدا می‌بینم
این عجب بین که چه نوری ز کجا می‌بینم

In the ruins, in the most unlikely place, I see the light of God.
Marvel at this: what a light, from what an unexpected source.

— Hafez of Shiraz, Ghazal 357, fourteenth century

To the young Iranians who survived what happened in March 2026, and to the young Americans, Israelis, Britons, and Canadians who will spend decades living with its consequences:

I am making an argument. Arguments have sides. This one has tried to be honest about its position: that the war was illegal, that the diplomacy was functional until it was destroyed, that the civilian deaths were not justified by the military objectives that were achieved, and that the long-term consequences of how this war was conducted are likely to be worse than the problem it purported to solve. These are assessments based on evidence. They are not delivered in anger, though anger would be understandable. They are delivered with the conviction that the truth, stated plainly, is the precondition of anything better following.

But an argument is not the same as a reckoning, and a reckoning is not the same as a direction. Unlike the preceding chapters, this letter is an attempt to describe, as specifically as possible, what "good" looks like from where we stand: what it would mean for the choices made in 2026 to produce conditions worth living in rather than conditions that were merely endured.

To the Young Iranians

You did not choose the circumstances of your birth. You did not choose to come of age in the specific political and economic conditions that shaped your generation. You did not choose to be bombed or to have your country's transition managed by people in Washington who have never been to Tabriz or Ahvaz or Rasht, who know Iran as a strategic location and not as a civilization.

What you have, and what nothing can take from you, is the civilization itself. The Persian literary tradition survived the Arab conquest of the seventh century, the Mongol invasion of the thirteenth century, the Safavid theocracy, the Qajar decline, the Pahlavi modernization, and forty-seven years of the Islamic Republic. Ferdowsi wrote the همانهاش (*Shahnameh*)—sixty thousand couplets that preserve the Persian language and civilization—at a time when Persian culture seemed to be disappearing. It was not a political act in the narrow sense. It was an act of civilizational faith: the belief that what is worth preserving will be preserved if someone decides to preserve it.

Forugh Farrokhzad wrote her poems in the 1950s and 1960s—poems about a woman's inner life, about desire, grief, and political awareness, that were considered scandalous in their time and that are now recognized as among the greatest literary achievements of the twentieth century in any language. She was not asking permission. She was not waiting for conditions to improve. She was doing the work.

The Woman, Life, Freedom movement—the generation that chanted ژن، ژیان، ئازادی—*Jin, Jiyan, Azadi* in Kurdish, and *Zan, Zendegi,*

Azadi in Farsi, in the autumn of 2022 and that rose again in January 2026—is the most recent expression of something that has been present in Iranian political life since the Constitutional Revolution of 1905: the insistence that Iran belongs to its people, that its people are capable of self-governance, and that the argument about what Iran should become is Iran's argument to have.

The bombs interrupted that argument. They did not end it. The argument will resume. It will be harder to have in the aftermath of destruction than it would have been had the destruction not occurred. But it will be had, because the impulse behind it is not contingent on favorable conditions. It is structural. It is what happens when an educated, cultured people with a four-thousand-year tradition of self-examination are kept from governing themselves.

To the Young Americans

You inherited a republic designed around a specific theory of how power should be constrained. The men who wrote the Constitution had read their history. They knew what unchecked executive power produces. They put the war power in Article I—in Congress, the branch closest to the people—deliberately because they had seen what it looked like when a king could make war at his pleasure.

That design has been eroded steadily since 1945. Operation Epic Fury is the lowest point in that erosion. A major war was launched against a large sovereign nation. At the same time, negotiations were active, without congressional authorization, on intelligence that did not support the stated rationale, with immediate civilian casualties, including children in schools. The constitutional architecture provides mechanisms for accountability. Whether those mechanisms are used is a political choice that belongs to you.

The Americans who opposed this war—the 43 percent who told pollsters they disapproved within seventy-two hours, the members of Congress who introduced War Powers resolutions, the military officers who privately questioned the intelligence basis, the diplomats who knew about the Geneva breakthrough and watched the bombs fall anyway—all exist. Theirs is not the story that was told loudly during the first days of the conflict. They are part of the American tradition too: the tradition that said the country can rise above its worst impulses, that the rules matter precisely because they are hardest to follow when it's most tempting to ignore them.

Your father's generation was told that Iraq had weapons of mass destruction. The intelligence was wrong, or was misrepresented, or both. The war cost 4,500 American lives, hundreds of thousands of Iraqi lives, and two trillion dollars, and produced an Iraq that is less stable and less democratic than the country it replaced. That lesson was available. It was not learned, or not learned completely, before 2026. Whether it is learned now is the question that the next generation of Americans will answer.

To the Young Israelis

Your country was built on the principle that the Jewish people, after what was done to them in Europe in the twentieth century, needed and deserved a safe place to exist as a people. That principle is not negated by what Israel did in February 2026. Principles of that magnitude are not canceled by single actions, however consequential. They endure, and they require reckoning.

The reckoning your generation faces is whether the security Israel sought through the 2026 strikes is more or less available now than before. The Iranian nuclear program, the stated primary justification for the strikes, has been set back at a cost. The Iranian motivation to acquire nuclear deterrents, across the entire population, has never been higher. The regional architecture that provided Israel with normalized relationships with Arab states is under stress. The international legitimacy that Israel requires for long-term security in a world of democratic public opinion has been substantially reduced. These are not liberal talking points. They are strategic assessments made by serious security analysts who support Israel's right to exist and have genuine concerns about what the 2026 war did to the actual security of the Israeli people.

Benjamin Netanyahu said that what he had yearned for had come. He may be right that he yearned for it. The question for your generation is whether it has made you safer. The answer to that question is not yet available, but the evidence suggests it will not be comfortable.

There is a piece of history that asks to be held alongside that statement. Cyrus the Great, the Persian king who freed the Jewish people from Babylonian captivity in 539 BCE, is honored by name in the Hebrew Bible. Isaiah calls him "the Lord's anointed." The Jewish community has carried the memory of Persian generosity across twenty-five centuries. For more than two millennia, the Persian-Jewish bond was one of history's most durable examples of two peoples who remembered each other well.

That history does not resolve what happened in February 2026. But it asks something of the generation that must now live with the consequences. What was destroyed in this war includes not just infrastructure and lives, but the possibility of a relationship rooted in what Cyrus did and Isaiah recorded. That possibility is not gone permanently. But it will require work, and honesty, and the willingness to hold the whole record—not just the chapter that ends with bombs, but also the one that begins with a king who freed captives and sent them home.

What the Persimmons Mean

There is a story about a woman who grew a garden and always left the highest persimmons unpicked. Not because she forgot them or could not reach them, but because they were not hers to take. The birds would come. The neighbors would benefit. The restraint was a form of generosity, and also a form of civilization: the acknowledgment that you exist in relationship, that not everything you could take is yours to take, that the space you leave unclaimed is itself a gift.

This book is a reckoning with what happens when that restraint is abandoned—when power takes what it can because it can, when the strong country makes a decision that will be paid for in blood by people who were not consulted, when the negotiating table is bombed because the negotiation was moving too slowly. The costs of that abandonment are measured in the chapters of this book: the casualties, the legal violations, the economic shocks, the five possible futures of Iran, of which only one is good, and the others range from difficult to catastrophic.

What good looks like, from where I stand, is not a policy prescription. It is not a ceasefire proposal, a reconstruction plan, or a legal brief. It is simpler than that, and harder. It is the decision made again, by every generation that inherits the consequences of the previous one, to behave as if the rules apply to you. As if the other person's life has the weight of your own. As if the high persimmons are not yours to take.

Iran is a civilization that is four thousand years old. It has survived what no civilization should have to endure and still produced beauty. Its people have been trying to govern themselves democratically for more than a century and have been stopped three times by outside forces that believed they knew better. My argument is that you do not know better. If the bombs stop falling, the sanctions are lifted, and the outside world stops making their choices for them, the Iranian people are capable of building what they want to build. That is what good looks like: a space cleared, not a system imposed.

The systems scientist Donella Meadows, writing about the dynamics of complex systems, described what she called the drift to low performance: a process in which a system's standards decline incrementally, each decline normalized by its proximity to the previous one, until the system is operating far below what it was designed to produce. No one inside it remembers what it was originally built for. The drift she described in environmental systems is visible in democratic institutions. The standard for congressional war authorization has drifted from a declaration of war to a blank-check AUMF to an implicit claim that the commander in chief can order any military action he chooses, as long as he does so before Congress can object. The previous step normalized each step. The drift is now so extensive that fifty-three senators voted to allow a war to continue without authorization, and the vote was not the lead story in most American newspapers.

The Persian social ritual of تعارف (*ta'arof*) is sometimes described by Westerners as a form of deception: people say things they do not mean, offer things they do not intend to give, and perform a social script rather than expressing a direct preference. That reading misses what *ta'arof* is actually doing. It is maintaining the relationship at a moment of potential conflict by creating space for both parties to retreat from a collision without losing face. It is the social technology of a civilization that has survived twenty-seven centuries in a geopolitically contested location by being smarter than its enemies at preserving relationships under pressure.

The Hafez line that opens this book's conclusion was written in the ruins of a tavern, in a poem about finding the light of God in the most disreputable possible place. Hafez was a mystical poet who understood that the divine presence is not found in the palaces of the powerful or in the proclamations of the triumphant. It is found in the ruins, in the unexpected source, in the voice that connects for six minutes through a VPN and says what needs to be said before the connection drops. The blogger in Tehran who wrote "They did not ask us." The civil society signatories who drew the line. The woman who chanted ژن، ژیان، ئازادی (Women, Life, Freedom) in the streets and have been chanting it, in one form or another, since 1905. These are the lights in the ruins. They were there before the bombs. They will be there after the bombs. That is not poetry. It is the historical record of a civilization that has survived Alexander, the Mongols, the British, the Shah, and forty-seven years of the most comprehensive sanctions in modern history. It will survive this, too.

Hafez wrote: in the ruins, in the most unlikely place, a light appears from an unexpected source. That possibility—light where no one thought to look—is what every generation that refuses despair has kept alive. I write within that refusal. The light is not guaranteed. It is possible. Possibility, maintained against the evidence to the contrary, is what civilization is made of.

The people who this quarrel has made worms' meat of did not choose to be in it. They were born into it, or they walked into it through a checkpoint or a negotiating room. Mercutio's curse—"a plague o' both your houses"—is not a metaphor in this book. It is the historical record of what happens when the feuding houses send their armies into streets that belong to neither of them. The houses survive. The people in the streets do not. Or if they do, they are fundamentally changed, diminished, made into something they did not choose to be. That is the plague. It falls on all the houses. It always has.

In 539 BCE, Cyrus the Great walked into Babylon and freed the enslaved people. He declared that every person could worship their own gods. He sent the Jewish people home to Jerusalem and funded the rebuilding of their Temple. This is recorded in the Cyrus Cylinder—the oldest known declaration of human rights—and in the Hebrew Bible itself, where Cyrus is called the Lord's anointed. The bond between the Persian and Jewish civilizations is ancient, real, and documented in texts that both peoples hold sacred. Every act of this war adds to a debt against that history. Every bomb on a Persian city, every child pulled from rubble, compounds an obligation that no military objective can discharge. Debt paid in violence does not close the account. It opens a new one. Honor the debt Cyrus earned. Do not add to the one being accumulated now. Instead leave a space amid the ruins where light can come through and spread.

The plague falls on all the houses. It always has. The people inside them did not build the feud.

That is the only thing I am certain of. Everything else is contested: the intelligence, the legal justifications, the sequence of events in Geneva, the counterfactual history of what might have been. But the certainty is this: the people who will live with the consequences are not the people who made the decision. They never are. And the minimum obligation of anyone who witnesses that asymmetry is to name it, as clearly and as honestly as they can, for as long as the record can be kept.

Chronology: Key Events – 2009 to 2026[5]

2009

June 12: The Iranian presidential election returns disputed results: the incumbent Mahmoud Ahmadinejad is declared winner over reformist Mir-Hossein Mousavi. Widespread fraud is alleged. Millions take to the streets in the largest protests since 1979—the Green Movement (Jonbesh-e Sabz). Security forces kill at least seventy-two protesters; some estimates range higher. Neda Agha-Soltan, who was shot on June 20, became a global symbol of the movement. The uprising is suppressed by the summer; Mousavi and fellow reformist Mehdi Karroubi are placed under house arrest in 2011, where they remain for years. The Green Movement is the direct political precursor to the Woman, Life, Freedom uprising of 2022—the generation that filled those streets in 2009 trained the generation that filled them again thirteen years later.

2015–2018

July 14, 2015: Joint Comprehensive Plan of Action (JCPOA) signed in Vienna. Iran agrees to cap uranium enrichment at 3.67percent,

5 Dates are not neutral. Some causes and sequence listed here are contested.

reduce its enriched stockpile by 98percent, and accept the most extensive inspection regime in arms control history. In exchange, international sanctions are lifted. IAEA verifies Iranian compliance in January 2016. The deal represents the high-water mark of Iran-US diplomatic engagement in the post-revolutionary era.

May 8, 2018: President Trump withdraws the US from the JCPOA over objections from European allies, the IAEA (which had certified Iranian compliance eight times), and the US intelligence community. A "maximum pressure" sanctions campaign begins. Iran had approximately 300 kg of low-enriched uranium stockpiled at the time of US withdrawal. By 2026, that figure had risen to 440.9 kg at 60percent purity—every kilogram of the increase was a direct consequence of the diplomatic rupture.

2019–2020

November 2019: Fuel price protests erupt across Iran after the government triples gasoline prices overnight. Protests spread to at least 100 cities within 72 hours. The government imposes a near-total internet blackout for five days. Human rights organizations document at least 1,500 killed, the deadliest suppression of civilian protest in post-revolutionary Iranian history. Approximately 7,000 were arrested. The internet blackout becomes a template for information control used during every subsequent wave of protests.

January 3, 2020: US drone strike at Baghdad airport kills IRGC Quds Force commander Major General Qasem Soleimani, the most powerful military figure in Iran after the Supreme Leader. Soleimani had overseen Iran's regional proxy network for two decades. Iran retaliates on January 8 with ballistic missile strikes on US bases in Iraq; no American fatalities. Hours after the retaliation, Iranian air defenses shot down Ukraine International Airlines Flight PS752 by mistake, killing all 176 aboard, including 57 Canadian citizens and 82

Iranian nationals. The government initially denies responsibility; the admission three days later, under pressure from satellite evidence, triggers a new wave of domestic outrage.

2022

September 16: Mahsa Amini, 22, dies in Tehran following her detention. The Women, Life, Freedom movement begins—the largest protests in Iran since 1979.

September 17–November 2022: Woman, Life, Freedom protests spread to all thirty-one Iranian provinces. Security forces kill at least 500 protesters; approximately 20,000 are arrested.

2023

January: IAEA reports Iran has enriched uranium to near weapons-grade 83.7percent purity at Fordow, calling it a "significant development" in nuclear escalation. Iran disputes the characterization but does not deny the level of enrichment.

March: Iran and Saudi Arabia announce normalization of diplomatic relations, brokered by China. Beijing's first major diplomatic achievement in the Middle East signals a shift in regional architecture.

July: IAEA Board of Governors passes resolution censuring Iran for failure to cooperate with the agency's safeguards investigation. Iran responds by further restricting inspector access.

2024

April 1: Israeli airstrike kills Iranian generals in Damascus, Syria. Iran retaliates with unprecedented direct missile and drone attack on Israel (April 13–14); most are intercepted.

April–December: Diplomatic back channel begins through Oman. Iran and the US hold indirect talks on the nuclear framework. Iran's enrichment reaches 440.9 kg at 60percent purity.

May 19: President Ebrahim Raisi was killed in a helicopter crash in East Azerbaijan province, along with Foreign Minister Hossein Amir-Abdollahian. First Vice President Mohammad Mokhber becomes acting president. Raisi was the first Iranian head of state to die in office since 1981.

July 5: Iranian reformist Masoud Pezeshkian wins presidential runoff election, defeating hardliner Saeed Jalili. Inaugurated July 28. Campaigns on nuclear diplomacy and sanctions relief; first reformist president since Mohammad Khatami left office in 2005.

November: Donald Trump wins the US presidential election. Iranian government signals cautious willingness to negotiate.

2025

January: The Trump administration reimposes maximum-pressure sanctions, including secondary sanctions on Iranian oil purchasers.

March: IAEA cameras at Fordow disconnected. Continuous monitoring ends.

June 13–24: The Twelve-Day War. Israeli strikes on Iranian nuclear facilities; Iran retaliates against American bases and Israeli cities. Six Americans killed at Al Udeid, Qatar—ceasefire brokered by Gulf states. Oil reaches $110/barrel.

July–December: Iran rebuilds nuclear infrastructure faster than projected. Oman resumes back-channel mediation. Four rounds of indirect US–Iran talks conducted.

December 28: Iranian rial collapses. Protests begin in Tehran, Isfahan, Mashhad, Rasht, and Tabriz.

2026

January 8: Mass protests across all major Iranian cities. Security forces respond; death toll estimated 3,000–36,000 (range reflects the information blackout that severely limited independent verification).

February 14–26: Fifth and sixth rounds of Oman-brokered negotiations in Geneva. US represented by Steve Witkoff and Jared Kushner; Iran by Foreign Minister Abbas Araghchi.

February 24: Oman's Foreign Minister Badr Al Busaidi announces a "breakthrough"—Iran has agreed to zero stockpiling of enriched uranium and full IAEA verification.

February 27: Al Busaidi flies to Washington and briefs Vice President Vance on the breakthrough. A fourth round of talks is being calendared.

February 27, late evening: Strike decisions made in the White House Situation Room.

February 28, 1:15 a.m. ET: Operation Epic Fury begins. B-2 bombers from Whiteman AFB, Missouri, strike Iranian targets in tandem with Israeli Operation Roaring Lion. Supreme Leader Khamenei was killed. Over 40 senior Iranian officials killed. Over 1,200 munitions deployed in the first 48 hours across 24 of 31 Iranian provinces.

February 28, 8:15 a.m. local time: Strike hits Shajareh Tayyebeh girls' elementary school, Minab, Hormozgan Province. More than 168 children and teachers killed.

March 1–3: Iranian mosaic defense activates. Over 400 ballistic missiles and 1,000 drones fired at regional targets. US Fifth Fleet HQ in Bahrain struck; US Embassy in Riyadh struck; Dubai airport closed. Oil reaches $143/barrel.

March 2: Secretary Rubio states: "There absolutely was an imminent threat, and the imminent threat was that we knew that if Iran was attacked—and we believed they would be attacked—that they would immediately come after us." International law scholars characterize the justification as "legally untenable."

March 3: Reuters/Ipsos poll: 27percent approve of strikes; 43percent disapprove; 29percent unsure. UN Secretary-General condemns use of force. 36 countries sign a joint statement.

War Powers and Constitutional Timeline

February 28: Congress was not notified of the strikes beforehand. Speaker Johnson briefed after the fact and characterized the operation as "defensive."

March 1: War Powers resolutions introduced in both the House and the Senate.

March 2: Senate Minority Leader Schumer, after classified briefing, states: "I found the legal justification for this action to be extremely thin."

March 3: President invokes emergency war powers. The Administration argues that the War Powers Resolution does not apply to ongoing defensive operations.

March 4: Senate votes 53–47 against a War Powers resolution to halt operations. Debate reveals a near party-line split, with several Republican senators nonetheless expressing concern about the legal basis for the strikes. Representative Ro Khanna of California: "The American people are tired of regime change wars that cost us billions of dollars."

Israeli F-35I Adir shoots down an Iranian Air Force Yak-130 light attack aircraft over Tehran—the first manned air-to-air kill by an F-35 in history, and the first Israeli-Iranian dogfight of the war. The engagement is confirmed by the Israel Defense Forces, which publishes footage of it. Iran's air force had attempted fighter sorties in response to the strikes; this intercept effectively ended organized Iranian air force resistance.

March 5–12: Iran's mosaic defense continues autonomous operations despite the degradation of centralized command. Multiple US MQ-9 Reaper drones were lost over Iran, most to passive infrared air defense systems that emit no radar signal, making them undetectable by the aircraft's threat warning systems. The Reaper losses are not publicly announced by the Pentagon, but are confirmed to *Air & Space Forces Magazine* by officials familiar with the matter. Approximately twelve MQ-9s have been lost in total as of mid-March.

March 12: A US Air Force KC-135 Stratotanker refueling aircraft crashes in western Iraq after a midair collision with a second KC-135 during combat operations, killing all six airmen aboard. The second KC-135 sustains severe tail damage and lands safely. The loss is the deadliest single accident for US personnel in the conflict to this point.

March 13: US Central Command announces 13 American service members killed in combat operations against Iran, approximately 200 wounded; 10 considered seriously injured. The figure does not include the KC-135 crew lost on March 12. General Dan Caine, Chairman of the Joint Chiefs, acknowledges Iran "retains some missile capabilities" and that US forces are "striking deeper into Iranian territory every day."

March 19–20, 2026—Nowruz and the F-35 Incident

March 19: A US Air Force F-35A Lightning II is struck by suspected Iranian fire at approximately 2:50 a.m. local time during a combat mission over central Iran and forced to make an emergency landing at a US air base in the Middle East. US Central Command spokesperson Capt. Tim Hawkins confirms: "The aircraft landed safely, and the pilot is in stable condition. This incident is under investigation." This is the first confirmed instance of an F-35—the most advanced fifth-generation stealth fighter in the US inventory, worth over $100 million—being struck by enemy fire in its operational history. The F-35's stealth design minimizes its radar cross section, but does not reduce its infrared (heat) signature, which passive systems can track without emitting any detectable signal.

Iran's Islamic Revolutionary Guard Corps releases video footage purporting to show the strike and claims responsibility. The IRGC states it used the Majid short-range air defense system (also designated AD-08), a domestically produced, passive infrared-guided missile system first unveiled at a military parade on April 18, 2021. The Majid operates without radar emissions; its electro-optical seeker tracks the heat signature of aircraft engines rather than relying on radio signals, which means it does not trigger an aircraft's radar warning receiver. Because the F-35's threat detection systems are designed to detect incoming radar signals, not infrared-guided weapons, the pilot would have received no electronic warning before impact. Independent analysis of the IRGC video by open-source intelligence analysts finds no evidence of digital fabrication; the post-impact physics are assessed as consistent with an authentic engagement. The US military has not confirmed the extent of damage to the aircraft or the specific weapon system involved; the investigation is ongoing as of this writing.

What is confirmed and what is not: Confirmed by US Central Command—the F-35 was struck and made an emergency landing; the pilot is in stable condition. Confirmed by the IRGC—claims responsibility and has released footage. Under investigation: the weapon system used, the extent of aircraft damage, and whether the aircraft can be returned to service. Not confirmed: Iranian claims that the aircraft was destroyed or crashed; IRGC statements are routinely overstated and should be treated as claims pending independent verification. Not supported by evidence: the role of Chinese or Russian defense systems in this incident. No strategic common defense pact exists between China, Russia, and Iran for active combat operations; any such transfer of advanced systems would require months of training, integration, and delivery. Multiple defense analysts, including *Air & Space Forces Magazine*, assess the most likely weapon to be an Iranian-developed passive infrared system, consistent with Majid's documented specifications.

Strategic significance: The F-35 was designed on the assumption that radar evasion provides effective air superiority over defended airspace. The use of passive infrared guidance to defeat stealth is not a new concept—defense analysts and the Air Force itself have identified the F-35's thermal signature as a potential vulnerability since the program's early stages—but this incident provides the first confirmed operational data point. It has immediate implications for the conduct of deep-penetration strikes into Iranian airspace, and broader implications for F-35 operational planning across the more than twenty allied nations that have acquired the aircraft. Air campaigns, as this event illustrates, cannot permanently suppress a capable, distributed, passive air defense network. This reinforces the core argument of this book: that airstrikes cannot substitute for verified diplomatic agreements, and that the destruction of radar-based air defenses does not produce uncontested airspace when the adversary has invested in systems that require no radar to operate.

March 20, 2026—Nowruz: The Persian New Year, Sal-e 1405, begins at the moment of the spring equinox: 14:46 UTC on March 20, 2026. It is the oldest continuously observed New Year celebration in the world, marked for more than 3,000 years across Iran and the Persian cultural sphere, now extending from Azerbaijan to Afghanistan, from Turkey to Tajikistan, and celebrated by more than 300 million people worldwide. *Sabzeh,* the sprouted wheat shoots, is the first of the seven items of the Haft-sin table: it represents renewal and the persistence of life. This year, as Iranian cities have been under bombardment since February 28, the *sabzeh* is growing in homes without roofs. It is still growing.

Nowruz has survived Alexander's conquest, the Arab invasion of the seventh century, the Mongol destruction of the thirteenth century, and forty-seven years of the Islamic Republic. It survived the bombs of February 28, 2026. A civilization that has kept the same new year for three thousand years is not a civilization that can be bombed into submission.

March 21: Trump posts on Truth Social at 7:44 p.m. ET, threatening to "hit and obliterate" Iran's power plants, "STARTING WITH THE BIGGEST ONE FIRST," if Iran does not fully reopen the Strait of Hormuz within 48 hours. Iran's Revolutionary Guards respond that the Strait will be "completely closed" if strikes on energy infrastructure proceed. Iranian missiles strike the Israeli cities of Arad and Dimona—near Israel's main nuclear research center—injuring more than 180 people and piercing Israel's air defense array. Netanyahu describes it as "a very difficult evening."

March 22: Iran strikes Riyadh with ballistic missiles; Saudi Arabia intercepts one, and two fall in uninhabited areas. Saudi Arabia orders Iran's military attaché and four embassy staff to leave the country. Israel launches new strikes on Hezbollah infrastructure in southern Lebanon and hits the Qasmiyeh Bridge near Tyre. Iraq extends its airspace closure by 72 additional hours. CENTCOM commander Admiral Brad Cooper states the Strait of Hormuz is "physically open" but that Iran is keeping ships away through missile and drone attacks on vessels. Iran's Foreign Minister Araghchi: "Freedom of Navigation cannot exist without Freedom of Trade. Respect both—or expect neither."

March 23: In a dramatic reversal hours before his own deadline expired, Trump announces the US has had "very good and productive conversations" with Iran toward a "complete and total resolution" and instructs the Defense Department to postpone "any" strikes on Iranian power plants and energy infrastructure for five days, "subject to the success of the ongoing meetings and discussions." Markets surge; oil prices drop. Iran's Foreign Ministry denies that any direct negotiations have taken place since the war began, characterizing Trump's announcement as an attempt to lower energy prices and "buy time." Trump tells reporters the strait "will be open very soon" and that US objectives include Iran halting uranium enrichment and surrendering its existing enriched stockpile. Iran's conditions—a permanent end to the war, reduction of US military presence in the region, compensation for damages, and a new Hormuz status quo reflecting Iranian interests—remain publicly unchanged. The war enters its 24th day unresolved.

March 29–30: Thousands of soldiers from the US Army's 82nd Airborne Division have started arriving in the Middle East, with about 2,500 Marines also arriving over the weekend. Forces include division headquarters elements, a brigade combat team, and two Marine Expeditionary Units positioned within striking distance of Kharg Island and the Strait of Hormuz. Total US ground-capable force in theater: approximately 57,000 to 60,000 personnel.

March 31: At least 15 US troops have died since the beginning of Operation Epic Fury, including six killed in a drone strike on Port Shuaiba, Kuwait. More than 520 US personnel have been wounded. The Intercept reports that CENTCOM has been providing outdated and undercounted casualty figures, citing a defense official who described a "casualty cover-up." Iran rejects the US Fifteen-point ceasefire proposal. Back-channel communications continue through Pakistan and Egypt.

Cumulative casualty record as of April 1: HRANA, the US-based Human Rights Activists News Agency, documents at least 3,519 killed in Iran since February 28, including at least 1,598 civilians, 1,212 military personnel, and 709 unclassified. Of the confirmed civilian dead, at least 244 were children. Iran International reports at least 4,700 Iranian security forces killed as of March 31. In Lebanon, at least 1,268 people have been killed and more than 1.2 million displaced by Israeli strikes. In Iraq, at least 105 people have been killed, the majority members of the Popular Mobilization Forces. US Central Command states it has struck over 11,000 targets in Iran since the beginning of the conflict. More than one million people have been displaced inside Iran. Oil stands above $108 per barrel.

The Strait of Hormuz remains effectively closed to commercial shipping, with over 1,000 vessels stranded.

April 1: President Trump addresses the nation from the Cross Hall of the White House at 9 p.m. Eastern—his first formal public address since the conflict began on February 28. He states the war's "core strategic objectives are nearing completion" and announces the US will "hit Iran extremely hard over the next two to three weeks." He declares "complete regime change" has occurred. He claims the nuclear objective "has been attained." Iran's Foreign Ministry calls his claim of a ceasefire request from Tehran "false and baseless." The Strait of Hormuz remains closed. The enriched uranium stockpile at Isfahan remains unaccounted for. The UN investigation into the Minab school strike remains ongoing.

April 3: An F-15E Strike Eagle from the 494th Fighter Squadron, RAF Lakenheath, is shot down over the Zagros Mountains by an Iranian shoulder-fired missile. It is the first manned US aircraft lost to Iranian fire in Operation Epic Fury. Both crew members ejected. The pilot is recovered within hours. The weapons systems officer, a US Air Force colonel, evades capture in mountainous terrain and signals his position using an emergency beacon.

April 5: The weapon systems officer is rescued after a 155-aircraft search-and-rescue operation, the largest combat search-and-rescue effort in modern US military history. Confirmed US losses during the operation include an A-10 Thunderbolt II, two MC-130J special operations transports destroyed by US forces after becoming bogged down in wet sand at an improvised airfield in Isfahan province, and four MH-6 Little Bird helicopters destroyed at the same site.

April 6: Trump's grid-strike deadline passes without action. Backchannel negotiations continue through Pakistan and Egypt. No ceasefire. No congressional authorization vote. IAEA continuous monitoring of Iranian enrichment facilities remains suspended. Status of 440.9 kilograms of uranium enriched to 60 percent at Isfahan: unverified.

April 7: Pakistan brokers a two-week ceasefire between the United States and Iran. Iran agrees to allow conditional shipping passage through the Strait of Hormuz. Israel states the ceasefire does not cover its operations in Lebanon and continues strikes within hours of the announcement.

April 11–12: Vice President Vance leads the US delegation to Islamabad for direct talks with Iran—the first face-to-face negotiations between the two countries in more than a decade. The Iranian delegation, led by Parliament Speaker Mohammad Bagher Ghalibaf and Foreign Minister Abbas Araghchi, arrives dressed in black. After twenty-one hours of talks, Vance announces that no agreement has been reached. The stated breaking point: the United States required Iran to commit to not pursuing a nuclear weapon; Iran's proposal included the right to enrichment as a non-negotiable condition. Both sides state that negotiations will continue. Iranian sources say the United States was looking for a pretext to leave. The ceasefire, technically, remains in effect.

April 16: The ceasefire holds, unevenly. Strait traffic has partially resumed under contested terms. IAEA inspectors remain outside Iran's surviving nuclear facilities. Back-channel contacts continue through Pakistani and Egyptian intermediaries; no second round of talks has been formally confirmed. Oil remains near $95 per barrel. Congressional opposition to further military action without authorization has grown.[6]

---

6 The nuclear situation is important to state clearly. Airstrikes have not constrained Iran's program. They have dispersed it. The decision to reject the JCPOA is the most expensive one in this record.

In Minneapolis, federal immigration enforcement operations drew organized legal and civic resistance. Courts intervened. Local officials held their positions. CBP and ICE operations were walked back. The administration that threatened a civilization abroad encountered, in a midwestern American city, institutions built to last.

Appendix: Poems of Witness

Persian poets have borne witness to their civilization through invasion, occupation, theocracy, and exile. This appendix collects the poems quoted or referenced in this book, with brief contextual notes. They are gathered here so the narrative chapters may proceed without interruption—but they are not supplementary. They are a key part of the argument.

The Fire-Crowned Woman[7]

Written in witness of the Women, Life, Freedom uprising (2022–2026)

She walks through rooms
that wanted her small.

She became fire.

The state security apparatus characterized her as a problem.
She called herself a citizen.

7 All poems in the first section are written by the author.

The law said: cover.
She said: Look.

They burned her headscarf.
They could not burn her.

She is still walking.
She has always been walking.
The fire is hers.
The crown is hers.
The future is being built.
In the rooms, they tried to make them as small as possible.

★★★

(On War, Silence, and the Unfinished Painting of History)

I stood before Picasso's *Guernica* in a silent gallery, utterly transfixed. The massive canvas loomed in stark blacks and fractured whites, a visual record of the 1937 bombing of a Basque town during the Spanish Civil War. There was no color in it, no hope, just the raw language of grief.

Only when I finally stepped back did I notice how quiet the room had become, as though we viewers had collectively entered a covenant of silence.

The Canvas of Ash

A mother wails—
her child limp in her arms,
a mouth frozen mid-cry
for a god who does not answer.

A horse rears—
eyes wild, legs thrashing,
caught between life and death
in the fire's white glow.

A bull stands—
not in defiance, not in fear,
but watching.
It has seen this before.

Walls crack—
not from time,
but from the weight of bombs
that do not know mercy.

They said it was strategy.
They called it necessary.
The dead call it nothing.

The Warning

Guernica is not history.
It is the present staring back.

The brushstrokes shift,
the weapons evolve,
the justifications change,
but the suffering remains.

The cycle does not break.
One war ends, another begins.
The canvas is repainted,

the names are rewritten,
but the lesson waits, unlearned.

Somewhere, even now,
the sky is burning again.

Do not turn away.

The Final Silence

The streets are quiet now.
The buildings are gone.
The names have faded.

Only the shadows remain,
burned into the pavement
like ghosts who do not know they are dead.

★ ★ ★

When Power Turns on Truth

In letters old, a warning told,
Of leaders who seek to hold
Their grip on power, hearts grown cold,
Their words are like poison, and lies unfold.

Truth tangled, twisted, marred,
By those whose motives dark are scarred,

But truth endures—
it always does.

The republic bends
but does not break
when citizens refuse to forsake
the covenant
that holds us all.

The Death of Siavash, from the *Shahnameh* (Book of Kings)

Abolqasem Ferdowsi, the sage of Khorasan, composed the Shahnameh between 977 and 1010 CE and completed it on the eighth of March, 1010. The poem runs to nearly fifty thousand couplets and is the national epic of Iran. The story of Siavash is among its most tragic and most instructive passages:

I. The command — Afrasiab orders the execution
Sever his head from his body with a dagger
on a stretch of earth where no grass will ever grow.
Spill his blood on that warm soil—
do not wait. Do not hesitate.

II. The warning—Piran counsels Afrasiab, and is ignored
A head that wears a crown—
that is not a head to cut, O wise king.
Why take a head that is innocent,
when Kavus and Rostam will be the ones who seek the reckoning?

III. The prayer—Siavash speaks before he dies
Let one branch appear from my seed,
shining like the sun before the assembly,
who will seek my reckoning from these enemies
and renew my tradition in the land.

IV. The blood—what power tried to prevent, and could not
The blood of Siavash must not reach the earth,
or on the day of reckoning, grass will grow from it.
At that very hour, a plant grew from that blood.
Only God knows how it grew.

In Persian:

سیاوش در شاهنامهٔ فردوسی

ابوالقاسم فردوسی • شاهنامه • داستان سیاوش ۳۵۸–۴۰۰ هجری قمری / ۹۷۷–۱۰۱۰ میلادی

فردوسی حکیم توس، شاهنامه را در فاصلهٔ سال‌های ۳۵۸ تا ۴۰۰ هجری قمری سرود و در روز هشتم مارس سال ۱۰۱۰ میلادی به پایان رساند. این اثر بزرگ که نزدیک به پنجاه هزار بیت دارد، حماسهٔ ملی ایران است. داستان سیاوش یکی از تراژیک‌ترین و پرمعناترین بخش‌های آن به شمار می‌رود.

سیاوش، شاهزادهٔ ایران، از دربار پدرش کاووس گریخت — نه به دلیل ترس، بلکه به دلیل وجدان. کاووس از او خواسته بود معاهدهٔ صلح را نقض کند، گروگان‌ها را بکشد و جنگی را از سر بگیرد که سیاوش خود پایانش داده بود. سیاوش نپذیرفت. به توران، سرزمین دشمن، پناه برد. افراسیاب او را به گرمی پذیرفت، دخترش را به همسری‌اش داد، و زمینی برای ساختن شهری نو بخشید.

اما گرسیوز، برادر افراسیاب، از رشد و محبوبیت سیاوش در دربار توران رشک برد. با دروغ و تهمت، ذهن افراسیاب را برضد سیاوش مسموم کرد. پیران، وزیر خردمند، هشدار داد. کسی نشنید.

یک — فرمان افراسیاب

کنیدش به خنجر سر از تن جدا
به شخی که هرگز نروید گیا
بریزید خونش بران گرم خاک
ممانید دیر و مدارید باک

دو — هشدار پیران نشنیده ماند

سری را کجا تاج باشد کلاه
نشاید برید ای خردمند شاه

چه بری سری را همی بی‌گناه
که کاووس و رستم بود کینه‌خواه

سه — دعای سیاوش پیش از مرگ
یکی شاخ پیدا کن از تخمِ من،
چو خورشید تابنده بر انجمن،
که خواهد از این دشمنان کینِ من؛
کند تازه، در کشور، آیینِ من.

چهار — خون و گیاه آنچه قدرت نتوانست باز دارد
نباید که خون سیاوش زمین
ببوید؛ بروید گیا روز کین
به ساعت گیاهی از آن خون برست
جز ایزد که داند که آن چون برست

فردوسی در این داستان نه فقط خیانت افراسیاب را محکوم می‌کند. او کاووس را نیز محکوم می‌کند — پدری که فرمان‌هایش پسر بی‌گناه را از وطن راند. سیاوش میان دو قدرت بی‌وجدان له شد: قدرتی که ادعا می‌کرد پدر اوست، و قدرتی که ادعا می‌کرد میزبان اوست. هر دو به منافع خود اندیشیدند. هر دو بی‌گناهان را هزینهٔ اهداف خویش کردند.

افراسیاب حتی از خون می‌ترسید. دستور داد خون را در تشتی زرین بگیرند تا به خاک نرسد — چون می‌دانست خون بی‌گناه در خاک بماند. اما خون به خاک رسید. گیاهی رویید. فردوسی می‌گوید: جز ایزد که داند که آن چون برست.

این همان الگویی است که شاهنامه نام می‌برد و این کتاب نیز نام می‌برد. نه یک خانه. هر دو خانه. مردم ایران در اسفند ۱۴۰۴ میان دو منطق گیر افتادند: حکومتی که شهروندانش آزادی‌های مدنی‌ای را که می‌خواستند نداشتند، و قدرت خارجی‌ای که همان شهروندان را تلفات قابل قبول عملیات نظامی خود می‌دانست. سازوکارها در هزار سال تفاوت دارند. منطق یکسان است.

زنی که در سال ۱۴۰۱ در خیابان‌های تهران با تابلوی «زن، زندگی، آزادی» ایستاده بود، همان شاخه‌ای بود که سیاوش خواسته بود. او از هیچ قدرت خارجی نخواسته بود آزادش کند. او آیینش را در کشور تازه می‌کرد. بمب‌هایی که در بیست و هشتم فوریه ۲۰۲۶ بر شهرش فرود آمدند، پاسخ ندای او نبودند. آن را قطع کردند.

خون سیاوش بر زمین ریخت و گیاهی رویید. ایرانیان آن گیاه را به نام او نامیدند. آنچه به خاک رسید، از یاد نرفت.

★★★

On the Epigraphs

Two poetic epigraphs frame this book. The first appears at the front:

"Someone will come who will spread the light."

—Forugh Farrokhzad, "Kasi Mi-Āyad" ("Someone Is Coming"), from Tavallodi Digar (Another Birth), 1964

This rendering condenses Farrokhzad's poem into a single line. The poem describes the arrival of an unnamed figure—someone better, someone like no one else—and ends with the repeated refrain "How good the light is." The compression is deliberate.

The second epigraph opens the Conclusion:

"In the ruins of the Magian tavern, I see the light of God—marvel at this: what a light, and from where I see it come."

—Hafez of Shiraz, Ghazal 357, fourteenth century

The *kharabat* (ruins, tavern) in Hafez carries a double meaning: physical desolation and the site of unexpected spiritual revelation.

Acknowledgements

Books do not emerge from silence, and this one less so than most.

This book was written in the middle of events that were still unfolding—which means it was written with the particular difficulty of not knowing the ending. The people who helped me think through its arguments, challenged its conclusions, read its drafts, and sustained me through its composition deserve more thanks than I can adequately say here.

To the memory of my parents, whose lives are the argument I am trying to make. My father operated on patients who could not pay. My mother built schools in the villages near her father's birthplace. They told me to do good and throw it in the river, and to leave the high persimmons for the birds. I have tried.

To my wife, Lindsay, who met me in the fire and stayed when the world turned. To my daughter, Nahid, and stepdaughters, Natalie and Charlotte: you are why the future matters.

To my colleagues at the University of Minnesota, at Renewable Energy Partners, at Energy Policy and Security Associates, and in the broader academic and policy community who have challenged, supported, and sustained me across four decades: I am grateful for the arguments. I am more grateful for the friendships.

With deep thanks to my editor at Calumet Editions, whose clarity, care, and discipline strengthened every page of this work.

To Mr. Ian Graham Leask, Publisher of Calumet Editions, who encouraged and invited me to write this book, read this manuscript with the seriousness it demanded, and committed to bringing it into the world without delay.

To the Iranian people—inside Iran and in the diaspora, in the streets and in the silence that precedes speech—whose resilience, creativity, and insistence on living fully in conditions that would have broken lesser cultures has been, for me, the great lesson of my adult life. Iran is not its government. It never has been. It is the مشاعره (*moshaereh*) games at the dinner table. It is the persimmons left on the high branches.

And to the tens of millions of people—people who did not choose this war, did not sit in the rooms where the decisions were made, and are living inside the consequences anyway.

This book is for all of them.

Glossary of Key Terms and Institutions

The following terms and institutions appear throughout this book. Many carry meanings that differ depending on who is using them and in what context. Where relevant, I have noted those contested meanings.

Article 110 (Iranian Constitution): The constitutional provision enumerating the sweeping powers of the Supreme Leader, including command of the armed forces, the power to declare war and peace, and the appointment of senior military and judicial officials. It is the legal architecture of *Velayat-e Faqih* (guardianship of the jurist) as a governing principle.

Article 111 (Iranian Constitution): The provision governing succession of the Supreme Leader. In the event of death or incapacity, an interim council assumes leadership duties until the Assembly of Experts selects a successor. This provision became operationally significant in February 2026.

Ashura: The tenth day of Muharram in the Islamic calendar, commemorating the martyrdom of Hussain ibn Ali at the Battle of Karbala (680 CE). The central holy day of Shia Islam and, in Iran, a major civic as well as religious occasion. The Karbala narrative that Ashura commemorates functions as both a political and a theological framework—see the Karbala Paradigm.

bonyad: A class of parastatal religious and charitable foundations in Iran, often controlling significant economic assets with limited public accountability. The largest include Setad (controlled by the Supreme Leader's office, originating from property confiscated after 1979) and Astan Quds Razavi (which controls the Imam Reza shrine complex in Mashhad). Their economic scale and opacity are central to the postwar economic architecture described in this book.

The Constitutional Revolution (1905–1911): Iran's first major democratic movement, which produced a constitution, a parliament (Majlis), and the first articulation of rights-based governance in Iranian history. It was eventually suppressed with the assistance of the Russians and the British.

Guardianship of the Jurist (Velayat-e Faqih): The political-theological doctrine developed by Ayatollah Khomeini, which holds that in the absence of the Hidden Imam (the Twelfth Imam of Twelver Shia Islam), supreme political authority belongs to the senior Islamic jurist. This doctrine is the constitutional and ideological foundation of the Islamic Republic's governing structure. It is contested within Shia Islamic jurisprudence: several major Shia scholars have challenged or rejected it.

JCPOA (Joint Comprehensive Plan of Action): The nuclear agreement reached in 2015 between Iran and the P5+1 powers (United States, United Kingdom, France, Germany, Russia, China), under which Iran agreed to significant limitations on its nuclear program in exchange for sanctions relief. The United States withdrew from the agreement in May 2018 under President Trump's first administration, citing its alleged insufficiency. Iran subsequently began expanding its nuclear program beyond the agreement's limits. Diplomacy aimed at reviving or replacing the agreement continued intermittently through 2025, before negotiations collapsed twenty-four hours before Operation Epic Fury began.

Karbala Paradigm: The term introduced by scholar Michael Fischer to describe how the Battle of Karbala (680 CE)—in which Hussain ibn Ali chose death over submission to a ruler he considered illegitimate—functions as a political and moral template in Shia culture. The paradigm frames every encounter with unjust power through the lens of the Karbala narrative: the righteous few, the overwhelming opposing force, the moral imperative to resist rather than submit.

Majlis: The Iranian parliament. Established under the 1906 Constitutional Revolution. Continues to operate under the Islamic Republic, though the Guardian Council must approve candidates before standing for election, and legislation is subject to Guardian Council and Expediency Council review. Its practical authority is constrained, but it remains a site of factional politics and occasional significant debate.

Operation Epic Fury: The name given to the joint US-Israeli military campaign against Iran that began on February 28, 2026. The operation included strikes on nuclear facilities, missile manufacturing and launch infrastructure, naval assets, and leadership targets, including the strike that killed Supreme Leader Ayatollah Ali Khamenei on March 1, 2026.

Operation Midnight Hammer: The US military strikes on Iranian nuclear facilities conducted in June 2025, following the Twelve-Day War between Israel and Iran.

postwar economic architecture: My analytical framework for describing a political-economic system in which governing institutions extract value from the population they nominally serve rather than providing services in exchange for consent. Distinguished from a Social Contract, in which legitimacy flows from the governed.

SAVAK: The intelligence and security service of the Pahlavi monarchy (Shah's Iran), active from 1957 until the 1979 revolution.

Setad: The organization formally known as Setad Ejraiye Farmane Hazrat Emam (Headquarters for Executing the Order of the Imam). Originally established to manage property confiscated from citizens who fled or were expelled after the 1979 revolution, it grew into one of Iran's largest economic conglomerates, with holdings in real estate, telecommunications, oil and gas, pharmaceutical manufacturing, and financial services. It operates under the authority of the Supreme Leader's office.

Strait of Hormuz: The narrow waterway between the Persian Gulf and the Gulf of Oman, through which approximately 20 million barrels of oil pass daily—roughly 20 percent of global oil consumption. It is the world's most important energy chokepoint, with no readily accessible alternative route for most Gulf oil exporters. Iran controls the northern shore. Iranian threats to close the strait have historically caused significant energy market disruption; actual closure would represent one of the most economically consequential single actions available to any state actor.

Supreme Leader (Rahbar): The highest political and religious authority in the Islamic Republic of Iran, with powers enumerated in Article 110 of the constitution. Ayatollah Ruhollah Khomeini served as the first Supreme Leader from 1979 until he died in 1989. Ayatollah Ali Khamenei held the position from 1989 until he died in the US-Israeli strikes of March 1, 2026.

tārājdi **(**from tārāj, Persian: تاراج**):** Plunder; the stripping of what belongs to others. The word carries more weight in Persian than the word for simple theft: it implies the act of those who believe that what they want is already theirs by right.

Third Current: My term for the political and social forces in Iran that are distinct from both the governing establishment and the exile politics of regime change: the labor organizers, teachers' unions, lawyers' associations, environmental activists, women's rights advocates, Kurdish and Baloch civil society organizations, student movements, and reformist religious voices that have been organizing across decades within Iran itself.

War Powers Resolution (1973): The US law requiring the president to notify Congress within forty-eight hours of committing US forces to hostilities, and limiting unauthorized military engagements to sixty days without congressional authorization. Executive branches of both parties have contested its practical scope and enforceability since its passage.

Woman, Life, Freedom: The slogan—and the name—of the uprising that began in Iran in September 2022, following the death of Mahsa Amini following her detention. The most sustained and geographically widespread protest movement in Iran since the 1979 revolution, it was driven primarily by women but supported across gender, class, ethnic, and religious lines. Its central claim was that the state's assertion of authority over women's bodies is not a religious obligation but an exercise of political power.

Selected Bibliography and Sources

Primary Sources and Official Documents

Central Intelligence Agency, *Iran: A History of Meddling, Repeated*, General CIA Records, 1979.

Constitution of the Islamic Republic of Iran , Articles 110 and 111, 1979.

Fourth Geneva Convention, *Article 147* (defining grave breaches, including extensive destruction of civilian property not justified by military necessity), 1949.

Office of the Historian, US Department of State. "Statement of Policy Proposed by the National Security Council," *Foreign Relations of the United States, 1952–1954, Iran, 1951-1954*, 1952.

United Nations, *UN Charter Article 51* (on the right of self-defense), 1945.

UN Human Rights Council, *Resolution A/HRC/S-39/L.1* (on Iran protests), 2026.

UN Security Council, *Resolution 1441* (on Iraqi disarmament), 2002.

UN Security Council, *Resolution 2573* (condemning attacks against critical civilian infrastructure as violations of international humanitarian law), 2021.

United States Congress, *War Powers Resolution*, 1973.

US Energy Information Administration, "World Oil Transit Chokepoints," (2024–2025).

Testimony Before the Senate Finance Committee, 119th Cong. (2026) (statement of Scott Bessent).

Supplementary Fundamental Laws to the Constitutional Law (1907). Translated by Edward G. Browne, *The Persian Revolution of 1905–1909*, Cambridge University Press, 1910.

Human Rights Documentation

Amnesty International. *Iran.* Amnesty International Publications, 1976.

Amnesty International. "Iran: Deaths and injuries rise amid authorities' renewed cycle of protest bloodshed," (January 12, 2026).

Amnesty International, "What happened at the protests in Iran?" (January 26, 2026).

Human Rights Activist News Agency in Iran (HRANA), *Annual Report on Execution in Iran 2024–2025,* (October 8, 2025).

HRANA, *The Crimson Winter: A 50 Day Record of Iran's 2025–2026 Nationwide Protests* (February 23, 2026).

Human Rights Watch. "Iran: Human Rights Situation Spirals Deeper into Crisis," (February 4, 2026).

International Commission of Jurists. *Annual Report*, 1976.

Iran Human Rights (IHRNGO). "At Least 3,428 Protesters Killed in Iran," (January 14, 2026).

Testimony before the Human Rights Council Special Session on the Situation of Human Rights in Iran. (2026) (Statement of UN Rapporteur).

News and Journalistic Sources

Barnes, Julian, and Eric Schmitt, Tyler Pager, Malachy Browne and Helene Cooper, "*U.S. at Fault in Strike on School in Iran, Preliminary Inquiry Says," The New York Times,* (March 11, 2026).

Copp, Tara, and Alex Horton, Ellen Nakashima, and Lior Soroka. "In surprise daytime attack, US, Israel take out Iranian leadership," *The Washington Post* (February 28, 2026).

Editorial Board of Iran International, "Thousands of protest deaths missing from Iran's official tally," Iran International. (February 2, 2026).

Gordon, Chris and Stephen Losey, "MQ-9s Over Iran: Striking and Finding Targets—But Taking Some Losses," *Air & Space Forces Magazine.* (March 11, 2026).

Kaul, Greta, and Jake Steinberg, Amanda Anderson and Anna Boone. "A close examination of the shooting of Renee Good," *Minneapolis Star Tribune.* (January 10, 2026).

Siamdoust, Nahid. "An Anguished Debate Among Iranians, " *New Lines Magazine.*(March 25, 2026).

Lange, Jason. " Just 1 in 4 Americans Say They Back Us Strikes on Iran," *Reuters,* multiple reports on Operation Epic Fury, Iran's retaliation, and diplomatic background (March 1, 2026).

Lum, Devon and Haley Willis, Alexander Cardia, Dmitriy Khavin and Ainara Tiefenthäler, "New Video Analysis Reveals Flawed and Fatal Decisions in Shooting of Pretti," *The New*

York Times. (January 6, 2026).

Price, Michelle and Mary Clare Jalonick, Stephanie Liechtenstein, and Sam McNeil. "Early US intelligence report suggests US strikes only set back Iran's nuclear program by months," *The Associated Press,* (June 25, 2025).

Serwer, Adam. *The Atlantic.* "Minnesota Proved MAGA Wrong," (January 26, 2026).

Wintour, Patrick. "'Death to the dictator': Iranian students hold protests for third day," *The Guardian.* February 23, 2026).

Policy and Academic Analysis

Carothers, Thomas, and Benjamin Press. *Understanding and Responding to Global Democratic Backsliding.* Carnegie Endowment for International Peace, 2022.

Chenoweth, Erica, and Maria J. Stephan. *Why Civil Resistance Works: The Strategic Logic of Nonviolent Conflict.* Columbia University Press, 2011.

CSIS. "Operation Epic Fury and the Remnants of Iran's Nuclear Program," (February 28, 2026).

Economist Intelligence Unit. *Democracy Index 2024.* The Economist Group, 2024.

GAMAAN (Group for Analyzing and Measuring Attitudes in Iran). *Iranians' Political Preferences in 2024: An Analytical Report.* Tilburg, 2025.

GAMAAN. *Iranians' Attitudes Toward the 12-Day War.* September 24–28, 2025.

GAMAAN. *Iranians' Attitudes Toward Religion: A 2020 Survey Report.* August 2020.

RAND Corporation. *The Rise of the Pasdaran: Assessing the Domestic Roles of Iran's Islamic Revolutionary Guards Corps.* (January 8,

2009).

Stimson Center. "Experts React: What the Epic Fury Iran Strikes Signal to the World" (March 2026).

Tamimi Arab, Pooyan, and Ammar Maleki. "The Secular-Religious Divide in Iran: An Analysis of GAMAAN's Online Surveys." In Jack D. Eller and Natalie Khazaal, eds., *Nonbelievers, Apostates, and Atheists in the Muslim World.* Routledge, 2024/2025.

Historical and Background Sources

Abrahamian, Ervand. *Iran Between Two Revolutions.* Princeton University Press, 1982.

Axworthy, Michael. *A History of Iran: Empire of the Mind.* Basic Books, 2008.

Encyclopedia Iranica. "SAVAK," "Constitutional Revolution." Columbia University. https://www.iranicaonline.org.

Fischer, Michael M. J. *Iran: From Religious Dispute to Revolution.* University of Wisconsin Press, 2003.

Gasiorowski, Mark J., and Malcolm Byrne, eds. *Mohammad Mosaddeq and the 1953 Coup in Iran.* Syracuse University Press, 2004.

Ghamari-Tabrizi, Behrooz. *Foucault in Iran: Islamic Revolution after the Enlightenment.* University of Minnesota Press, 2016.

Hiro, Dilip. *The Longest War: The Iran-Iraq Military Conflict.* Routledge, 1991.

Keddie, Nikki R., with a section by Yann Richard. *Modern Iran: Roots and Results of Revolution.* Yale University Press, 2006.

Milani, Abbas. *The Shah.* Palgrave Macmillan, 2011.

Mishra, Pankaj. *Age of Anger: A History of the Present.* Farrar, Straus and Giroux, 2017.

Mottahedeh, Roy P. *The Mantle of the Prophet: Religion and Politics in Iran.* One World Publications, 2008.

Nafisi, Azar. *Reading Lolita in Tehran: A Memoir in Books.* Random House, 2003.

Nasr, Vali. *The Shia Revival: How Conflicts within Islam Will Shape the Future.* W.W. Norton, 2006.

Shuster, W. Morgan. *The Strangling of Persia.* Mage Publishers, 1987.

Takeyh, Ray. *Hidden Iran: Paradox and Power in the Islamic Republic.* Times Books / Henry Holt, 2006.

Wurtsbaugh, Wayne A., et al. "Decline of the World's Saline Lakes." *Nature Geoscience* 10 (2017): 816–821.

About the Author

Massoud Amin was born in Iran and came to the United States as a teenager, arriving shortly before the Iranian Revolution. He attended university in the United States where he built his academic career.

He comes from a family with deep roots in Iranian professional and cultural life.

He is Professor Emeritus of Electrical and Computer Engineering at the University of Minnesota, where he served as Director of the Technological Leadership Institute and held the Honeywell/H.W. Sweatt Chair in Technological Leadership. He is widely known as the "father of the smart grid" for his foundational work on intelligent power systems. After September 11, 2001, he founded and directed EPRI's infrastructure security and protection programs, leading research and development on critical infrastructure for North American utilities.

He has advised the White House, Congress, the Department of Defense, the Department of Energy, the Department of Homeland Security, and other federal agencies on technology policy, infrastructure security, and national resilience. He is Chief Technology Officer of Renewable Energy Partners and President and Chairman of Energy Policy and Security Associates. He has authored more than 300 peer-reviewed publications, eight research volumes, and several books.

He has never stopped being Iranian. He has never stopped being American. He does not take lightly the distance between where he was born and where he is now, or the obligations that distance creates. He does not expect to resolve the tension between these identities, and no longer tries. He has learned, instead, to use it as a lens for seeing clearly and as a source of the kind of grief that produces honesty.

He lives near Minneapolis, Minnesota, with his wife and daughters.

www.ingramcontent.com/pod-product-compliance
Lightning Source LLC
LaVergne TN
LVHW091107080826
845145LV00008B/1834